Media Activism in the Digital Age

Media Activism in the Digital Age captures an exciting moment in the evolution of media activism studies and offers an invaluable guide to this vibrant and evolving field of research.

Victor Pickard and Guobin Yang have assembled essays by leading scholars and activists to provide case studies of feminist, technological, and political interventions during different historical periods and at local, national, and global levels. Looking at the underlying theories, histories, politics, ideologies, tactics, strategies, and aesthetics, the book takes an expansive view of media activism. It explores how varieties of activism are mediated through communication technologies, how activists deploy strategies for changing the structures of media systems, and how governments and corporations seek to police media activism. From memes to zines, hacktivism to artivism, this volume considers activist practices involving both older kinds of media and newer digital, social, and network-based forms.

Media Activism in the Digital Age provides a useful cross-section of this growing field for both students and researchers.

Victor Pickard is an Associate Professor at the University of Pennsylvania's Annenberg School for Communication. He is the author of *America's Battle for Media Democracy* (2014), and co-editor of *Will the Last Reporter Please Turn Out the Lights* (2011) and *The Future of Internet Policy* (2015).

Guobin Yang is a Professor at the University of Pennsylvania's Annenberg School for Communication and Department of Sociology. He is the author of *The Power of the Internet in China: Citizen Activism Online* (2009) and *The Red Guard Generation and Political Activism in China* (2016). He has also edited several books.

Shaping Inquiry in Culture, Communication and Media Studies
Series Editor: Barbie Zelizer

Dedicated to bringing to the foreground the central impulses by which we engage in inquiry, the *Shaping Inquiry in Culture, Communication and Media Studies* series attempts to make explicit the ways in which we craft our intellectual grasp of the world.

Explorations in Communication and History
Edited by Barbie Zelizer

The Changing Faces of Journalism:
Tabloidization, Technology and Truthiness
Edited by Barbie Zelizer

The Politics of Reality Television:
Global Perspectives
Edited by Marwan M. Kraidy and Katherine Sender

Making the University Matter
Edited by Barbie Zelizer

Communication Matters:
Materialist Approaches to Media, Mobility and Networks
Edited by Jeremy Packer and Stephen B. Crofts Wiley

Communication and Power in the Global Era:
Orders and Borders
Edited by Marwan M. Kraidy

Boundaries of Journalism:
Professionalism, Practices and Participation
Edited by Matt Carlson and Seth C. Lewis

Place, Space, and Mediated Communication:
Exploring Context Collapse
Edited by Sun-ha Hong and Carolyn Marvin

Media Activism in the Digital Age
Edited by Victor Pickard and Guobin Yang

Media Activism in the Digital Age

Edited by Victor Pickard and Guobin Yang

LONDON AND NEW YORK

First published 2017
by Routledge
2 Park Square, Milton Park, Abingdon, Oxon OX14 4RN

and by Routledge
711 Third Avenue, New York, NY 10017

Routledge is an imprint of the Taylor & Francis Group, an informa business

© 2017 selection and editorial matter, Victor Pickard and Guobin Yang; individual chapters, the contributors

The right of Victor Pickard and Guobin Yang to be identified as the author of the editorial material, and of the authors for their individual chapters, has been asserted in accordance with sections 77 and 78 of the Copyright, Designs and Patents Act 1988.

All rights reserved. No part of this book may be reprinted or reproduced or utilised in any form or by any electronic, mechanical, or other means, now known or hereafter invented, including photocopying and recording, or in any information storage or retrieval system, without permission in writing from the publishers.

Trademark notice: Product or corporate names may be trademarks or registered trademarks, and are used only for identification and explanation without intent to infringe.

British Library Cataloguing-in-Publication Data
A catalogue record for this book is available from the British Library

Library of Congress Cataloging-in-Publication Data
Names: Pickard, Victor W., editor. | Yang, Guobin editor.
Title: Media activism in the digital age / edited by Victor Pickard and Guobin Yang.
Description: London ; New York : Routledge, 2017. | Includes index.
Identifiers: LCCN 2016057652 | ISBN 9781138228016 (hardback : alk. paper) | ISBN 9781138228023 (pbk. : alk. paper) | ISBN 9781315393940 (ebook)
Subjects: LCSH: Mass media—Social aspects. | Mass media—Political aspects. | Social media—Political aspects. | Digital media—Political aspects.
Classification: LCC HM1206 .M38733 2017 | DDC 302.23—dc23
LC record available at https://lccn.loc.gov/2016057652

ISBN: 978-1-138-22801-6 (hbk)
ISBN: 978-1-138-22802-3 (pbk)
ISBN: 978-1-315-39394-0 (ebk)

Typeset in Sabon
by Integra Software Service Pvt. Ltd.

Contents

List of illustrations viii
List of contributors ix
Acknowledgments xiii
Foreword: What is media activism? xiv
W. LANCE BENNETT

Introduction 1
VICTOR PICKARD AND GUOBIN YANG

SECTION I
Communication for social change 7

Introduction: Conceptualizing media activism: Intent,
process, and action 8
SANDRA RISTOVSKA

1 The future of digital enfranchisement 10
  JEFF LANDALE AND SASCHA MEINRATH

2 Media in action: A field scan of media and youth organizing in
  the United States 28
  SASHA COSTANZA-CHOCK, CHRIS SCHWEIDLER, TERESA BASILIO, MEGHAN
  MCDERMOTT, AND PUCK LO

3 Studying media at the margins: Learning from the field 49
  CLEMENCIA RODRÍGUEZ

4   The online translation activism of bridge bloggers, feminists,
    and cyber-nationalists in China   62
    GUOBIN YANG

SECTION II
Policy interventions   77

Introduction   78
TIMOTHY LIBERT

5   The battle over diversity at the FCC   81
    MARK LLOYD

6   Feminist activism and US communications policy   100
    CAROLYN M. BYERLY

7   A return to prime-time activism: Social movement theory and
    the media   120
    DES FREEDMAN

SECTION III
New political genres   135

Introduction: New media dialectics   136
JONATHAN PACE

8   *Cahiers de doleance* 2.0: Crowd-sourced social justice blogs
    and the emergence of a rhetoric of collection in social media
    activism   139
    PAOLO GERBAUDO

9   Data activism as the new frontier of media activism   151
    STEFANIA MILAN

10 The use of the geoweb for social justice activism   164
    LESLIE REGAN SHADE, HARRISON SMITH, AND EVAN HAMILTON

SECTION IV
Feminism's digital wave   183

Introduction   184
ROSEMARY CLARK

11 Feminists, geeks, and geek feminists: Understanding gender and
    power in technological activism   187
    CHRISTINA DUNBAR-HESTER

12 Analog girl in a digital world: Hip hop feminism and media
    activism   205
    AISHA DURHAM

    Index   216

Illustrations

Figures

2.1	Organization media activities in which youth are engaged	34
2.2	What brought you to this work?	35
2.3	Stories youth want to tell media	36
2.4	Where organizations see the impact of the media they produce	38
2.5	Media increases youth engagement	40
2.6	The most important target audience	40
2.7	Organizations conduct media analysis	41
2.8	Make, distribute, and consume media across platforms	43
2.9	Top supports needed for media work to continue	43
3.1	Fetus cookies courtesy of activist bakers	53
5.1	US Gender 2010 Census	84
5.2	Full-power TV ownership by Gender 2014	85
5.3	US population by race/ethnicity 2014 Census	85
5.4	Full-power TV ownership by Hispanic Demo 2014 Census	85

Tables

6.1	Comparative broadcast ownership data	102
6.2	Gender representation on the boards of the largest diversified media companies in the US	103
6.3	Gender representation on the boards of technology companies	104
6.4	Female ownership by media format	112

Contributors

Teresa Basilio is a Brooklyn-based artist, activist, and educator originally from San Juan, Puerto Rico. She is former Co-Director at Global Action Project and her latest production, *Voces de Fillmore*, is a short documentary on the impact of gentrification on Puerto Rican families in Los Sures in Williamsburg, Brooklyn.

W. Lance Bennett is Professor of Political Science and Ruddick C. Lawrence Professor of Communication at the University of Washington, Seattle, US. His research focuses on how communication processes affect citizen engagement with politics. He is author of *Civic Life Online: Learning How Digital Media Can Engage Youth* (2008), and co-author of *The Logic of Connective Action: Digital Media and the Personalization of Contentious Politics* (2013).

Carolyn M. Byerly is Professor and Chair of the Department of Communication, Culture and Media Studies at Howard University. She takes a political-economy approach to her research on issues in mass media. She is the editor of the *Palgrave International Handbook of Women and Journalism* (2013), and the co-author of *Women and Media: A Critical Introduction* (2006).

Rosemary Clark is a doctoral candidate at the University of Pennsylvania's Annenberg School for Communication. Her research examines the dynamic relationship between feminist social movements and media in the United States, focusing specifically on popular media's appropriation of feminist rhetoric, digitally mediated feminist activism, and the do-it-yourself media tactics of grassroots feminist collectives.

Sasha Costanza-Chock is Associate Professor of Civic Media at MIT. She is a Faculty Associate at the Berkman-Klein Center for Internet & Society at Harvard University, and creator of the MIT Codesign Studio (codesign.mit.edu). She is the author of *Out of the Shadows, Into the Streets: Transmedia Organizing and the Immigrant Rights Movement* (2014).

Christina Dunbar-Hester is Assistant Professor at the Annenberg School for Communication and Journalism at the University of Southern California and an ethnographer who studies the intersection of technical practice and political engagement. She is the author of *Low Power to the People: Pirates, Protest, and Politics in FM Radio Activism* (2014).

Aisha Durham is an Associate Professor of Communication at the University of South Florida. Her research about black popular culture explores the relationship between media representations and everyday life. She is the author of *Home with Hip Hop Feminism: Performances in Communication and Culture* (2010).

Des Freedman is a Professor of Communications and Cultural Studies at Goldsmiths, University of London. He is the author of *The Politics of Media Policy* (2008) and *The Contradictions of Media Power* (2014), and co-author of *Misunderstanding the Internet* (2nd edition, 2016).

Paolo Gerbaudo is Lecturer in Digital Culture and Society at King's College London. His research focuses on social movements, social media, protest culture and youth. He is the author of *Tweets and the Streets: Social Media and Contemporary Activism* (2012), and of *The Mask and the Flag Populism, Citizenism and Global Protest* (2016).

Evan Hamilton is journalist and graduate of the Masters of Information program at the University of Toronto. His research explores how data driven journalism plays a role in community development, civic engagement and digital literacy, and critically examines journalists as advocates for government transparency and openness.

Jeff Landale is a researcher for X-Lab at Penn State University, where he writes on surveillance reform, telecommunications, and technology from a civil liberties perspective. Before joining X-Lab, Jeff researched telecommunications companies' human rights policies and practices at the international NGO Access Now, and supported victims of child abuse through various programs in Massachusetts.

Timothy Libert is a doctoral candidate at the Annenberg School for Communication at the University of Pennsylvania. His research focuses on privacy-compromising information flows on the web, and he is the author of the open source software platform webXray.

Mark Lloyd is Professor of Professional Practice of Communication at the USC-Annenberg School. Lloyd has been an associate general counsel at the FCC, a visiting scholar at MIT, the General Counsel of the Benton Foundation, an attorney at the DC law firm Dow, Lohnes & Albertson and an Emmy Award-winning broadcast journalist. He is the author of *Prologue to a Farce: Communication and Democracy in America* (2007).

Puck Lo is a filmmaker, non-fiction writer, and researcher currently based at Stanford University. She has worked with social movement groups since 2001 to make media for radical political change.

Meghan McDermott is senior lead for Mozilla Education, at the Mozilla Foundation, where she directs city-based peer learning networks and grantmaking for digital equity. Prior to this role, she was the executive director of Global Action Project (2003–2013) and a researcher with the EDC Center for Children & Technology. She earned her masters at the Harvard Graduate School of Education. She is an avid, rabid fan girl for RAD.

Sascha Meinrath is the Palmer Chair in Telecommunications at Penn State University and director of X-Lab. He is a renowned technology policy expert and is internationally recognized for his work over the past two decades. Meinrath's research focuses on distributed communications, Digital Feudalism, Digital Craftsmanship, telecommunications and spectrum policy, cybersecurity and privacy, and disruptive technology.

Stefania Milan is Assistant Professor of new media and digital culture at the University of Amsterdam, the Netherlands, and the Principal Investigator of the DATACTIVE project. She is the author of *Social Movements and Their Technologies: Wiring Social Change* (2013), and the co-author of *Media/Society* (2011).

Jonathan Pace is a PhD candidate in the Annenberg School for Communication at the University of Pennsylvania, where he writes on digital media, political economy, and critical theory. His work centers on the electronic exchange of commodities and the role of new media in contemporary capitalism.

Leslie Regan Shade is Associate Dean, Research, and Professor of Information at the University of Toronto. Her research focuses on the social, policy, and ethical aspects of information and communication technologies (ICTs), with particular concerns toward issues of gender, youth, and political economy.

Sandra Ristovska is a documentary filmmaker and a George Gerbner Post-doctoral Fellow at the Annenberg School for Communication, University of Pennsylvania. In addition, she is a Visiting Fellow at the Information Society Project and Advisor for the Visual Law Project at the Yale Law School. Her work examines issues of visual evidence, human rights, and global media activism.

Clemencia Rodríguez is Professor in the Department of Media Studies and Production at Temple University. Her research explores how people living in the shadow of armed conflict use media to shield their communities from armed violence's negative impacts. She is the author of *Fissures in the Mediascape: An International Study of Citizens' Media* (2001), and *Citizens' Media Against Armed Conflict: Disrupting Violence in Colombia* (2011).

Chris Schweidler is co-founder of Research Action Design, a worker-owned cooperative that partners with grassroots organizations on research, tech, and media. Chris has spent more than a decade supporting rigorous community-led research and popular communication as a part of social justice advocacy and movement building.

Harrison Smith holds a PhD from the University of Toronto's Faculty of Information. His research focuses on the political economies of geospatial media, surveillance, and mobile digital culture. His thesis explores the economic and cultural implications of location data to inform new methods of audience targeting and clustering for mobile and location-based marketing.

Acknowledgments

This book is the product of a great team project. We thank our inimitable colleague Barbie Zelizer for inviting us to organize one of the annual symposia in her Scholars Program in Culture and Communication. The symposium took place on December 5, 2014 with the support of Dean Michael Delli Carpini and the unparalleled staff at the Annenberg School for Communication, as well as the support of our students and colleagues. As coordinator of the Scholars Program, Emily Plowman ran the show with grace, dedication, and exquisite skills in every administrative detail. Several of the stellar doctoral students at the Annenberg School—Rosemary Clark, Tim Libert, Jonathan Pace, and Sandra Ristovska—provided indispensable help in organizing and running the symposium. They moderated panels and each wrote an introduction to one section of this volume. David Berman, who was later joined by John Remensperger, played an essential role in communicating with our contributors. David also prepared and formatted the volume for production with great care, and we could not have finished the book without his tremendous help. Sanjay Jolly gave the entire book a close read and provided invaluable assistance with final editing details. Jamie Askew, our editorial contact at Routledge, sent us numerous gentle reminders, nudging us to complete the final submission. Needless to say, we are grateful to all the authors for contributing to the volume and for their diligence in helping us to meet the deadlines. We also want to thank the anonymous reviewers of the manuscript for providing valuable feedback. Last but not least, we thank Lance Bennett for delivering a keynote speech at our symposium and kindly writing a preface to this volume. We alone, of course, are responsible for any errors that might remain.

Foreword
What is media activism?
W. Lance Bennett

Judging by the diverse and interesting ideas in this book, the field of media activism has become vibrant and timely. As with any rapidly emerging field, it makes sense to think about its boundaries, its core precepts, and areas in which more work would be welcome. First and most obviously, media activism suggests a focus on how activists use media and communication strategies to advance various causes (including media access and media rights policies). Communication media of various kinds have long been essential for helping activists coordinate among themselves and reach broader publics. The ubiquity and networking capacity of digital media have, in many ways, changed the political game. At least since the pioneering *indymedia* collective came of age during the WTO protests in Seattle at the end of the last century, activists have embodied the call to "be the media." This does not mean that the many different kinds of politics discussed in this volume are free of the shadow of legacy media, with the select crew of social and political actors who are granted voices in it. Nor do sophisticated uses of activist media necessarily guarantee successful outcomes. History tells us that political struggles against more powerful forces in society require endless vigilance and commitment on the part of many people, often over generations.

While media platforms and access to them do not represent a magic bullet for activists, the range of political work enhanced by insurgent media is' impressive. From creating public spaces for exploring gender identity to protesting corporate rule on a global level, activists have made their presences known, and developed their places in society and popular consciousness. Even though the transparent nature of much of the media in these spaces opens activists up to surveillance and repression, the legacy of many movements suggests that large distributed networks are hard to shut down. Given the range and "spreadability" of digital content, the struggles of local activists may attract large and geographically dispersed audiences to bear witness and join in solidarity.

In addition to studying how activists for different causes use media, and with what effects, the field of media activism also looks at the broad set of policy questions surrounding access, privacy, security, and the development and ownership of all forms of media. As those involved with the media reform movement have said so often, whatever one's first cause may be, fighting for public media access should be a companion concern. This said, the media reform movement has also experienced various tensions, such as different priorities regarding a local as opposed to a national focus and questions about race, gender, and movement agendas. Thus, the common concern for media access does not automatically resolve the factional struggles that run through most movements.

The internal conflicts found in any form of activism also exist in realms of media activism. In addition, many activists are skeptical about the role of media strategies. My own studies of the Occupy Wall Street protests from a few years back showed that for many core activists, the experience of direct, deliberative democracy was paramount, and the social media barrage surrounding their protests was, at best, a way of making their presence felt, and, at worst, a noisy distraction that made it difficult to distinguish the truly committed from the casual spectator.

This brings me to another question about the field. There seems to be a persistent split between those old-school activists who learned that proper movements have strong leadership, formal organization, resource streams, and collective identity, while many other media activists see communication technologies as organizational resources that enable new models of movements that are less bureaucratic, require fewer resources, and rely less on central leaders. The field can benefit from exploring these differences, and showing how different models of movements arise, how they interact, and which ones may work best in particular contexts.

I think it is fair to say that many scholars who study activism are activists themselves—or adopt supportive stances toward the causes they study. This does not mean a loss of critical perspective. To the contrary, most scholar–activists seek to understand how things work and what happens when they don't. It may be useful for the development of the field, however, to add more explicit normative frameworks: principles of democratic activism, evaluation standards for various media strategies, and ways of talking about outcomes that enable comparisons across different sectors. These standards will help a field that is deeply concerned about values be more explicit about what those values are, and how to raise them to analytical frameworks.

Another question for this emerging field is what to make of the activism of less progressive stripes than the ones studied in this volume. Studying the media practices of neo-Nazis, racists, or climate deniers, among other groups, may be less appealing than examining social justice activism. As my own work has also neglected these topics, I point no fingers here. However, it seems imperative that we look at activists who oppose progressive causes, and understand how they view their own media activism. As I write these words, I am following the most baffling presidential campaign of my lifetime. Donald Trump has shunned conventional models of political organization in favor of activating a multimedia network through which flows a steady stream of "alternative facts" and the ambiguous promise to "Make America Great Again." Whether by some far-(alt-)right plan, or the self-styled "truthful hyperbole" of the candidate in chief, the result has been a daily challenge to the reality of evidence and journalism. It was a campaign that so profoundly attacked the integrity of the nation's most important democratic ritual that much of that ritual was exposed as a fragile symbolic narrative depending on faithful reenactment by those who live inside it every four years. Trump elected to burn down the house. But he could not have disrupted the symbolic core ritual of the national civil religion so thoroughly without an uncanny set of media practices.

Trump is an interesting case of media activism—both because he engaged the legacy media in ways no candidate ever has, and at the same time condemned the bias of a lying press that formed a conspiracy with Hillary Clinton to steal the election. His middle-of-the-night Twitter storms typically made, and often dominated, the next news cycle. In the process, he exposed the taste of legacy journalism organizations for tawdry spectacle, even as they often made efforts to condemn it. Does the field of media activism have a place for Trump? Does it look at the workings of *Breitbart*, and the likes of its chief operative, Steve Bannon, who became the CEO of Trump's campaign? Indeed media activism would also seem to include the long history of operations like Breitbart–Bannon–Trump. Witness the story of Citizens United, or the law–media–politics complex (i.e. "the vast right wing conspiracy") that has scandalized the Clintons since the 1990s, and smeared Barack Obama throughout his term. These have all been notable successes on the right. Indeed, *Citizens United* was able to turn a tawdry film about Hillary Clinton into a democracy-shaking legal ruling, with a little help from the Supremes. It may be that while looking at how the progressive left uses media activism to promote social justice and democratic values, we are missing the big story of how media activism on the right is debasing the larger democratic public sphere.

The point here is that media activism is a broad field that would prosper with the expansion of its research scope, and by developing more explicit theoretical and normative frameworks. This will enable a growing field to look beyond case studies of particular struggles and locate them in the broader context of the media and democratic life. Perhaps we can develop—or make more explicit—a shared story about the importance of media in helping citizens understand the value of living in more open, egalitarian societies, and how various media and communication strategies may advance or undermine that goal.

Introduction

Victor Pickard and Guobin Yang

How do we make sense of the theories, histories, politics, ideologies, tactics, and aesthetics underlying various types of media activism? The growing subfield of media activism studies has gained wide attention in recent years, but little consensus exists regarding its central questions and concerns. Discussion often focuses on large events or processes related to mobilization. This edited collection takes a more expansive view to explore varieties of activism mediated through communication technologies, activists' strategies for changing the structures of media systems, and government efforts to regulate or police media activism. From memes to zines, hacktivism to artivism, this book considers activist practices involving both older kinds of media and newer digital, social, and network-based forms. The book provides case studies of activists using media to make political interventions in different historical periods and at local, national, and global levels.

The book is divided into four thematic sections: communication for social change, policy interventions, feminism's digital wave, and new political genres. Under the first theme, several of the contributors look at how communication technologies are or should be marshaled to effect social change. Sascha Meinrath and Jeff Landale draw attention to the various entrenchments of digital disenfranchisement and strategies for overcoming them. Their analysis shows that we should be particularly concerned about new feudalistic relationships between users and a handful of tech companies. Drawing from a rich corpus of data generated by mixed research methods, Sasha Costanza-Chock and members of his research group show how LGBTQ and Two-Spirit activists produce vibrant cultural and media work across diverse technological platforms. These activists "tell their own intersectional stories" while successfully changing the broader culture. Clemencia Rodríguez proposes that we focus on grassroots activists who produce "media at the margins." This shift in focus, she suggests, gives us purchase on the complexity of media ecologies and activists' deployment of media technologies in everyday life. Guobin Yang's study of online translation activism in China draws attention to a different type of "media at the margins"—the uses of translation by activists and online communities in their struggles for information transparency, recognition, and the performance of collective identities. The chapter highlights the importance of language and translingual practices in transnational online activism.

Another set of contributors focus on policy-related activist interventions aimed at changing the media system at the structural level. Their work considers the tactics, structures, and normative foundations necessary for creating media that are accessible to all, provide a forum for diverse views and voices, and scrutinize and contest concentrated power. These scholars analyze the politics of media policy with an eye toward changing it. For example, Mark Lloyd historicizes the decades-long struggles around the Federal Communications Commission to create a more diverse media system, underscoring the structural barriers that such activist campaigns continue to face. Carolyn Byerly writes about feminist media interventions at the policy level, particularly around media ownership. Drawing from historical cases, she provides a compelling account of the unique challenges that women face in confronting barriers to policy changes, and she suggests strategies for mobilizing feminist engagement with media policy. Similarly, Des Freedman asks us to consider the vital social movement work around policy engagement, and how grappling with these larger power structures is a necessary endeavor for any activist project.

Under a third theme of "feminism's digital wave," chapters by Aisha Durham and Christina Dunbar-Hester bring to light yet another important question in the study of media activism—its gendered and racialized dimensions. Through her studies of FM radio activism and diversity advocacy in free and open source software (F/OSS) and hacker spaces, Dunbar-Hester shows that technology is a site of gender production and maintenance. Durham maps the emergence of hip hop cyber feminism through a case study of the 1997 Philadelphia Million Woman March. These two chapters suggest that studies of media activism should not focus narrowly on either media or activism per se, but should analyze instances of media activism in broader social and cultural contexts. Both chapters show clearly that scholars might also examine whether and how media activism might be constitutive of new collective identities and agencies.

The fourth theme concerns what we refer to as new political genres. By this, we mean forms of activism associated with the use of new communication technologies. Our use of this concept is inspired by Lievrouw's work on alternative and activist new media, where she writes that "Genres have both *form* and *purpose*: that is, they have typical material features or follow certain format conventions, and they allow people to express themselves appropriately, and to achieve their various purposes or intentions, in a given situation."[1] While Lievrouw studies five genres—culture jamming, alternative computing, participatory journalism, mediated mobilization, and commons knowledge—several authors in this volume cast light on newer genres. In his chapter on crowdsourced blogs, Paolo Gerbaudo approaches this form of social media activism as a new political genre. Based on an analysis of the Wall Street Tumblr blog "We are the 99%" and the "No Nos Vamos, Nos Echan" ("We Don't Go, They Send Us Out") blog in Spain, Gerbaudo argues that crowdsourced blogs break with the network logic of communication and testify to the rise of a new communicative logic which he calls the "rhetoric of collection."

The chapters by Stefania Milan and Leslie Regan Shade, Harrison Smith, and Evan Hamilton present additional new political genres of media activism. For Milan, data activism interrogates the politics of big data by examining, manipulating, leveraging, exploiting, resisting or meddling with the creation and use of data. Data activists recognize that the collection and uses of big data are not neutral but carry socio-political agendas. Through an examination of several cases of social justice activism using geospatial media such as participatory mapping or crowdsourced information, Shade, Smith, and Hamilton's chapter provides insights into the new frontiers of activism and a critical assessment of the challenges inherent in these new political forms, especially issues of privacy, surveillance, and inclusion. In addition, these two chapters raise the crucial question of media activism surveillance. Activists have always faced risks of state policing, but in the age of digital media, surveillance has become an increasingly vital new dimension of policing. Sociologist Patrick Gillham and his colleagues find that compared with earlier periods, the policing of protest during the Occupy Wall Street movement emphasized the control of public spaces, high-tech surveillance, the management of information and intelligence about activists, and the shaping of information available to the public.[2] These new features signal the emergence of a new mode of protest policing, which centers on the use of surveillance and intelligence to manage risks and preempt potentially illegal activities. This suggests that research on media activism should also pay more attention to the role of surveillance in shaping media activism.

There are a number of questions and quandaries that the emergent subfield of media activism studies might address. First, there is a definitional question: how do we define media activism when so much activism is increasingly mediated? Is this kind of activism a meaningful distinction? Perfect typologies are elusive and typically fall apart under scrutiny, suggesting that perhaps we should leave it undefined. Second, as with all forms of communication research, we need to further internationalize and historicize media activism. Internationalize in terms of providing not just global case studies, but also comparative research that can cast into relief strengths and weaknesses, tensions and contradictions, and other salient features of different activist models. Historicize by not just providing historical case studies, but also by tracing out lineages, continuities, and disjunctures over time within particular activist models, theories, and practices. For example, we need more work on the connections between the global justice movement of the late 1990s and early 2000s and the more recent Occupy Wall Street movement.[3] Erasures of race, class, and gender hierarchies associated with "structurelessness," which often emerges in horizontalist forms of activism, affected both movements.[4]

Third, are there distinct theories of media activism? Social movement theories seem ready-made for media activism studies, but are they sufficient? We might follow John Downing's advice for a political economy of social movements and media activism, one that looks for power inequities not just within the activist projects themselves, but also expands our notion of social movements to include the everyday struggles that are not always visible.[5] We might also heed sociologist Andrew Walder's call to go beyond the study of mobilization processes and pay more attention to the influence of ideologies, political culture, and social structural conditions in media activism.[6] Just as activists benefit from a diversity of tactics, media activist scholars benefit from a diversity of theories and methodologies.

Fourth, to develop theories of media activism, a first step might be to write histories of media activism—not necessarily general histories, but histories of specific genres of media activism or of media activism in specific historical periods or countries. For example, how much do we know about activism associated with the use of bulletin board systems (BBS) in the USA or in China? What might a history of hashtag activism look like? How about histories of global media activism in the 1960s, when an alternative activist press flourished in many countries where student radicalism and anti-colonial struggles were at their peak? Fortunately, we do not have to start from scratch. Important works already exist on some earlier periods, such as Robert Darnton's study of the underground publications of the French Revolution[7] and Todd Gitlin's analysis of television and student activism in the 1960s.[8]

And finally, this brings us to the role of the activist scholar. Scholars are often drawn to the aesthetics of media activism and the creative uses of new digital technologies. But is it enough to simply describe media activism? Should we also be contributing to media activist projects that advocate for social justice? Many scholars in this subfield think we should, especially among the contributors to this book. But while activist scholarship has obvious virtues, it also brings with it obvious tensions that must be negotiated through radical reflexivity.

The following essays by leading scholars and activists help shed light on these and many other questions. The fact that this collection does not arrive at any clear answers is a healthy sign. The subfield of media activism studies is still cohering. It is in flux, which makes it vibrant and interesting. Hopefully we can maintain that dynamism going forward.

Notes

1 Leah Lievrouw, *Alternative and Activist New Media* (London: Polity, 2011), 20.
2 Patrick F. Gillham, Bob Edwards and John A. Noakes, "Strategic Incapacitation and the Policing of Occupy Wall Street Protests in New York City, 2011," *Policing & Society* 23, no. 1 (2012): 81–102.

3 Victor Pickard, "Assessing the Radical Democracy of Indymedia: Discursive, Technical and Institutional Constructions," *Critical Studies in Media Communication* 23, no. 1 (2006): 19–38; Todd Wolfson, *Digital Rebellion: The Birth of the Cyber Left* (Urbana: University of Illinois Press, 2014).
4 Jo Freeman, "The Tyranny of Structurelessness," *Berkeley Journal of Sociology* 17, (1972): 151–164.
5 John Downing, "Towards a Political Economy of Social Movement Media," *Democratic Communiqué* 26, no. 1 (2013): 17–28.
6 Andrew Walder, "Political Sociology and Social Movements," *Annual Review of Sociology* 35, (2009): 393–412.
7 Robert Darnton, *The Forbidden Best-Sellers of Pre-Revolutionary France* (New York: WW Norton, 1995).
8 Todd Gitlin. *The Whole World Is Watching* (Berkeley: University of California Press, 1980).

Section 1

Communication for social change

Introduction
Conceptualizing media activism: Intent, process, and action

Sandra Ristovska

Communication practices weave the social fabric of daily life. They are, therefore, at the heart of social change processes. In this sense, Jesús Martín-Barbero sought to orient the debate in communication studies away from the dominant focus on media to mediations, which, in his view, is a conceptual framework better suited to capture "the articulations between communication practices and social movements and the articulations of different tempos of development with the plurality of cultural matrices."[1] Following him, I argue that mediation is a useful concept for thinking about unfolding manifestations of media activism because it provides a theoretical lens that insists on the cultural, social, political and historical specificities of the contexts in which communication processes create meaning and generate possibilities for social change.

A focus on mediation also sheds light on how a healthy body politic is constituted not only by people who subscribe to democracy by virtue of their direct participation in the system, usually expressed through voting or social protest, but also by communities who endorse democratic values as a sensibility and experience even in the seemingly mundane, day-to-day communicative practices.[2] Mediation, therefore, accommodates broader thinking about media activism—and its constituent parts—in its broader spectrum as an intent, process, and action. Tackling mediated forms of activism through this tripartite notion captures the varied impulses that drive social change: the interplay between action and acting, horizontal and vertical dynamics, transformative and transactional outcomes, the interchanges between centers and margins, urban and rural communities, as well as the underpinnings of local and global forces.

Each of the authors in this section embraces the complexities of activist instantiations and the multiple social change mechanisms through which communities, often excluded from mainstream dialogue, claim cultural and political agency. Thinking about activism as an intent and process undergirds Clemencia Rodríguez's as well as Sasha Costanza-Chock, Chris Schweidler, Teresa Basilio, Meghan McDermott, and Puck Lo's essays. They highlight both the plurality of media-making at the margins and the uses of media as determined by the lived experiences and needs on the ground. Whether it is baking cookies to counter controlling narratives about women's bodies and reproductive rights in Norman, Oklahoma, or the media-making practices of LGBTQ and Two-Spirit organizations in the U.S., fighting against discrimination across multiple and intersectional axes of identity, media activism surfaces both as an intent and as a gradual, rhizomatic, and transformative process. Guobin Yang's chapter broadens our understanding of the spectrum of communicative practices as social change processes by studying online translation activism in China as a doubly mediated political form. It shows how online communities of translation, facilitated by new network technologies, are mobilized for politicizing information and performing identities. Jeff Landale and Sascha Meinrath, on the other hand, shift gears to thinking about activism as action. By reframing the debate on the digital divide away from mere access and connectivity to the capacity for active participation and empowerment, they see digital enfranchisement through a call for political action measured by policy outcomes that can better protect the values of participatory democracy and freedom of expression.

What these four essays show is how mediated forms of activism in their various permutations have become an important vehicle for seeking participation in public culture, claiming agency, and shaping democratic processes. Furthermore, the authors in this section demonstrate a theoretical and methodological commitment that moves away from popular technological, political, commercial, or ahistorical determinations when discussing media activism in order to capture the complexities and richness of communication processes for social change. Together, then, they contribute to a broader debate about how we can conceptualize the nuances and specificities of media activism studies.

Notes

1 Jesús Martín-Barbero, *Communication, Culture and Hegemony: From the Media to Mediations* (London & Newbury Park: Sage, 1993).
2 Chantal Mouffe, *Dimensions of Radical Democracy: Pluralism, Citizenship, Community* (London: Verso, 1992).

Chapter 1

The future of digital enfranchisement

Jeff Landale and Sascha Meinrath

Traditional notions of the digital divide and how to bridge this persistent gulf are increasingly antiquated and out of touch with a series of even more nefarious practices that are generating myriad new areas of discrimination and marginalization.[1] Civil society's failure to update normative goals and minimal requirements for digital equality are creating dangerous new avenues for undermining social and economic justice on a global scale.[2] Today, meaningful civic participation and participatory democracy increasingly require access to virtual realms where members engage with information, rather than passively receiving it.[3] And at the same time, for all our broadband-connectivity self-congratulations, the majority of the world's population (especially in rural, poor, and traditionally underdeveloped regions) continues to be excluded from digital resources.[4] As we will show, even the so-called "solutions" to these very real problems may end up locking billions of people into new feudalistic relationships that, for the first time, span both their in vivo and virtual lives—with the very acts of storytelling and the fundamentals of imagination being colonized by new, discriminatory platforms. Our aim is to shed light on the growing importance of *meaningfully* bridging the digital divide. We put forward a positive conceptualization for how to do this—digital enfranchisement—while also underscoring how the impacts of information and communication technologies (ICTs) on participatory democracy must embrace the complex interplay of limited thinking spanning technological, political, economic, and civil society domains. While these same technologies can frequently be harnessed to strengthen social movements, "we should not adapt compliantly to whatever technologies happen along, but commit ourselves to supporting technologies that are 'compatible' with citizenship and democracy."[5]

The digital divide is currently conceptualized as a lack of meaningful access to online networks, with a concomitant solution of providing connectivity (and occasionally, digital literacy skills).[6] However, this digital divide framework recognizes only one core facet of an increasingly complex ecosystem predicated on commercializing personal information,[7] creating vendor lock-in,[8] and otherwise removing agency from end-users.[9] To address the creation of these new digital divides, we need to expand our conceptualization of the problem in two key ways: first, we need to address the super-linear detriments that accrue to the underserved and disconnected as the migration of civic discourse and the public sphere writ large becomes an expected norm;[10] and, second, we must prevent seemingly easy, marginal "solutions," from becoming the goal of governmental, civil society, corporate, and philanthropic initiatives. If left unchecked, those programs create even more insidious digital divides that fundamentally undermine the civic and economic benefits of connectivity and access to digital resources.[11]

The costs of exclusion from digital networks are increasing dramatically for the shrinking percentage of the global populace not meaningfully online—this is the dark side of Metcalfe's Law,[12] which states that just as the value of a network increases supralinearly, the costs of network exclusion accrue to those unconnected in even greater supralinearity.[13] New plans to bridge the divide require a framework that encompasses both the online/offline dichotomy, which still dominates current debate, as well as an acknowledgment and addressing of the problems of different and inherently unequal forms of connectivity (a digital "separate but equal" problem that new forms of prioritization, surveillance, and commercialization are driving). Within this context, meaningfully bridging the digital divide requires a solution that provides both connectivity and the tools and resources for latecomers to meaningfully organize, self-govern, and attain truly equitable access.

While we call out several deficiencies in current efforts to bridge the digital divide through limited "walled-garden" forms of connectivity, this is certainly a non-exhaustive list of shortcomings.[14] Not all connectivity is created equal[15] and our goal is to expand the criteria by which we judge efforts to address digital divides and meaningful connectivity, writ large.

1. History of the digital divide and digital inclusion

The divide between those with access to ICTs and Internet connectivity and those without is a decades-old concern for both the developed and developing worlds.[16] The digital divide has received attention from state agencies, international agencies, NGOs, and academics, as well as popular and specialized press outlets. A full overview of the previous literature is beyond the scope of this article, but we provide a brief review of several sources that originated or transformed the idea of the digital divide.

Originally, the digital divide focused on the geographic and demographic topology separating those who were online from those who were not. This gap has been analyzed under the demographic rubrics of age, race, and class, and the geographic rubrics of country and the urban/rural divide. Research has shown a digital divide between the young and the old,[17] the rich and the poor,[18] racial minorities and majorities,[19] developed countries and formerly colonized and underdeveloped countries,[20] as well as urban areas and the countryside.[21] Policy makers have attempted to bridge each divide with a range of strategies: developed countries like the United States offer funds and incentives to private corporations to extend broadband networks in order to bridge the urban/rural divide, such as the Federal Communications Commission's (FCC) Universal Service Fund,[22] while underdeveloped countries have achieved huge increases in connectivity through mobile connections.[23]

The impact of the digital divide was and continues to be measured across two main domains, economic and civic. As developed countries transition to post-industrial "knowledge economies," and developing economies jostle to be integrated into global production and distribution networks, economic security and prosperity have become increasingly predicated on access to, and knowledge of, digital communications networks.[24] In the United States, the economic digital divide concerns the detrimental impacts of a workforce untrained in ICT. This mindset is exemplified by the National Telecommunications and Information Administration's (NTIA) 1999 report, "Falling Through the Net: Defining the Digital Divide," which states "Information tools, such as the personal computer and the Internet, are increasingly critical to economic success and personal advancement."[25] However, the surge in NTIA's interest quickly waned, with the original Technology Opportunity Program being shut down just one decade after it began.[26] The reverberating detrimental impacts of these far-too-short-term government programs affected community programs in every state. The Computer Technology Center Network (CTCnet) grew out of this same focus, increasing in size to over 1000 CTCs at its height, before disbanding in the mid-2000s due to dramatic cuts in government support for community technology and digital literacy training.[27] Sadly, this exact same process is currently playing out following the introduction of the Broadband Technology Opportunities Program (BTOP) in 2010 (and the subsequent elimination of additional BTOP support only 4 years later). Despite public support, powerful telecom corporate interests have often ignored incentives and multi-million dollar government subsidies to assist in closing the digital divide, preferring to pursue higher profit margins in cities and other well-serviced areas.[28] NTIA's 1999 report also focuses on the digital divide as an issue of connectivity alone, something NTIA corrected in its 2010 BTOP funding priorities, defining the digital divide as "the divide between those with access to new technologies and those without."[29]

In addition to economic and labor concerns, the digital divide also always had substantial political implications—something that policy makers, media scholars, and advocates have had to grapple with at local, state, and national levels. Network penetration rates have increased globally across all demographics, yet the rate of increase has varied, often along the same lines as the digital divide. As cyberpunk author and "cyberspace" coiner William Gibson presciently observed, "The future is already here—it's just not very evenly distributed."[30] In many cases, the implementation of broadband access (and concomitant digital resources) has led to the development of even wider gaps between constituencies with connectivity, and those without. As network penetration rates increase and access to them is seen as the norm, the basic goods, services, and information required for an informed, economically successful, and active citizenry are rapidly migrating online.[31] These goods, services, and information, and participatory access are becoming harder for those left behind, and this is transforming what was "just" inequality into a crisis of exclusion from civic and economic society.

Rahul Tongia and Ernest Wilson explain this phenomenon and its effects in their paper "The Flip Side of Metcalfe's Law."[32] Metcalfe's Law states that "as more people join a network, they add to the value of the network non-linearly." The "flip side", or dark side in their original formulation, of Metcalfe's Law states that, "It's precisely when only a minority of the population is not in the network that the costs of exclusion rise dramatically."[33] As a higher percentage of people get online and receive the (supra-linear) benefits that the Network Effect provides, the gulf between these same online and offline constituencies will expand exponentially. As Tongia and Wilson summarize, "The costs of network exclusion are not trivial in modern society, and grow higher as more essential services for citizenship, economic transactions and quality of life migrate from the traditional world of 'atoms and molecules' to the online universe."[34] Thus, our own successes in lessening certain facets of the digital divide are causing even more harm to those on the wrong side of the growing gulf in access to digital resources than existed even ten years ago. "Once a network includes the majority of the population, the *disadvantage* is held only by a few."[35]

According to the International Telecommunications Union's statistics, the developed world has passed a key tipping point, with the majority of the population online, and the developing world is on its way there.[36] With the costs of exclusion rapidly increasing, it is more imperative than ever to *universally* bridge the digital divide. The increasing costs associated with exclusion from digital communications networks has put pressure on government and development agencies to improve access—but also to play fast and loose with reports that are increasingly painting overly rosy pictures of the true state of connectivity in order to appear to be solving this persistent problem. An early indication of the fudged figures that agencies responsible for ensuring expanded access would put out can be seen in the FCC's statistics on broadband access in the United States, which misleadingly claim that "290 million Americans—95 percent of the US population—live in housing units with access to terrestrial, fixed broadband infrastructure capable of supporting actual download speeds of at least 4Mbps."[37] The catch is that "access" is officially defined to mean that if a single house in a census tract has access to advertised speeds of over 4Mbps, then all houses in that census tract are considered to have broadband connectivity—a massive overstatement of real connectivity, to say the least. Even the FCC's 2014 report on official broadband speeds showed that more than half of Americans receive more than their advertised broadband speeds (and that 95 percent of Americans get more than their advertised speeds for Cable and Fiber—something that numerous independent analyses have systematically found to not be the case).[38]

Questions about what precisely constitutes "access" have troubled analysts for decades. A 2003 article on the digital divide and community informatics outlined the complexity in concretely defining "access," stating that:

> the nature of that "access" is not without ambiguity, whether for example, the concern is for simple "access" as, through multiple user environments such as telecenters, or whether there is a concern to provide in-home "personal" access; and, what about the quantity, quality and format of that access—Broadband, WiFi, dial-up, bandwidth—which "access" is sufficient to "bridge the DD" [digital divide] and how or when do we know this?[39]

Despite these long standing concerns, it is only recently that questions about what constitutes access have expanded beyond official (quantitative) methodologies that were created to overstate "success," to include conceptualization about fundamentally changing the *qualitative* measures of access to connectivity. Most measures of the digital divide have taken for granted that all network access is created equal for all users—ignoring most factors beyond network speed and (occasionally) pricing. With the exception of the coverage of heavy-handed Internet censorship in certain hot spot countries, few questions were raised about what content, services, applications, and user experiences clients actually had.[40]

Traditional views toward the digital divide and its solutions need to be challenged in light of content-limited *walled-garden connectivity*, such as Facebook's Internet.org application.[41] Facebook's program aims to provide free mobile connectivity to users—but this connectivity is heavily restricted to a list of pre-approved websites which are then described as "basic internet services." While technically "connectivity" in the narrowest sense, this program significantly limits the utility of Internet access and transforms the Internet from a participatory, open-ended medium to one more geared to being a conduit of curated information that is consumed by users who are also placed under totalizing surveillance in the form of Facebook's "identity infrastructure." In essence, there's no privacy within Facebook's walled garden—this system is, without a doubt, exactly what authoritarian regimes around the globe would love to see in their own back yards.

While two of the three pillars of the Internet.org program are laudible—"making internet access affordable by making it more efficient to deliver data" and "using less data by improving the efficiency of the apps and experiences we use"—the third platform muddies the waters and undermines these benefits: "helping businesses drive internet access by developing a new model to get people online."[42] Internet.org's new model is actually an old one: fundamentally, it is a form of price-discrimination wherein customers are not charged for data-usage on predefined applications. This is not only a clear violation of the FCC's recent Open Internet rules,[43] but also one that threatens Internet freedom in regions where this model is implemented by requiring network monitoring and shaping tools to be in place, and discouraging or outright banning encryption and anonymizing software—doubly disadvantaging the world's poor while laying claim that this is some sort of "solution."[44]

As Facebook CEO Mark Zuckerberg wrote, "this is good for people because they'll have an affordable way and a reason to connect to the internet and join the global knowledge economy."[45] However, zero-rated plans like Internet.org offer a second-class form of Internet connectivity, where content not approved by Facebook is off-limits, and where no one has the ability to reshape or innovate on the network-architecture layers of this system in any meaningful way. In fact, due to the severe limits placed upon users by the Internet.org application, many of the qualities assumed to be intrinsic to the Internet, such as an expanded possibility for technological innovation, civic participation, and general Internet craftsmanship, are squelched.[46] Worse, programs like Internet.org allow governments, international agencies, non-governmental organizations (NGOs), and the philanthropic arms of corporations to claim that the digital divide has been addressed—even if this means officially redefining the digital divide and its solutions in ways that erase many of the crucial social, economic, and civic advantages of Internet access in the first place.

While Facebook's program is currently in the media spotlight, programs like Internet.org are rapidly expanding all around the globe, introducing new qualitative complexities into the traditional digital divide debate. What used to be a simple, dichotomous variable (you either had connectivity or you did not), has grown in recent years to encompass questions of speed, reliability, and latency, and is now rapidly transforming into a multi-dimensional array of qualitative assessments about the *kind* of connectivity available and where the locus of control over use and online innovation resides.

Unsurprisingly, this degraded form of access is proposed as the solution for bringing "the next billion"—who were unable to afford, or who were not even offered—full connectivity. Whereas a true altruistic endeavor might seek to provide baseline connectivity to all (for example, baseline connectivity with no use restrictions at all), these endeavors are really about how to create new extractive business models, such as monetizing the privacy and personal data of the world's poor. In announcing Facebook's initiative, Zuckerberg admitted as much, stating that a new business model was required because "it may not actually be profitable for us to serve the next few billion people for a very long time, if ever."[47] Thus, the underlying drive is really to find new ways to maintain, rather than eliminate, telcos' profit margins, as Zuckerberg readily admits, "[e]ven though projections show most people may soon have smartphones, the majority of them still won't have data access. This is because [...] the cost of a data plan is vastly more expensive than the price of a smartphone."[48] The commonality is that most walled-garden "solutions" are often explicitly geared toward the *economic* aspects of Internet access—bringing people into the "knowledge economy"[49]—rather than the civic, participatory, or liberatory aspects of connectivity.

Contemporary work on the digital divide needs to meaningfully address both shortcomings of the architected solutions. Whether Internet.org or One Laptop Per Child,[50] the failure to deploy empowering solutions has been systematically undermining efforts to bring digital resources to billions of people who are not currently meaningfully connected. Like efforts that tend to (sometimes literally) airdrop technology into communities with no useful support for training on use or maintenance, walled-garden access removes agency—eliminating the possibility of owning, changing, hacking, improving, revising, or self-governing communications networks and ICTs. As Michael Gurstein describes:

> While considerable development resources have been spent on creating ICT infrastructure and access points (e.g. local telecenters), few of these initiatives have been directed toward expanding local capacity for developing, managing and maintaining ICT capabilities.[51]

Degraded forms of connectivity, pushed by corporate and state interests, are guaranteed to *exacerbate*, and not address, the digital divide. As Gurstein underscored, the effective use of ICTs necessitates "[t]he capacity and opportunity to successfully integrate ICTs into the accomplishment of self or collaboratively identified goals."[52] This is not just about access to a resource, it's about the freedoms granted by that access.

Unequal forms of access cannot help but be discriminatory—they are a method for controlling their users as well as information. While in-depth contemporary research into the digital divide has focused on crucial discrepancies based on race, class, geography, and the urban/rural divide,[53] due to current digital divide efforts, we now need to ensure we address the mechanisms of how the operationalization of connectivity affects civic participation and political engagement, writ large. As Gurstein wrote in 2003, "Without attention being paid to these issues, 'access' ... is about being able to consume and receive rather than produce and distribute."[54]

Internet.org explicitly works toward generating more data—privately owned and for sale—about its users: "while operators know some information about their customers, the pre-paid model prevents them from knowing who their customers are. Giving people the ability to link their Facebook or other accounts with operators could help solve these problems."[55] If the next billion are brought online through walled gardens that limit user ability to access information on pre-approved, universally surveilled platforms, the democratic potential of the Internet will be weakened. These "solutions" forego a true public sphere in lieu of a one-way producer/consumer dynamic in which users consume information while producing the raw material (in the form of data generated by their online activities such as posts, likes, and so on) for companies like Facebook to profit from. As Anna Malina warned in 1999,

> the unequal gaps that already exist between rich and poor in civil society will widen dramatically if ICTs are designed primarily in support of information held as privately owned property for sale in a highly commercialized and competitive "electronic" public sphere.[56]

For civic media advocates and proponents of Internet freedom, zero-rated connectivity models that offer degraded forms of access represent a case where "ICTs used ostensibly for emancipatory purposes can also support structures that represent anti-democratic formations."[57] This is an unacceptable outcome, and one that need not occur.

2. Democratic implications: The need for holistic solutions, equitable access, and liberatory ICTs

Degraded forms of connectivity result from thinking that conceptualizes the digital divide as a technical problem, rather than a political–economic one. Too often, this mindset drives technical solutions—extended Wi-Fi coverage, build-out of fiber optic cables, and training for individuals on how to use ICTs—while glossing over the far more important relationships amongst technology, civil society, and the political and economic topology they're enmeshed in. Thus, these "solutions" tend to recreate a fractal of ever-repeating digital divides rather than fundamentally altering the underpinnings that caused these divides in the first place.

If, however, we understand the digital divide in the context of a politically fraught public sphere, we can illuminate the social, economic, and political barriers that are working to prevent a positive, participatory, democratic, and liberatory digital enfranchisement outcome. Rather than identifying a nebulous and changeable idea of "access" as the goal for an empowered citizenry, we need to outline criteria for communications technologies that empower users, amplify underrepresented voices, and enable meaningful engagement with and participation in online public spheres. This is our tentative definition of digital enfranchisement. The democratic implications of ICTs supporting digital enfranchisement rest on three core qualities:

(1) enabling users to transcend spatial diversity and temporal synchronization to engage in public discourse;
(2) lowering the costs of disseminating information and democratic deliberation to near-zero; and
(3) transforming media into a fundamentally dialogical, transactive, participatory, and liberatory process.

Democracy has always been limited by in vivo requirements that create spatial and temporal barriers that alienate and marginalize. Harkening back to the birth of modern democracy, political enfranchisement in ancient Greece was *de facto* limited to the free citizens who lived in the city-states, or those with the ability to make the sometimes days long journey from the countryside to take part in the deliberations in the agora.[58] Representative forms of democracy are also lauded and defended as being practical solutions to the problem of bringing together constituents to debate and decide on issues; yet, even today, the size of the US House of Representatives is limited by thinking how best to make decisions using the technologies and geospatial limits of the 1920s, with little regard for the detrimental impacts this thinking has on representative democracy.[59] ICTs have the potential to bypass these antiquated barriers, allowing constituents to participate in discussion, deliberation, and decision-making without the need to be in the same place at the same time, opening the public sphere to those who are geographically isolated or who are unable to devote specific fixed periods of time to civic engagement.

New media was preceded by old media and old media was preceded by the printed word, which was simply a medium for transmitting information, and was the raw material out of which a democratically engaged civil society, albeit a limited one, was formed. While the printing press has facilitated a wider public sphere than ever before, prohibitive costs remain for the production and distribution of information in this form.[60] The per unit cost of information over ICTs is exponentially lower, and continues to decrease each year as broadband speeds continue to grow at roughly 50 percent a year.[61] While these developments potentially open the public sphere to those unable to afford the costs of printing and distribution, new barriers to entry (such as bundling, bandwidth caps, the anti-tethering requirements of acceptable use policies, and artificial scarcities) are constantly being introduced to thwart the commoditization of connectivity. It is an open secret that both spectrum licensure and interconnection as well as peering points between networks have become key locations for creating artificial scarcity in broadband markets and have led to rent-seeking behavior by dominant market players.[62]

The technologies that enabled old media were predominantly a one-way street, with messaging *from* broadcasters (a word broadly used to describe both the technologies of the medium and the organizations that produced and distributed the content) *to* receivers.[63] The Internet is still used to distribute many forms of old media: Sandvine Inc.'s report on "global internet phenomena" noted that 50.9 percent of US aggregate Internet traffic came from the Real-Time Entertainment traffic category, "applications and protocols that allow 'on demand' entertainment that is consumed (viewed or heard) as it arrives."[64] Yet even these platforms remain relatively open to review, revision, and manipulation (and displacement by new media if they fail to meet consumers' needs). The same medium that allows users to receive content can often also allow them to produce and distribute it.[65]

The dialogical nature of digital communications, combined with constantly lowered marginal costs, caused cyber-utopians to predict a revitalization of democracy in the wake of widespread access to digital communications networks. They conceptualize the Internet as a new Gutenberg press enabling borderless public fora to be accessible to all, a place where discussion and debate would take place on the basis of merit and not certification or pre-existing social status.[66] Twenty-first century democracy would be digital democracy—the Internet would be the harbinger of a global liberal democracy during this "end of history,"[67] serving liberal democracies by universalizing the bourgeois public sphere—what Jürgen Habermas, philosopher of communicative rationality and the public sphere, called "the sphere of private people come together as a public ... to engage them in a debate over the general rules governing relations in the basically privatized but publicly relevant sphere of commodity exchange and social labor."[68] The promise of a universal democracy would finally be fulfilled by dramatically reducing the costs of producing and disseminating information (and therefore differing opinions, points of view, and interests) to nearly zero. In liberal democracies, this would allow for the inclusion of even more members of a polity into the conversations and debates that would shape society's future,[69] while a new generation would "use technology to displace old modes and orders," breaking down the information control upholding the remaining authoritarian regimes in the world.[70]

This view is, of course, not without its skeptics,[71] who point out similarly optimistic views on the utopian impact of technologies over the past century.[72] While the unbridled enthusiasm of the cyberutopians is not fully justified, there are numerous positive facets of current efforts that should be celebrated. And regardless of one's optimism or skepticism, civic engagement is increasingly dependent on access to online communications. Older, offline public spheres are in the process of being vacated (as seen by the widely commented-on decline of traditional news media and decline of soapbox oratory to near-on non-existence starting at the end of the Progressive Era), while virtual public spheres continue to expand and online communications, blogs, citizen journalism, and social media, are all thriving.[73] Techno-utopians and techno-pessimists will reiterate their usual arguments, but it remains the case that technology is merely a tool that *mediates* democratic practice, whether the technology is the *ostraka*, shards of pottery used in a system of voting by ancient Athenians to exile (or ostracize) members of the political elite deemed too powerful to remain within the city,[74] or Wordpress-enabled citizen journalism blogs. As civic participation and democratic practice migrate online, the platforms and institutions which underpin connectivity will be crucial for the success of democracy in the twenty-first century.

Addressing concerns over the forms that communications technologies take and who exercises control over telecommunications infrastructure and the public spheres these networks undergird is a crucial task as the "next billion" come online. Unlike older media (which had intrinsic technological roles for broadcasters and receivers), digital communications are able to function as a *dialogical* and democratic communications media, not just in terms of content, but in terms of control over the medium itself. "Access" should be more than just "access to information"; it should be access to the tools to create and disseminate information, collectively build identity, and efficaciously act within a twenty-first century public sphere.[75]

In their seminal 2006 work and follow-up 2008 paper, "The New Network Neutrality: Criteria for Internet Freedom," Meinrath and Pickard presented a definition of network neutrality geared toward strengthening and empowering this virtual public sphere.[76] Nearly a decade later, the importance and relevance of these ten criteria still hold,[77] as can be seen by the heightened political struggles around net neutrality, common carriage,[78] and online privacy.[79] Their criteria span many of the key issues including Internet governance—with criteria #10 espousing that the network "is run by its users." While the 2008 paper advocated for the devolution of the "Amerocentric" control over Internet governance, and for a more multistakeholder governance process, today it is also possible for users to run last-mile connectivity infrastructure, both by installing the infrastructure and by using it as a platform to govern itself.[80]

When it comes to expansion of Internet connectivity, there are two likely trajectories that digital communications technologies may take. Both have pronounced implications for media activists and democracy advocates around the globe. These communications technologies can become sites of pervasive (corporate and state) surveillance, strengthening the authoritarian tendencies of states, with overt and subtle content filtering.[81] They can become media that ever-increasingly deepen the divide between existing identities, exacerbate intra- and international crises, and undermine the functioning of democratic processes and states.[82] Alternatively, cyberspace could become a site which offers the tools to construct new, broader identities that can overcome sectarian and racial conflicts, expand the domains for active public representation of the marginalized and disenfranchised, and create non-localized and transnational fora for discourse.

With over half of humanity offline, the immediate question is whether the "next billion" will be brought online via walled gardens where civil discourse and Internet craftsmanship are secondary to corporate advertisers' business models. What happens to the more than three billion people who simply have no meaningful disposable income and are of no economic worth to the bottom lines of traditional business models? Our current trajectory, whether we look at the activities of Internet.org, NSA.gov, or many far more innocuous privacy-invasive practices and content-curating walled gardens, is toward a form of connectivity that disempowers end-users and strengthens authoritarian tendencies. But, with concerted effort and intervention, this is not a fait accompli—it is possible to create forms of universal connectivity whereby individuals and communities are in control of their identities, democracies, and digital destinies.

Qualitatively degraded connectivity depends on a fundamental misunderstanding of democracy's relationship to digital communications. Not all connectivity is equivalent, and instituting two-track forms of connectivity risks creating first- and second-class citizens via one of the most powerful tools ever created. Because the costs of expanding broadband to achieve universal access are substantial, proponents of limited or walled-garden varieties often argue that their efforts are a necessary first step that is better than nothing. However, limited access to privately owned social media platforms (with a few NGO services usually thrown in for public relations cover)[83] creates platforms that are even more insidious than the marginalization created by antiquated one-way broadcast media. These new digital surveillance platforms (and, to be clear, their function is first and foremost to commercialize information collected on their users) also act to sublimate the empowering civic aspects of online communications in favor of the consumerist and profit-maximizing priorities. Digital democracy cannot thrive under the yolk of massive data collection of people's personal information and private communications. If recent history has taught us nothing else, these systems, even if set up initially for great good, become rapidly corrupted and turned into tools for great ill.

3. Digital enfranchisement

Solutions to the digital divide must be both holistic and realistic: connectivity with the tools for civic participation, self-direction, and self-government. What are needed are platforms for access as well as the tools that enable full and active digital enfranchisement. Digital enfranchisement is ensured not only when people are brought into the network, but when the network is for and of its users and constituents.

Historically, endeavors to bridge the digital divide have often failed due to their reliance on top-down approaches that only offer the potential of connectivity without the potential for changing the underlying conditions that necessitate these interventions in the first place. When it comes to technology, we are addicted to treating symptoms without acknowledging—much less addressing—the root problem. Nearly all current approaches to addressing the digital divide fail to meaningfully enfranchise those excluded because they aim for connectivity rather than active participation and empowerment. Digital Enfranchisement is ensured not only when people are brought into the network, but when the network is both for and of its participants.

The dark side of Metcalfe's Law examined above shows how the costs associated with exclusion from many networks increase dramatically as the percentage of the populace served by that system increases. This is why universal service provision (and, more importantly, equitable access) must become a part of all of our broadband goals and interventions. Current regulatory structures and mandates enable a dominant ISP business model that actually reinforces this digital divide. Inefficiencies and artificial scarcities are driving networks with high capital requirements and operating expenses that then necessitate high Average Returns Per User (ARPUs) to maintain the historically high profit margins of these corporations. In turn, this high ARPU service provision model all but guarantees that the poorest quintiles of the over seven billion people on the planet will lack meaningful access to online connectivity and digital resources and opportunities.

Today, many of the "solutions" being proposed would both maintain this current market structuring while simultaneously creating a "separate but equal" connectivity regime where the very platforms for social and public engagement are privately owned and controlled. Traditional theories of civic engagement ground it in access to a public sphere, yet meaningful civic engagement and political enfranchisement threaten many of the same institutions and players that are now determined to bring their form of connectivity to the masses. At best, this creates a substantial conflict of interest (for example, what happens when a government demands information from Internet.org about its users?). But this process also creates a platform whereby surveillance is a mandatory component of the use of these "resources"—opening up new threat vectors and uncertainties for constituencies that are already operating at the margins.

Meaningfully bridging the digital divide requires a solution that provides not just connectivity, but the tools and resources for latecomers to this new public sphere to meaningfully organize and engage. In much the same way that society has historically engaged in major interventions to address prior structural inequality (e.g. from the Magna Carta and Habeas Corpus, to the Fifteenth and Nineteenth Amendments to the Constitution, and the Voter Rights Act of 1965), we now need to accomplish this same society-shifting evolution in thinking. A twenty-first century civil society must, of necessity, engage in a new global effort to ensure full digital enfranchisement.

This coming decade will set the trajectory for our democratic ideals for generations to come; it is a critical juncture for setting new norms for what it means to live in a twenty-first century civil society. As we have shown, digital technologies will enable contemporary society to make tremendous improvements in quality of life for billions of people. We caution, however, that our widespread failure to maintain a critical stance toward the supposed benefits, as well as a general ignoring of the downsides of the Faustian bargains that profit-maximizing behavior often brings to philanthropic and development work, are creating entirely new digital divides that may, in fact, be far worse than anything we've faced thus far. As enthusiastic supporters of the liberatory potential of digital resources, we believe that a far more nuanced stance—one that explicates both the benefits and costs of various interventions—is crucially needed and too often missing from contemporary debates. We also worry that we are entering an era that, without technological vigilance, will resemble a digitally mediated, feudalistic consumer society more than a golden era for participatory democracy and freedom of expression. And we hope that by shedding light on these issues, we can avoid these coming pitfalls and fully enfranchise the entire global populace.

Notes

1 Leo Mirani, "Millions of Facebook Users Have No Idea They're Using the Internet," *Quartz*, 29 February 2015, http://qz.com/333313/milliions-of-facebook-users-have-no-idea-theyre-using-the-internet/
2 For example, the woefully modest national broadband goals in the United States National Broadband Plan, which aim to provide 4Mbps download speeds (1Mbps upload) by 2020, placing the US *last* amongst highly industrialized nations in our broadband speed aspirations. Federal Communications Commission, *Connecting America: The National Broadband Plan*, 2010, http://download.broadband.gov/plan/national-broadband-plan.pdf
3 Alberto Ibargüen and Walter Isaacson, "Foreword" in *Knight Commission on the Information Needs of Communities in Democracy, Informing Communities: Sustaining Democracy in the Digital Age* (Washington, DC: Aspen Institute, 2009), https://assets.aspeninstitute.org/content/uploads/files/content/docs/pubs/Informing_Communities_Sustaining_Democracy_in_the_Digital_Age.pdf
4 International Telecommunications Union, *The World in 2014: ICT Facts and Figures*, 2014, www.itu.int/en/ITU-D/Statistics/Documents/facts/ICTFactsFigures2014-e.pdf
5 Anna Malina, "Perspectives on Citizen Democratization and Alienation in the Virtual Public Sphere," in *Digital Democracy: Discourse and Decision Making in the Information Age*, Eds. Barry N. Hague and Brian D. Loader (London: Routledge, 1999), 27.
6 Alliance for Affordable Internet, *Affordability Report 2014*, 2014, http://1e8q3q16vyc81g8l3h3md6q5f5e.wpengine.netdna-cdn.com/wp-content/uploads/2015/03/a4ai-affordability-report-2014.pdf
7 Federal Trade Commission, *Data Brokers: A Call for Transparency and Accountability*, May 2014, iv–vii, https://www.ftc.gov/system/files/documents/reports/data-brokers-call-transparency-accountability-report-federal-trade-commission-may-2014/140527databrokerreport.pdf
8 Sascha D. Meinrath, James W. Losey, and Victor W. Pickard, "Digital Feudalism: Enclosures and Erasures from Digital Rights Management to the Digital Divide," *CommLaw Conspectus* 19, no. 2 (2011): 423–479.

9 James Losey and Sascha D. Meinrath, "The Digital Craftsman: How Centralized Control of Communications Technologies is Foreclosing 21st Century Craftsmanship," *Journal of Peer Production*, no. 9 (2016).
10 Rahul Tongia and Ernest J. Wilson III, "The Dark Side of Metcalfe's Law: Multiple and Growing Costs of Network Exclusion," Conference paper for the Center for the Study of Science, Technology, and Policy (2 December 2009). The conference paper was later revised and published as Rahul Tongia and Ernest J. Wilson III, "The Flip Side of Metcalfe's Law: Multiple and Growing Costs of Network Exclusion," *International Journal of Communication* 5 (2011): 665–681. We prefer the original conference paper's description of this as "the dark side," rather than "the flip side."
11 Seeta Gangadharan, "Digital Inclusion and Data Profiling," *First Monday: Peer-Reviewed Journal of the Internet* 7, no. 5 (2012), http://firstmonday.org/ojs/index.php/fm/article/view/3821/3199
12 Metcalfe posits that "the value of a network goes up as the square of the number of users." Carl Shapiro and Hal R. Varian, *Information Rules: A Strategic Guide to the Network Economy* (Cambridge, MA: Harvard Business Press, 1999), 184.
13 Tongia and Wilson, "The Flip Side of Metcalfe's Law," 667.
14 Detroit Digital Justice Coalition, *Principles*, http://detroitdjc.org/principles/
15 Srikanth Sundaresan, Walter de Donato, Nick Feamster, Renata Teixeira, Sam Crawford, and Antonio Pescapè, "Broadband Internet Performance: A View from the Gateway," Proceedings of the ACM SIGCOMM Conference (SIGCOMM '11), ACM, New York, NY (2011), 134–145, doi:10.1145/2018436.2018452
16 A 1995 RAND Corporation study discusses the worrying trend of information "haves" leaving the "have-nots" further behind. Robert Helms Anderson, "Universal Access to E-Mail: Feasibility and Social Implications," *RAND Corporation Center for Information Revolution Analysis* (1995).
17 Peter Millward, "The 'Grey Digital Divide': Perception, Exclusion and Barriers of Access to the Internet for Older People," *First Monday: Peer-Reviewed Journal of the Internet* 8, no. 7 (2003), http://firstmonday.org/ojs/index.php/fm/article/view/1066
18 Lee Skallerup Bessette, "It's About Class: Interrogating the Digital Divide," *Hybrid Pedagogy: A Digital Journal of Learning, Teaching, and Technology*, 2 July 2012, www.hybridpedagogy.com/journal/its-about-class-interrogating-the-digital-divide/
19 Robert W. Fairlie, "Are We Really A Nation Online? Ethnic and Racial Disparities in Access to Technology and Their Consequences," *Report for the Leadership Conference on Civil Rights Education Fund*, 2005, www.freepress.net/sites/default/files/fp-legacy/lccrdigitaldivide.pdf
20 The International Telecommunications Union's 2014 statistics showed 78 percent of the population of the developed world was using the internet, while only 32 percent of the developing world was. International Telecommunications Union, *The World in 2014*.
21 Federal Communications Commission, *Closing the Digital Divide in Rural America*, 2014, https://www.fcc.gov/blog/closing-digital-divide-rural-america
22 Federal Communications Commission, *2015 Broadband Progress Report*, 2015, 7–16, https://apps.fcc.gov/edocs_public/attachmatch/FCC-15-10A1.pdf
23 GSMA, *GSMA Mobile Economy Report 2015*, 2015, 10–11, www.gsmamobileeconomy.com/GSMA_Global_Mobile_Economy_Report_2015.pdf
24 Alliance for Affordable Internet, *Affordability Report 2014*, 2014, http://a4ai.org/affordability-report/report/#table-of-contents
25 National Telecommunications and Information Administration, *Falling Through the Net: A Report on the Digital Divide*, 1999, xv, www.ntia.doc.gov/legacy/ntiahome/fttn99/FTTN.pdf

26 National Telecommunications and Information Administration, *Falling Through the Net*.
27 US Department of Education, *Programs, Funding Status, Community Technology Centers*, www2.ed.gov/programs/comtechcenters/funding.html
28 Gerry Smith, "AT&T, Verizon Reject FCC Funds To Close Digital Divide," *Huffington Post*, 30 July 2012.
29 National Telecommunications and Information Administration, *Falling Through the Net*, xiii.
30 National Public Radio, *NPR: Talk of the Nation, The Science in Science Fiction, Interview with William Gibson*, 30 November 1999, www.npr.org/templates/story/story.php?storyId=1067220
31 Knight Foundation, *Informing Communities: Sustaining Democracy in the Digital Age*, 2009, www.knightfoundation.org/media/uploads/publication_pdfs/Knight_Commission_Report_-_Informing_Communities.pdf
32 Tongia and Wilson, *The Flip Side of Metcalfe's Law*.
33 Tongia and Wilson, *The Flip Side of Metcalfe's Law*, 674.
34 Tongia and Wilson, *The Dark Side of Metcalfe's Law*, 3.
35 Tongia and Wilson, *The Flip Side of Metcalfe's Law*, 675.
36 International Telecommunications Union, *ITU Releases 2014 ICT Figures*, 2014, www.itu.int/net/pressoffice/press_releases/2014/23.aspx#.VHy_LzHF9b0
37 Federal Communications Commission, *Connecting America: The National Broadband Plan*, 2010, 20, http://download.broadband.gov/plan/national-broadband-plan.pdf
38 Federal Communications Commission, *Fixed: Measuring Broadband America*, 2014, Chart 22.1f, http://data.fcc.gov/download/measuring-broadband-america/2014/2014-Fixed-Measuring-Broadband-America-Report.pdf
39 Michael Gurstein, "Effective Use: A Community Informatics Strategy Beyond the Digital," *First Monday: Peer-Reviewed Journal of the Internet* 8, no. 12 (2003), http://firstmonday.org/ojs/index.php/fm/article/viewArticle/1107/1027&quot%3B&gt%3B
40 Though, in 2015, as the row over Facebook's Zero Rating program in India has exemplified, questions are now beginning to be raised about what "Internet connectivity" and "access" really mean. Matthew Wall, "Facebook's Mark Zuckerberg hits back in Internet.org India row," *BBC*, 17 April 2015, www.bbc.com/news/technology-32349480#_blank
41 Guy Rosen, "Introducing the Internet.org App," *Internet.org*, 31 July 2014, http://internet.org/press/introducing-the-internet-dot-org-app. At the time of writing, the apps available on the first implementation (in Zambia) of the Internet.org App are AccuWeather, Airtel, eZeLibrary, Facebook, Facts for Life, Google Search, Go Zambia Jobs, Kokoliko, MAMA (Mobile Alliance for Maternal Action), Messenger, Wikipedia, WRAPP (Women's Rights App), and Zambia uReport.
42 Mark Zuckerberg, "Is Connectivity a Human Right?" *Facebook*, 2014, https://www.facebook.com/isconnectivityahumanright
43 Protecting and Promoting the Open Internet, Report and Order on Remand, Declaratory Ruling, and Order, 30 FCC Rcd. 5601 (2015).
44 Sascha Meinrath and Sean Vitka, "Crypto Wars II," *Critical Studies in Media Communication* 31, no. 2 (2014): 123–128; Sascha Meinrath and Victor Pickard, "The New Network Neutrality: Criteria for Internet Freedom," *International Journal of Communications Law and Policy* 12 (2008): 225–241.
45 Mark Zuckerberg, *Is Connectivity a Human Right?*, 2013, https://scontent-lga3-1.xx.fbcdn.net/v/t39.2365-6/12057105_1001874746531417_622371037_n.pdf?oh=33769e62a21ae123b6f319991f02b471&oe=59292827
46 Losey and Meinrath, "In Defense of the Digital Craftsperson."

47 Zuckerberg, "Is Connectivity a Human Right?" 2.
48 Zuckerberg, "Is Connectivity a Human Right?" 2.
49 Zuckerberg, "Is Connectivity a Human Right?" 2.
50 Audrey Watters, "The Failure of One Laptop Per Child," *Hack Education*, 9 April 2012, http://hackeducation.com/2012/04/09/the-failure-of-olpc
51 Gurstein, "Effective Use."
52 Gurstein, "Effective Use."
53 Todd Wolfson, *Digital Rebellion: Birth of the Cyber Left* (Urbana, Chicago, and Springfield, IL: University of Illinois Press, 2014).
54 Gurstein, "Effective Use."
55 Zuckerberg, *Is Connectivity a Human Right?* 10.
56 Malina, "Perspectives on Citizen Democratisation," 28.
57 Malina, "Perspectives on Citizen Democratisation," 27.
58 Ancient Greek historian Thucydides estimated a mere 5,000 regular attendees at meetings, even during wartime when crucial decisions were made. Thucydides, *The Landmark Thucydides: A Comprehensive Guide to the Peloponnesian War*, Ed. Robert B. Strassler (New York: Free Press, 2008): 8.72.
59 The Reapportionment Act of 1929 set the number of representatives at 435. Up until that time, the number had been allowed to grow with the population; however, this artificial limitation was put in place because the decision-making space didn't have enough seats for the 483 members that would otherwise have been allotted. By comparison, if we had kept the same relative ratio of citizens to representatives that were suggested by Congress through the end of the 1800s, the US House of Representatives would be a far more representative governing body of over 5000 elected officials.
60 Richard R. John, *Spreading the News: The American Postal System from Franklin to Morse* (Cambridge, MA: Harvard University Press, 1999).
61 Jakob Nielsen, "Nielsen's Law of Internet Growth," *Nielsen Norman Group*, 5 April 1998, www.nngroup.com/articles/law-of-bandwidth. Note how the law applies to "high-end user's connection speed"—portending that those on the wrong side of existing digital divides might be facing far lower percentage growth rates.
62 Jon Brodkin, "Netflix War is Over, but Money Disputes Still Harm Internet Users," *Ars Technica*, 13 March 2015, http://arstechnica.com/information-technology/2015/03/netflix-war-is-over-but-money-disputes-still-harm-internet-users/
63 While a few will argue that radio and television are, in fact, a two-way medium and even more would agree that newspapers have feedback loops for two-way communication, we situate all of these media within a general "broadcast model" whereby active discussion between producer and consumer of that medium is extremely limited and perhaps even more so amongst the viewers/listeners/readers.
64 Sandvine Inc., *Global Internet Phenomena Report 1H 2014*, 2014, www.sandvine.com/downloads/general/global-internet-phenomena/2014/1h-2014-global-internet-phenomena-report.pdf
65 Which is, of course, exactly how YouTube has come to dominate the free video distribution market.
66 John Perry Barlow, *A Declaration of Independence in Cyberspace*, 1996, https://projects.eff.org/~barlow/Declaration-Final.html
67 Francis Fukuyama's notion of "the end point of mankind's ideological evolution and the universalization of Western liberal democracy as the final form of human government" which "has occurred primarily in the realm of ideas or consciousness and is as yet incomplete in the real or material world." Thus the internet is seen as the means of "extending those principles [of liberal democracy] spatially" to effect the "universal homogenous state." Francis Fukuyama, "The End of History?", *The National Interest* (Summer 1989).

68 Jürgen Habermas, *The Structural Transformation of the Public Sphere: An Inquiry Into a Category of Bourgeois Society* (Cambridge, MA: MIT Press, 1989), 27.
69 Knight Foundation, *Digital Citizenship: Exploring the Field of Tech for Engagement*, 2014, www.knightfoundation.org/media/uploads/media_pdfs/Digital-Citizenship-tech4engage-summit-report.pdf
70 Andrew Sullivan, "The Revolution Will Be Twittered," *The Atlantic*, 13 June 2009, www.theatlantic.com/daily-dish/archive/2009/06/the-revolution-will-be-twittered/200478/
71 Evgeney Morozov, *The Net Delusion: The Dark Side of Internet Freedom* (New York: PublicAffairs, 2011).
72 Ethan Zuckerman, "Is Cyberutopianism Really Such a Bad Thing?" *Slate Magazine*, 17 June 2013, www.slate.com/articles/technology/future_tense/2013/06/cyberutopianism_should_not_be_a_dirty_word.html
73 Though, it should be noted, this does not mean that online communications and public spheres are nearly as efficacious as in vivo media—tradeoffs are certainly being made and their implications only beginning to be understood.
74 Editors, "Ostracism," *Encyclopaedia Britannica*, 2013, www.britannica.com/EBchecked/topic/434423/ostracism
75 While technology, like the printing press and radio, lowered the cost barrier to addressing a public, the near-zero cost of duplication combined with the in-built dialogical nature of the internet challenges Habermas' model of publicity in unprecedented ways.
76 Meinrath and Pickard, "The New Network Neutrality."
77 Requires common carriage; is open architecture and supports open source driver development; is open protocol and open standard; supports an end-to-end architecture; is private; is application neutral; is low-latency and first-in/first-out; is interoperable; is business-model neutral; is run by its users.
78 Nilay Patel, "Net Neutrality and the Death of the Internet," *The Verge*, 15 January 2015, www.theverge.com/2014/1/15/5311948/net-neutrality-and-the-death-of-the-internet
79 Lee Rainie and Mary Madden, "Americans' Privacy Strategies Post-Snowden," *Pew Research Center*, 16 March 2015, www.pewinternet.org/2015/03/16/americans-privacy-strategies-post-snowden/
80 Ryan Gerety, Andy Gunn, and Will Hawkins, "Case Study: Mesh Sayada," *Commotion Wireless*, February 2014, https://commotionwireless.net/files/posts/041814-Case-Study-Sayada.pdf
81 Eli Pariser, *The Filter Bubble: What the Internet is Hiding From You* (London: Viking/Penguin Press, 2011).
82 For example, see the manifestation of nationalist sentiment on Weibo during the dispute between Japan and China over the Diaoyu/Senkaku islands in 2012. "In contrast to the righteous official diplomatic language of sovereignty and the rationalist reasoning about economic rights over the islands, the drive of grassroots actions were historically oriented nationalist emotions." Miao Feng and Elaine J. Yaun, "Public Opinion on Weibo: The Case of Diaoyu Islands Dispute," in *The Dispute Over the Diaoyu/Senkaku Islands: How Media Narratives Shape Public Opinion and Challenge the Global Order*, Ed. Thomas A. Hollihan (New York: Palgrave Macmillan, 2014), 128.
83 Privately, many ICT4D experts have disclosed that the utilization rates for most of these added NGO services are often woefully marginal, a reality that is usually far out of proportion with the public declarations of the stated purpose and intent of these interventions.

Chapter 2

Media in action: A field scan of media and youth organizing in the United States

Sasha Costanza-Chock, Chris Schweidler, Teresa Basilio, Meghan McDermott, and Puck Lo

Introduction: Youth-led media organizing in the US

> "Media—finding your voice and determining how to tell your own story—is the first essential step in your own liberation."
>
> Kim McGill, organizer with Los Angeles-based Youth Justice Coalition

In 2003, Kim McGill and 60 other people who had been jailed, imprisoned or deported got together to build a youth, family, and prisoner-led movement to end juvenile detention.[1] All had been through the system as young people, in a context where, according to McGill, "Los Angeles county was locking up more young people than anywhere else in the world. People told stories of lock-up, and coming home." The organization that they built, Youth Justice Coalition (YJC),[2] is one of dozens of groups in the US that use popular education[3] and other methods of critical inquiry to support young people from marginalized communities to become activists, conduct participatory action research,[4] and make media, often in the form of videos, written reports, and radio pieces. Through media-making practices, these youth organizers create new narratives; ultimately, they aim to organize and inspire young people to take political action. Kim notes:

> When we first formed, there were almost no organizations where formerly incarcerated people were speaking for ourselves. It was always professional advocates with graduate degrees and lawyers speaking for us. We found that in order to move policy we needed to create our own reports. Now we speak for ourselves and make our own demands. Creating alternative media has meant a lot to people's sense of independence.

YJC has collected video stories and created written reports to share with community members, elected officials, and law enforcement. They have successfully fought to improve conditions at juvenile detention centers, reduce LA county's use of imprisonment for youth, and challenge "war on gangs" policing policies that target low-income youth of color.[5] While Los Angeles' police department was touted as a "model" for reform in the era following the Rodney King beating, young people working with YJC published the county's first report to analyze all police killings since the year 2000, and to name all victims since 2007.[6]

In the early 2000s, as YJC was forming, other youth and their allies around the country also discovered the potential of youth-led media projects to build political organizing skills and incite action on issues that were ignored by adults and mainstream media. In New York City's historically queer-friendly West Village, LGBTQ youth working with the Manhattan-based organization, FIERCE!, created the video documentary *Fenced OUT* to document the loss they felt when they were forced by new, gentrifying residents to stop meeting at the Christopher Street Pier, a longstanding destination point for queer youth who had nowhere else to go.[7] In 2001, in rural Kentucky, in response to a growing local crisis at the time, youth made a short video documentary, *Because of Oxycontin*,[8] to expose the dangerous side effects of the prescription painkiller that they saw ripping apart their community. Ben Spangler, who worked with the young film producers at the Appalachian Media Institute in Whitesburg, Kentucky, put it this way:

> Students are on the ground and know what's going on. They tackled this issue before anyone else was talking about it. After they produced this they sent it to senators and representatives in the state. Soon after, it began being discussed, and they ended up putting regulations on that drug.

While young people have led and been part of most social movements in US history,[9] it was not until the 1990s and 2000s that youth organizing in the US cohered as a field. During that time, while the state slashed the social safety net and dismantled public programs, many community-based groups working with young people registered as nonprofit organizations with 501(c)3 tax-exempt status in order to receive funding from private foundations and other donors. According to the Funders' Collaborative on Youth Organizing, a group of grantmakers and youth organizers who have tracked developments in the youth organizing world for the past 15 years, "the field was largely created and designed by low-income young people and young people of color, with their cultures and ways of being in the forefront." Financial support for youth organizing, in particular youth of color from low-income communities, allowed emerging community leaders at the time to take on issues including police brutality, access to public education, and environmental justice. Overall, many organizers of that era recall, there was a heady sense of possibility in the growing youth organizing movement. "It was really exciting to see youth leadership around police violence," said Jesse Ehrensaft-Hawley, a youth organizer at the time. "But there wasn't an organized LGBTQ youth voice. We saw a void and decided to fill it." In

1999, four New York City police officers fired 41 bullets at Amadou Diallo, striking the unarmed 22-year-old immigrant 19 times and leaving him dead on the doorstep of his apartment in the Bronx. After the officers were acquitted, Jesse got together with 11 LGBTQ youth to form FIERCE!, an LGBTQ youth organizing group that fought against police violence and NYC Mayor Rudy Giuliani's "broken windows" policing practices that targeted homeless people and LGBTQ youth of color, especially trans women of color.[10] "Compared to today, it was much more possible to be a brand-new, fledgling youth organizing group and seek funding—and get it," recalled Jesse, who today is Co-Director of Global Action Project (G.A.P.),[11] a media-arts and leadership education organization for New York City youth.

Since then, many major donors have stopped funding both youth organizing and youth-led media work. During the 1990s and 2000s, as video and audio technology became more accessible, many youth groups began to offer training in arts and culture-based youth development programs, supported at times by foundation funding. By the mid-2000s, however, much of this funding had dried up. "The decrease in foundation funding for youth organizing is the single most important trend we have identified and poses a potential threat to the growth of the field and the health of the communities that groups support," the Funders' Collaborative on Youth Organizing wrote in a 2013 report surveying the youth organizing field.[12]

Today's funders shy away from the mix of "arts, culture and leadership development," said Ben Spangler at the Appalachian Media Institute. They're more likely to fund job training programs that teach computer coding and programming—"whether or not it makes sense," Ben added. Overwhelmingly, funders seem to believe that new digital tools are an equalizing force in an unequal world, and a natural catalyst for young people's civic engagement. Among funders, said Krystal Portalatin, who with Jesse co-founded FIERCE!, "There's the desire to use more multimedia strategy, but not to fund it." The technodeterministic idea that new digital tools will somehow level the playing field for marginalized youth because they are so-called "digital natives,"[13] even in a world of stark and steadily increasing inequality, fits well with the steady rise of neoliberalism both as an ideology and as a force that shapes policy in multiple arenas, including education.[14]

In direct contrast to popular assumptions that young people are magically imbued with multimedia production skills at birth, many youth organizers around the country argue that media is a critical arena of intentional struggle. To take one example, the Youth Media Council's work in challenging representations of youth of color on commercial radio offers an important model for how to communicate—and achieve—media justice. In 2006, YMC produced a report to document their work, evaluate the lessons learned from their first three years, and share their story.[15] In another study, Quiroz-Martinez, Pei Wu, and Zimmerman document how environmental justice organizations across the country are thoughtfully and ambitiously addressing multigenerational movement building. One of their key findings is that youth organizers are using the power of arts and culture to engage youth in the environmental justice movement, to reach the hearts of community members, to inspire dialogue around divisive topics, and to build community.[16] More broadly, pushing back against internet-centric master narratives about youth mobilization, Costanza-Chock argues that young people have been at the forefront of social movements throughout history, including those that took place before the internet age.[17] There is a growing body of research that explores how youth organizers work across social justice issues, the strategies they develop to empower themselves, their communities, and their movements, and the ways that youth organizing is a key site for the development of a leadership pipeline that leads to broader social movements.[18] This article contributes to that line of research, and concludes with thoughts about how educators working in schools may be able to forge stronger connections with youth organizers and incorporate transformative media strategies, ideas, practices, and materials into the pedagogy of digital media literacy.

Research design and participation

As a social justice youth media-arts organization that supports youth organizers to tell their stories, Global Action Project (G.A.P.) saw clearly that the media landscape was quickly changing. We wanted to hear more about, and support, youth media organizing practices that further visionary change. Between 2012 and 2014, G.A.P., in partnership with DataCenter and Research Action Design (RAD.cat),[19] conducted surveys, focus groups, and interviews with youth organizers across the country. We wanted to see how they use media as a tool to advance their activism, and what challenges they face. Our research questions were:

- *What stories do youth want to tell?*
- *How do youth organizing and media strategy fit together?*
- *How do youth organizers gage impact and reach audiences?*
- *What media tools are youth organizers using and how?*
- *What challenges do youth organizers face when using media as part of their organizing strategies?*

To address these questions, we employed mixed methods including a literature review, survey, focus groups, and interviews. First, we convened a diverse advisory board to advise, review our research design and instruments, and help with outreach. Advisory board members were recruited based on their experience with youth media and youth organizing, as well as geography and issue areas. Second, we conducted an extensive literature review in order to assess the state of research on the role of media in youth leadership development and organizing for social change. Third, we conducted six focus groups with a total of 49 youth, youth organizers, and adult allies. The focus groups captured rich data on the stories young people want to tell with their media, the best practices in the use of media in youth organizing, and the barriers that young people and youth organizers face in using media.

Findings from the focus groups also informed the next stage of research, a national online and in-person survey of youth organizers and allies. To recruit organizational respondents, we tapped our existing networks by emailing relevant listservs, posting to social media, and making phone calls. We collected 166 surveys from youth organizers at 106 diverse youth-focused organizations in more than 50 cities across the US. Respondents worked on a range of issues, with particular focus on immigration, gender and sexuality, and education. Survey participants were mostly people of color, and more than half self-identified as female. Over half were under 25 years old, and about 40 percent self-identified as youth. Three fifths identified as activists or as youth organizers. Most organizations participating in the survey were small, with three quarters of organizations reporting ten or fewer paid staff. More detailed demographic information about survey respondents is available from Global Action Project's website, at http://bit.ly/MIA-report-GAP.

Additionally, we conducted a series of participatory data analysis workshops with the preliminary findings from the survey and focus groups. Young people and adult allies reviewed, discussed, and contributed to analysis of the findings at hands-on workshops at the Allied Media Conference and at the Digital Media and Learning Conference.

Key findings: Transformative media for youth organizing—Media practices, impacts and challenges

Youth don't just participate, they lead organizational media work

One out of three respondents report that youth lead most of their organizational media work. We also found that youth are increasingly involved in all aspects of making media—from training peers to implementing a media strategy. When we asked about media activities in which youth were engaged, 63% said they were engaged in media production, 60% said political education, and 56% said training peers and members. Additionally, 50% conducted media analysis, while 49% took part in developing media strategy. Just 8% said that youth were not engaged in organizational media activities.

"Our stories are missing"—Why youth organizers work with youth and media

"Our stories are missing," said media literacy trainer Candelario Vazquez, who grew up in the agricultural fields of Florida.

I learned that from my own experience being a farmworker. The media romanticized the farm industry, but people like us didn't exist. When you look up the keyword, "day laborer," or "jornalero," the first thing that pops up is someone else's racist story about day labor. That's what kids see.

Vazquez spent years teaching media production and computer classes with the immigrant rights organization Encuentro in New Mexico. "Media is a storytelling tool," he said. "Making videos, sound bites, and art are important ways for our community to survive and to tell the stories that will make our kids proud."

Back in New Mexico around 2009, Candelario remembers, many mixed-status immigrant families and undocumented migrants were relocating from Arizona, fleeing laws such as SB 1070, which required police to work directly with immigration authorities and engage in racial profiling. At the same time, nationally, a campaign was mounting against CNN anchor Lou Dobbs, who regularly interviewed anti-immigrant vigilantes on his TV show, *Lou Dobbs Tonight*.[20] As part of the campaign to hold Lou Dobbs accountable for hate speech, Candelario recorded video testimony of community members speaking out against the anti-immigrant racism they saw in the media. Eventually, by the end of 2009, after being given an ultimatum by the company's president, Dobbs left CNN.[21] "I saw the spark going into folks," Candelario recalled of the Dobbs campaign. "People were really activated talking about the media. People said, 'We don't have control over our media.' These politicians are using media against our communities. But we can use it too."

Candelario began teaching a media literacy class, which covered basic computer skills, public speaking, video, and radio production. As a result, these days Encuentro's Latino/a and immigrant members regularly visit the state capitol to film legislative sessions with flip cameras and cell phones. They tweet and post short video clips on the organization's Facebook page, advocating for domestic workers' rights and driver's licenses for undocumented people. Their tactics have swayed lawmakers and inspired members to tell their own stories, Candelario said. "Encuentro sparked in me and others the need to make media," Candelario continued. Now, a team of youth and adult community reporters routinely shoot and edit videos discussing different laws and social issues. The organization hopes to host a new, low-power community radio station soon. "People want to use the tools available to them—whatever they have—and tell it like it is," Candelario said.

Candelario's experience resonates with many of our research participants. Nearly 60% of respondents, and half (47%) of youth, said they do media work because they want to advance social justice:

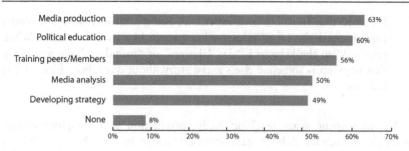

Figure 2.1 Organization media activities in which youth are engaged

About one in four survey respondents said that they came to the work because of personal experiences with injustice. Among youth organizers, one in four got started in media organizing and production work while enrolled in youth educational and employment programs.

"Mainstream and even alternative media is not in the hands of communities of color"

"Mainstream and even alternative media is not in the hands of communities of color," said Kim McGill from Los Angeles' Youth Justice Coalition. As a result, Youth Justice Coalition members found students of color are routinely portrayed by the press and in popular culture as being violent or criminal. When, following a spate of school shootings, including the 2012 tragedy at the Sandy Hook Elementary School in Newtown, Connecticut, many schools became increasingly policed, students of color suffered most, Kim said. While the national media focused on school shootings, Youth Justice Coalition gathered information about the effects of militarizing schools. A 2013 statement[22] the coalition released summarizes findings by other researchers on gun laws, delinquency rules, and disproportionate arrests of Black students at schools. It names President Nixon's zero-tolerance drug laws as a predecessor to post-Columbine school policies that have installed security guards in hallways and normalized routine locker searches. It calls for job creation, laws to punish gun manufacturers, and an end to police violence. "We can imagine the pain and suffering that the youth and families in Newtown, Connecticut are facing," reads the statement, which was signed by hundreds of young people of color from San Diego to the Bronx.

> As youth growing up on some of America's deadliest streets, we are all too familiar with gun violence and its impacts. But, we have also seen how attempts to build public safety with security systems, armed police and prisons have failed. Despite the fact that school shootings have

overwhelmingly happened in white schools, youth of color have paid the price.²³

Youth Justice Coalition's experience was echoed in our focus groups, where many participants articulated a deep desire to challenge and reframe how those outside of the community represent them. For example, about a fifth of survey respondents, and many focus group participants and interviewees, said that they created their own media to deliberately challenge narratives in commercial media that undermine the well-being of their communities.

Communication as a right: Access alone is not enough

Our research shows that youth need more than access alone to mass media and technology; they want to learn how to analyze and understand existing media, tell their own stories, and produce media to build power in their communities. Nearly two thirds (62%) of survey respondents also said that in their media work they tell their personal stories to achieve greater goals: from expressing hope to raising awareness about the conditions their communities face, from forming alternate visions for justice to contributing to direct policy change.

Some contend that all youth who make and use media are "engaged," and feel that "liking" a page on Facebook or posting a comment is a form of civic participation and activism. However, the young people we surveyed said that passive consumption of online content, or merely using social media, was not in itself activism. Storytelling for social change requires more than "Clicktivism," they said: it requires political organizing.²⁴

Media changes minds, hearts and policies

Research participants also say that they use media to document and share stories and visions for social change, shift social and cultural norms, reach broader audiences, and influence policy. Many were especially interested in

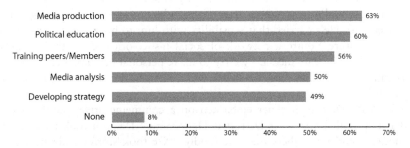

Figure 2.2 What brought you to this work?

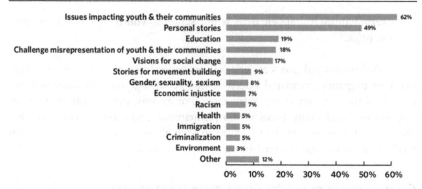

Figure 2.3 Stories youth want to tell media

using and making media to bring in more members, spark political dialogue, and create leadership opportunities for youth.

Organizations say that their highest priorities for their media work are to shift the way people think about issues (67%), to reach more youth and audiences (63%), to create youth leadership opportunities (57%), and to win campaigns (44%).

Media-making forges lasting bonds, intergenerational connections, and community ties

Our research shows that youth value being part of intentional learning spaces that foster storytelling, root cause analysis, and learning alongside adult allies as a means of leadership development. For example, as a teenager, Dakarai Carter, now 21, attended a web radio class at Youthville, a community youth center in Detroit, Michigan. When his instructor there stopped teaching the class, Carter recalled, "I was kind of devastated." The teacher encouraged him to get involved in Detroit Summer, a multi-racial, intergenerational collective founded by radical philosopher and activist Grace Lee Boggs.[25] Eight years later, Carter's still there. "I like the way that in Detroit Summer they are more of a family. They're good friends with each other and really care about personal problems and things going on," Carter said. He's carried that sensibility with him to his activist work with Detroit Future Youth, a network of social justice-oriented youth programs that teach and create media: "We try to make personal or human connections as much as possible, because that's what changes things: getting to know people."

In 2010, Detroit Summer embarked on a commemorative mural project that they called "Another Detroit is Happening." Dakarai took part in the endeavor and remembers the time fondly. "We took stories and interviews that we gathered, along with photography, and collaged all those together," he said. "We made environmentally friendly wheatpaste silk screens and went around the city, pasting them up. It was fun. It incorporated a lot of people." Each mural told a story about organizing, Dakarai recalled, highlighting a historical event, a significant place, or a local Detroiter. The most popular mural, Dakarai said, was one documenting a recent peace march that called for an end to violence and "restoring the neighbor back to the 'hood.'" Many locals requested copies of that screen printed poster, he said. "The emotion was captured," he said. "People like the message." After the murals were completed, Detroit Summer hosted a mural tour so that people in the community could meet and talk with the artists. "Some people were unaware of those problems or things we covered, so we brought it to the forefront," Dakarai said. "The murals brought people together around common issues."

Youth learn, teach, and stay involved when making media

"When youth work on media projects, they then don't want to do anything else," said Krystal Portalatin of New York City's LGBTQ youth organizing group, FIERCE!. "Just film. It comes up every couple of years." Back in the year 2000, Krystal and other young people in the group filmed interviews with queer youth who were being pushed out of a historically gay neighborhood in Manhattan that was being redeveloped. FIERCE!'s video survey quickly morphed into a half-hour long documentary, Krystal said, produced by some dozen youth members who felt an urgency to document the experience of their community as it became threatened and displaced by gentrification. The documentary, "Fenced OUT," in turn, inspired FIERCE!'s first organizing campaign: demanding a 24-hour drop-in center near the Christopher Street Pier for homeless and queer youth. "I thought it would be a lot of info-gathering," Krystal recalled of the video project.

> But what we caught on camera was what actually happened—footage of residents patrolling the neighborhood. A security guard told us, 'Residents don't want you here.' We caught it on film; this was proof. We're not just talking about these things, we're showing you.

During the process of shooting and editing the documentary, said Krystal, she and the other youth producers realized that if they wanted to make sure that young people could access the pier or other safe spaces, they would need to get together with other LGBTQ youth and their allies to confront the area's new residents, city planners, and police. "What the film process taught me was—what does it mean to organize? To talk to people and really listen and learn," recalled Krystal, who was a high schooler when she shot and edited the FIERCE! documentary.

These experiences were echoed by survey respondents, who shared that media-making increases youth engagement in many aspects of their work:

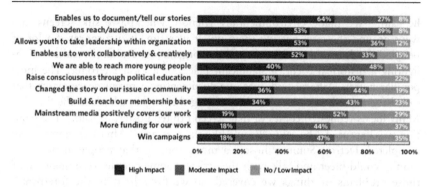

Figure 2.4 Where organizations see the impact of the media they produce

Four out of five respondents (79%) said they wanted the media they made to convince other youth to take social or political action, such as organizing in the community or testifying to legislators. Many (69%) wanted their media work to educate about issues like homophobia, net neutrality, and workers' rights—and to bring more youth into social justice activism.

Partnerships help media organizers do more

"The reason we were able to make 'Fenced OUT' happen was we worked with Paper Tiger TV," said Krystal. Paper Tiger TV is a nonprofit, volunteer-based artists collective that produces documentaries, studio shows and advocacy shorts in New York City. This experience is common across the field. Just over half (52%) of respondents stated that their organization partners with others on media work including production, analysis, peer-to-peer media literacy workshops, sharing press databases or communications staff, and cross-promoting or conducting campaigns together. More than three fifths (62%) said they want to scale up or continue partnerships.

Media is a critical tool for political education and youth leadership development

More than two thirds (73.4%) said that their organization conducts political education. For this study, political education is defined as a process of dialogue, activism, and inquiry that develops both an individual and a collective analysis of the root causes of injustice. Using and making media can facilitate a richer engagement by youth in the study of history, power, and resistance, which then informs their frames, messages, productions, and outreach strategies, respondents said. For example, while working on Fenced OUT, Krystal and other FIERCE! youth met elders, including longtime organizer and Stonewall riot veteran, Sylvia Rivera. FIERCE! screened its documentary at college campuses and facilitated conversations about the need for safe spaces for queer and trans people. "Through making the documentary, we realized that what we needed to talk about was the intersection of gentrification with criminalization, lack of services and homophobic violence," Krystal said. "So our campaign then literally fought with ideas of what space was and who has access to it."

Indeed, nearly three quarters (74%) of respondents said that their organization's political analysis includes an intersectional examination of power, representation, economic inequality, racial justice, public policy, gender and sexuality, and education reform, among other core issues. Additionally, a majority (69%) of those surveyed said that making media rooted in an organizing project has increased political consciousness among participating youth, as well as among their peers. Many youth organizers said that they saw young people grow as leaders and learn to critically analyze power while working on media projects. This dynamic between analysis, production, and purposeful inquiry expands the definition of "media impact" beyond traditional metrics, such as audience reach or products created, to include skills like listening, sharing, teamwork, and taking an idea from concept to fruition in a social justice context.

"Producing this sort of first-voice content challenges stereotypes"

Twelve years ago, as a teenager, Ben Spangler—now the Director of the Appalachian Media Institute—heard a punk rock show on the radio that would change his life. "They were playing all kinds of crazy stuff," he recalled. "It blew me away. I come from a small town. I didn't know anybody who liked that kind of music other than myself." Ben tracked down the radio station, which was run by Appalshop, a nonprofit multi-disciplinary arts and education center in the Appalachian mountains. Soon afterward, Ben was working on a documentary with other young people enrolled in Appalshop's documentary-making program. Their film, "Searching for an Appalachian Accent," looked at "how your accent affects people," he said, and in particular, "how having a Southern or mountain accent carries such heavy negative connotations." Ben and his peers interviewed locals who "carried a real pride with having a mountain accent and talked about how it gave them an identity ... Southeastern Kentucky is a part of the country that isn't treated very well by the media," Ben said. "Producing this sort of first-voice content challenges stereotypes."

Youth make media to reach their peers, families, and political allies

Despite assumptions that the purpose of making media is always to wrangle directly with the mainstream, the top three target audiences, according to youth organizers who responded to our survey, are: youth who are peers (81%), their parents/families (75%), and allies (74%):

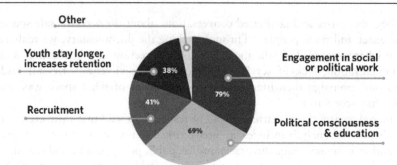

Figure 2.5 Media increases youth engagement

Additionally, two thirds (66%) of survey respondents say that in their organization, they currently analyze how the issues they work on are portrayed and framed by mass media, and that they think about who target audiences are:

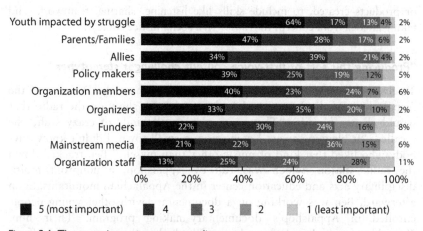

Figure 2.6 The most important target audience

Half of respondents say they would like to do more media analysis. A small, but significant group (about 10%) aren't sure what media analysis is, and about a fifth of respondents (18%) say they aren't sure whether their organization conducts political education.

Youth organizers are making, sharing, and using more media than ever across diverse platforms

Our research confirms that media is now a core component of the organizing landscape. Effective organizing with media is as much about process as product, respondents said. They noted that, ideally, organizations develop media strategy to work across platforms, engage youth in all aspects of media work, draw on the resources and skills of media partners, and target clearly defined audiences based on campaign goals. Respondents also said that they are creating their own media more than ever before, including video, photography, social media, and organizational websites. They use a wide range of platforms and strategies to distribute the media that they make, including via organizational websites, social media, and email, but also in face-to-face workshops, via printed materials, at fundraising events, and at schools and universities, among other methods. They also intentionally work across mediums and platforms, for example, by producing photography or video content, then distributing that content online via social media:

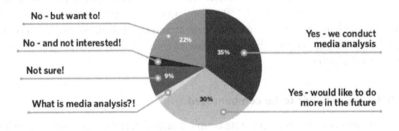

Figure 2.7 Organizations conduct media analysis

Barriers and challenges

Media is critical to movement building, yet young people face tremendous structural barriers to engaging in media work. Despite the rise of social media, survey respondents said that many communities still lack basic equipment, software, and technical training for making or using media. Many pushed back on the idea that all youth are "digital natives" whose access to and active participation in, new media spaces are guaranteed by virtue of being born after 1996. Additionally, they said, increasing racial and economic polarization has ensured that youth from marginalized communities have few opportunities to meaningfully access technology and media.

For example, in New Mexico, where the digital divide is the worst in the nation, "more than four of five (82%) of households with an annual income greater than $50,000 have internet access, while only 57% of households with annual income under $15,000 are connected to the internet," according to the University of New Mexico.[26] Encuentro, an immigrant advocacy group based in the central part of the state, trained young people to conduct video interviews asking other youth around the state how—or if—they were able to get online. "We found that one kid traveled 17 miles from one part of Albuquerque to another part of Albuquerque on a bike in order to use the internet," said Candelario Vazquez, who worked at Encuentro. "We heard from kids who had to buy internet from McDonald's in order to do their homework. Some families had to choose between paying the water bill or the internet bill."

Young people aren't taken seriously, and they demand accountability from adult allies

Within organizations, young people face additional challenges, such as not being taken seriously by adults. Although we heard from some organizations that they work to transform ageist structures and practices in order to foster productive intergenerational relationships, four out of ten (40%) of youth survey respondents noted that youth input generally "was not listened to or well-received." Respondents said they wanted more safe spaces, both peer-to-peer and intergenerational, as well as more accountability to young people who have chosen to share their stories as a catalyst for social change.

Media work needs to be compensated

Organizations want to keep young people engaged and increase their leadership within the organizations. Yet organizations find themselves increasingly vulnerable, let alone able to offer young people opportunities for continued engagement, stability, or even employment opportunities. Nearly 60% of organizations reported they did not have paid media staff and relied on volunteers to do communications or media work. As one respondent expressed, "we need more funding to hire paid staff. It would be great to have a dedicated media associate as part of our organization, but at the moment, our organization is so small, we're having interns handle most of our media work."

Organizations know what they need to turn the tide

Media is critical to movement building, but it is being de-funded. Organizers said that, increasingly, media is the means by which youth are best able to change discourse, share their artistry, raise political awareness, and connect to community-based organizing. Yet funding for youth-led media projects continues to dwindle, despite the fact that nearly all organizations (83%) said that the top support they needed to continue media work was more funding.

When asked what they need to scale up their media work, most said they need staff with the necessary skills (68%), followed by access to equipment or software (56%). Additionally, youth organizers said that their top priorities for training are in technical production (72%), distribution and outreach strategies (69%), and effective use of media for political education (65%).

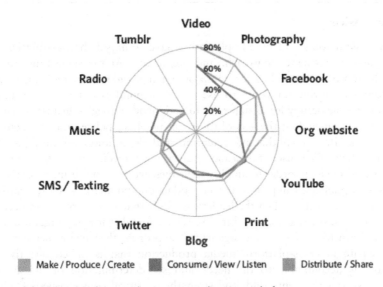

Figure 2.8 Make, distribute, and consume media across platforms

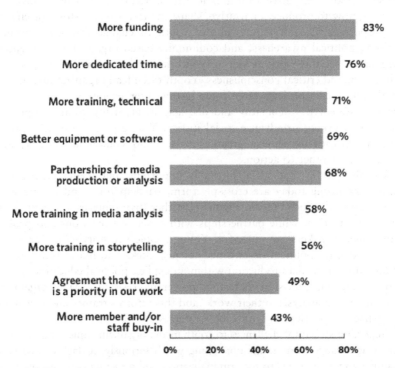

Figure 2.9 Top supports needed for media work to continue

Conclusions

New digital tools and mobile platforms have reshaped the possibilities of storytelling, aesthetics, outreach, and organizing. At the same time, there has been a drop in funding for youth organizing, right at the moment when conditions are ripe for youth to use media to build power on the ground. Young people occupy leadership roles in nationwide struggles against systemic inequalities, including the school-to-prison pipeline, police violence against Black and Brown youth, and detention and deportation policies, just to name a few. They use, make, and analyze mass media, alternative media, and social media in order to amplify their messages. Beyond using media as a means to publicize campaigns, media production and analysis is a formative, creative way to strengthen the leadership skills that youth organizers need.

In surveys, focus groups, and interviews we found that many organizations use a "transformative media organizing" approach: they invite members to participate in cross-platform media production that is linked directly to action, is accountable to the needs and self-determination of the group whose stories are being told, and strengthens critical consciousness.[27] This approach builds the knowledge, skills, leadership, and self-determination of participants as they create change with the media they make, be it campaign-driven, personal narrative, or dramatic fiction. Media work, when it involves learning how to produce a narrative, shape the terms of the story, or engage in purpose-driven storytelling, allows youth to change discourse through artistry, political awareness, and community-based organizing experiences. Organizers see this work as key for youth leadership development, political education, and critical consciousness. Youth often lead organizational media work, and media projects often forge lasting intergenerational bonds. Contrary to stereotypes of apathy and disengagement, many young people are explicitly working to advance social justice. Young people are telling their personal stories to achieve greater goals, build community power, and inspire one another to action.

We also found that social media is important, but media practices in youth organizing today are cross-platform, participatory, and in line with campaign goals. Social media augments, rather than replaces, other kinds of media production, while partnerships with other organizations and professional media makers are powerful. Young people say storytelling for social change requires political organizing, not just clicks and likes. Additionally, many said that media production within an explicit political education framework can facilitate the study of history, power and resistance. Many organizers conduct media analysis in their work, and this informs frames and messages, as well as production and outreach strategies.

Important structural challenges to youth media organizing must be addressed. Challenges range from adults not taking youth seriously, to lack of access to training and equipment, to the criminalization and targeting of youth of color.

Most agree that media is critical to movement building, but that explicitly politicized media work is being defunded. Besides funding for staff, equipment, and software, youth organizers want training in production, distribution, and outreach, as well as effective use of media for political education.

Our findings have important implications for funders, who we believe should re-invest in youth organizing. Along with general operating support for youth organizing, and in addition to restricted program dollars, it is crucial for funders to offer specific funds for *media strategy and production*, including for ongoing equipment upgrades and purchases, as well as to underwrite travel and registration fees that enable youth to attend trainings. This approach would support young people who are already organizing on a common issue to meet and plan with their peers, in order to move beyond individual campaign messages. We also note the importance of paid positions for youth organizers to work as media producers. According to our findings, one third of youth media organizations say that youth lead most of their media work, but nearly two thirds (60%) don't have paid media staff and struggle to keep youth involved over time. Additionally, there is a clear need to increase support for youth-friendly media, technical, creative, and strategy trainings and curriculum. Over half of respondents partner with other organizations to share media skills, but say they specifically need youth-focused curriculum and projects that can be youth-led. Many survey respondents and interviewees also talked about the need to *fund partnerships that enrich media capacity*. More than half (52%) of respondents stated that their organizations partner with others on media-making, media analysis, media trainings, media distribution, and mass media outreach, and in order to share equipment and resources. Overall, it is crucial to support youth-led media organizing that is cross-platform, participatory, and action-oriented. Our findings do not support the idea that social media replaces all other forms of media-making. Instead, social media is complementary to short and long form video and audio production, among other important forms. Great transformative media organizers work across platforms, to reach their communities where they are at, and do more than tell a compelling story: they invite community members to participate in media work and to take action. This approach needs to be better understood and resourced.

We also believe our study carries key lessons for educators. In particular, we note that youth organizers have found the pedagogy of digital media to be most effective in structured, purpose-driven contexts. Our findings suggest that educators work with young people to integrate digital media skills-building into engaged pedagogy. Digital media education can become part of what bell hooks calls education as the practice of freedom,[28] and can help develop powerful solutions to systemic inequalities, based in young people's lived experience and political analysis. Media-making education should not only provide job skills and badges, it should also transform consciousness, skills, and creative capacity. It remains important to teach media analysis in a political education framework, with root cause and intersectional analyses that build critical consciousness and youth leadership. Additionally, our findings suggest the need to challenge widespread assumptions that access to media tools such as smartphones is in itself transformative, that participation in social media automatically leads to increased civic capacity, and that all youth experience the world as "digital natives."

There remains a need to foster safe, peer-to-peer youth spaces for self-determination and leadership. In some cases, educators working in schools may be able to support the creation and maintenance of such spaces, as allies to youth leaders in their communities. We also note the need for educators and school administrators to move beyond an exclusive "job readiness" focus in digital media education, to recognize the benefits of an approach that links digital media skills to storytelling as a form of self-determination by young people in communities most affected by injustice. By self-determination, we mean that youth develop the power to demand better structural conditions and to put forward visions for change on their own terms. We also note the need for concrete accountability structures that support meaningful youth involvement in policy and administrative decision-making. Community lies at the heart of a transformative agenda, and solutions work best when they are rooted in the values, knowledge, expertise, and interests of that community. In many of our focus groups, youth organizers also described the power of positive intergenerational relationships to strengthen their organization's capacity to tell critical stories for change. Finally, it is crucial to ensure that media-making is seen as a core practice of leadership development in the digital age, and not merely as an add-on. Media-making is not only a key strategy for amplifying young people's messages, media production and analysis can also be formative, creative means to strengthen youth knowledge, engagement, and leadership.

Through this research, we have attempted to lift up the stories that youth want to tell about the role of media-making in their organizing work, especially young people who identify as Queer, Trans*, and/or People of Color (QTPOC). We have also tried to highlight how media-making, when it takes place within a political education and movement-building framework, can be a transformative experience for youth participants and their communities. We recognize that those who are most impacted by the issues we discuss here are the experts on the subject, and they are already transforming the world around us. We hope that our findings will generate increased support for youth-led, transformative media work that is explicitly embedded in community organizing.

Appendices

In the interests of space, rather than including a series of appendices here, we note that the following key additional information can be found in the full Media in Action report (http://bit.ly/MIA-report-GAP):

- Detailed demographics of survey and focus group participants
- An appendix of key terms
- More information about the organizations behind this research (G.A.P., DataCenter, and RAD).

Full acknowledgments of the many people who contributed to this research.

Notes

1 This article is based on primary research conducted by Global Action Project, Research Action Design, and DataCenter. Findings were first released online as: Meghan McDermott, Chris Schweidler, Teresa Basilio, and Puck Lo, *Media in Action: A Field Scan of Media & Youth Organizing in the United States* (New York: Global Action Project, Research Action Design, DataCenter, 2015).
2 Youth Justice Coalition, 2017, www.youth4justice.org
3 Paulo Freire, *Education for Critical Consciousness* (London and New York: Bloomsbury, 1973).
4 Orlando Fals-Borda, "Participatory Action Research," *Development: Seeds of Change* 2 (1984): 18–20.
5 See YJC reports at www.youth4justice.org/ammo-tools-tactics/yjc-reports
6 Youth Justice Council, *Don't Shoot to Kill: Homicides Resulting from Law Enforcement Use of Force within L.A. County, 2000–2014* (Los Angeles: Youth Justice Council, 2014), www.youth4justice.org/new-release-of-data-from-yjc-on-law-enforcement-use-of-force-resulting-in-a-homicide
7 For more about Fenced OUT, see: www.fiercenyc.org/fenced-out-fierces-youth-produced-documentary
8 Anna Bentley, Faith Colwell, Jessica Williams, and James Pigman, Because of Oxycontin, 2001, https://vimeo.com/31628436
9 Sasha Costanza-Chock, "Youth and Social Movements: Key Lessons for Allies," in *The Role of Youth Organizations and Youth Movements for Social Change*, Kinder & Braver World Project Research Series (Cambridge, MA: Berkman Center for Internet & Society, 2012), http://cyber.law.harvard.edu/node/8096
10 Bernard E. Harcourt, *Illusion of Order: The False Promise of Broken Windows Policing* (Cambridge, MA: Harvard University Press, 2009).
11 Global Action Project, 2016, https://global-action.org
12 https://fcyo.org/resources/2013-national-youth-organizing-field-scan-the-state-of-the-field-of-youth-organizing
13 Sue Bennett, Karl Maton, and Lisa Kervin, "The 'Digital Natives' Debate: A Critical Review of the Evidence," *British Journal of Educational Technology* 39, no. 5 (2008): 775–786.
14 Wendy Brown, *Undoing the Demos: Neoliberalism's Stealth Revolution* (Cambridge, MA: MIT Press, 2015).
15 Kristen Zimmerman, *Reframing Power: An Evaluation of the Youth Media Councils' First Three Years* (Los Angeles: Youth Media Council, 2006), www.centerformediajustice.org/wp-content/uploads/2014/10/Reframing-Power.pdf
16 Julie Quiroz-Martinez, Diana Pei Wu, and Kristen Zimmerman, "ReGeneration: Young People Shaping the Environmental Justice Movement" (Oakland, CA: Movement Strategy Center, 2005), www.issuelab.org/resource/regeneration_young_people_shaping_the_environmental_justice_movement

17 Costanza-Chock, "Youth and Social Movements."
18 For example, see Taj James and Kim McGillicuddy, "Building Youth Movements for Community Change," *Nonprofit Quarterly*, 8, no. 4 (2001): 1–3; Movement Strategy Center, "Bringing it Together: Uniting Youth Organizing, Development and Services for Long-term Sustainability" (Oakland, CA: Movement Strategy Center, 2005); Young Wisdom Project of the Movement Strategy Center & The Youth Speak Out Coalition, "Making Space Making Change: Profiles of Youth-led and Youth-driven Organizations" (Oakland, CA: Movement Strategy Center, 2004), www.movementstrategy.org/media/docs/1892_MSMC.pdf; S. Ginwright and James T, "From Assets to Agents of Change: Social Justice, Organizing, and Youth Development," *New Directions for Youth Development*, 96 (2002): 27–46; Shawn Ginwright, "Building a Pipeline for Justice: Understanding Youth Organizing and the Leadership Pipeline," Funder's Collaborative on Youth Organizing, Occasional Papers Series on Youth Organizing, no. 10, 2010, www.fcyo.org/media/docs/6252_FCYO_OPS_10_ScreenVersion.pdf
19 Research Action Design, http://rad.cat
20 Sasha Costanza-Chock, *Out of the Shadows, Into the Streets! Transmedia Organizing and the Immigrant Rights Movement* (Cambridge, MA: MIT Press, 2014).
21 Julie Hollar, "Dropping Dobbs: A Victory for Media Activism, and the Challenge Ahead," *NACLA Report on the Americas* 43, no. 1 (2010): 46.
22 Youth Justice Coalition, Statement by Youth of Color on School Safety and Gun Violence in America, 2013, www.youth4justice.org/wp-content/uploads/2013/04/04-0113YouthofColorResponsetoSchoolShootingsFinalStatement.pdf
23 Ibid.
24 David Karpf, "Online Political Mobilization from the Advocacy Group's Perspective: Looking Beyond Clicktivism," *Policy & Internet* 2, no. 4 (2010): 7–41.
25 Grace Lee Boggs, *Living for Change: An Autobiography* (Minneapolis, MN: University of Minnesota Press, 1998).
26 University of New Mexico Bureau of Business and Economic Research, *Broadband Subscription and Internet Use in New Mexico*, 2013, www.doit.state.nm.us/broadband/reports/NMBBP_bb_use_0613.pdf
27 Sasha Costanza-Chock, Chris Schweidler, and the Out for Change: Transformative Media Organizing Project, *Towards Transformative Media Organizing: LGBTQ and Two-Spirit Media Work in the United States* (New York: Ford Foundation, 2015). Strengths and needs assessment by the Ford Foundation's Advancing LGBT Rights Initiative, Research Action Design, and the MIT Center for Civic Media. Available online at http://transformativemedia.cc/research.
28 bell hooks, *Teaching to Transgress* (New York: Routledge, 2014).

Chapter 3

Studying media at the margins: Learning from the field

Clemencia Rodríguez

Introduction

In this essay I attempt to draw from specific research studies on community/alternative/citizens' media to reflect on how we theorize media at the margins. I am using the concept of "the margin" as a shortcut to speak of complex dynamics of power inequality. Processes of asymmetrical access to material and symbolic resources shape differentiated and unequal access to the public sphere.[1] In our societies, some communities have greater access to technologies as well as the necessary cultural capital to position their voices in the public sphere. Other communities struggle to empower their voices and position themselves in local, national, and international public spheres. Here, I call these sites of struggle "margins." Rather than an in-depth examination of power dynamics at the margins, I am interested in exploring how specific media ecologies develop in these sites of struggle.

In some cases I draw from my own research while in other instances I examine research done by others. In every case, however, all the research I look at is very localized in a specific geographic and historical context, thus it may or may not resonate with media at the margins in other localities. At the margins, media tend to be less universal, less driven by global trends and markets, and more grounded in local time, place, interest, and need; this is one of the first aspects we can identify as a major difference between media at the center and media at the margins. My journey through media at the margins has been fascinating from beginning to end; this is why I've never been tempted to switch gears and study media at the center. Investigating media at the margins is an adventure into uncertainty, surprise, wonder, and amazement. At the margins, media never look the way we expect; technologies are used in ways that differ from their originally intended purpose; media don't emerge or develop in a predictable manner. Journeying into media at the margins is stepping into "the land of otherwise."

1. Many margins, many media

First, media at the margins are positioned so otherwise that we cannot see them. At the margins, media have generally existed out of sight, rendered invisible by the glitter and excitement of media at the center; we've never had enough scholars, researchers, or policy makers paying attention to media at the margins. As a result, we tend to flatten media at the margins; we overgeneralize, overlooking key differences between distinct types of media. In the last twenty years numerous terms have emerged to name media at the margins, including alternative media, community media, citizens' media, grassroots media, autonomous media, indigenous media, pirate media, and social movement media. Accordingly, debates abound around which term is more appropriate and there is an explosion of theoretical arguments for and against each term, attempting to privilege one over the other. I have been an active participant in these debates and yet, today, I've come to think that we should shift gears. Media at the margins exist as a plurality. There are many different margins, and each margin produces its own type of media.

The geographic margin of Belén de los Andaquíes, a small town in southern Colombia where I have conducted research since 2004, is a case in point. This town of six thousand is home to the *Escuela Audiovisual Infantil de Belén de los Andaquíes* (Children's Audiovisual School of Belén de los Andaquíes [EAIBA]), a participatory media initiative where children produce their own audiovisual narratives. I was drawn to EAIBA for several reasons: first, EAIBA has developed its own, very idiosyncratic media pedagogy based on local languages and aesthetics; second, EAIBA maintains high production standards, something rare among participatory media initiatives that prioritize process over product; and third, EAIBA carefully designs the moment of media reception as much as the moment of media production.[2]

Belén de los Andaquíes and all of southern Colombia has been the target of stigmatization and demonization for decades. National and international media, politicians and policy makers in Bogotá, and "war-on-drugs" global narratives have framed the region as a far-away place, isolated and distant from order and civilization, a place plagued by violence and in need of taming and subduing by strong (mostly military) authorities. Southern Colombia is known as a place where everyone participates in the cocaine-production business, is a member of a guerrilla organization, or both.

These notions of self and place permeate local cultural imaginaries. In this geopolitical margin, EAIBA uses media to reconfigure local identities and counter mainstream media representations of the region and its people as violent and savage. As soon as a child walks in the school's door, EAIBA immerses him/her in a myriad of quotidian processes specifically designed to re-signify notions of self and place. In a series of playful activities, children are enticed to use media technologies to produce their own narratives of who they are and where they live. During excursions to the nearby river, children focus their cameras on the beauty of the surrounding Amazonian landscape; microphones capture local sounds—birds, street vendors, bicycles, the buzz of the local market. Each one of these processes alters the political agency of Belén's children. In other writing I coined the term "citizens' media"[3] to describe the transformative and empowering potential of participatory media. "Citizens' media" finds theoretical support in Chantal Mouffe's notion of citizenship as a fluid and embodied re-enactment of political agency in everyday life,[4] and also in Jesús Martín-Barbero's assertion that political agency requires voice.[5] In this sense, citizens' media "are communication spaces where men, women, and children learn to manipulate their own languages, codes, signs, and symbols, gaining power to name the world in their own terms. Citizens' media trigger processes that allow individuals and communities to re-codify their contexts and selves. These processes ultimately give citizens the opportunity to re-structure their identities into empowered subjectivities strongly connected to local cultures and driven by well-defined utopias. Citizens' media are the media citizens use to activate communication processes which shape their local communities."[6]

Comunas, working-class neighborhoods perched above the cosmopolitan and ultra-modern city of Medellín, constitute a very different margin. Here, a grassroots filmmaking organization called *Pasolini en Medellín* [PeM] believes in the performative power of the camera in the streets of these violent neighborhoods. In a context like Medellín's neighborhoods, where war has imposed meanings, ways of understanding, and cultural codes, media are used as performative tools to *make things happen*. PeM's leaders describe themselves as vultures, "flying in the periphery of what has been said, looking for stereotypes and established signifiers as carrion."[7] As a case in point, PeM's media practice "digests" and transforms the cultural code of young masculinity as a sign of aggression. Duvan Londoño, one of PeM's filmmakers, recalls:

> I remember seeing two kids playing guns in my neighborhood. They were representing *Bazuquito* and *Lucho*, two real thugs that terrified the neighborhood during the 90s. They were gang leaders of enemy militias. What struck me the most was that one of the kids yelled that bullets could not harm him, which is actually one of the myths that circulated in the neighborhood, that one of these thugs was protected by sorcery and spells and bullets could not harm him. The power these myths had over the neighborhood stayed with me; when *Bazuquito* and *Lucho* controlled the neighborhood, these kids were not even born.[8]

Years later, Duvan came back to his neighborhood to shoot *Click Obtura Gallo*, a documentary about VillaNiza, the neighborhood where he grew up. By this time, people in the neighborhood were used to seeing PeM's youth shooting in the streets, setting up lights, and arranging actors in a scene. What he found was a testimony to PeM's performative power:

> What I saw is that, over time, my role as a filmmaker began to attract the kids' attention in the neighborhood. Seeing what we were doing had

a seductive force on them. Toward the end of the shooting, I found several of these kids playing in the street. At first I thought they were setting up their usual games of guns and warriors, but I was surprised when I saw that the game was about a team making a film; it was quite a performance. When I saw that, I remembered those other kids I had seen, and I came to a new understanding, which is that our practice is displacing the violence that, unfortunately, has occupied such a central place in our neighborhoods.[9]

In this case, even before any media content is produced, PeM's media practice is making things happen in these communities. This is what I mean when I write about the performative power of media. Is this citizens' media? Or alternative media? Or do we need a new label to refer to this use of media technologies at a specific margin?

Now I would like to examine a different type of margin: the political margin at Zuccotti Park in New York City, where, despite being at the center of techno-capitalism, marginalized social movements elbowed their way into a place almost entirely colonized by technology, financial powers, and state apparatuses. In this context, politicized subjects use innovative information and communication strategies, including interpersonal communication, "traditional media," and social media, as they respond to multiple and diverse needs.

On September 20, 2011, Occupy activists had to figure out how to communicate after the New York City police arrested Justin Wedes for refusing to stop using a megaphone.[10] In order to control noise, the city of New York has an ordinance that bans "the use of any device or apparatus for the amplification of sounds … without a permit from the police commissioner,"[11] and the police used this ordinance to disrupt communication among Occupy protesters, banning all use of microphones and loud speakers. To address this newly encountered communication need, protesters implemented "the human microphone," or "successively wider rings of spoken repetition"[12] of a speaker's statements. Defined by Nardone as "organized vocal amplitude,"[13] the human mic is an excellent example of media at the margins: community communicators detect communication needs and use their know-how to figure out a way to solve the problem with whatever resources are at hand.[14]

The human microphone was not invented by Occupy protesters. As is typical in social movement media, processes of sharing best practices and cross-fertilization brought the human microphone from the anti-nuclear movements of the 1980s to the factory occupations in Argentina and the anti-globalization demonstrations of the early 2000s and on to Occupy.[15] In their analysis of protest camps, Feigenbaum, Frenzel, and McCurdy propose the term "promiscuous" to explain how ideas and strategies "travel and spread in multiple directions" in "often cunning and seemingly chaotic" processes of crosspollination, adaptation, hybridization, replication, etc.;[16] these authors warn against looking for linearity and large-scale structures in a process of social change, and suggest paying attention to micro-structures and sometimes imperceptible processes that connect one movement to another across time and space.[17] The human mic is yet another type of media at the margins, more in line with social movement media than citizens' media or performative media. Activists need information to travel fast, not just from a hub to the nodes, but from one node to another, and they use a multiplicity of communication strategies—including interpersonal communication—to this end.

A very different margin is experienced by my students at the University of Oklahoma, living in the center of the religious right where the public conversation about abortion takes on almost cultish overtones. My young students bake cookies in the shape of fetuses, to be used as part of their activist media to counter the efforts of Oklahoma politicians to regulate women's bodies and reproductive rights.

Figure 3.1 Fetus cookies courtesy of activist bakers

The simple, domestic cookie is used to defy convention, position counter-cultures in the public sphere, and break away from tradition into experimentation, newness, and movement. This type of media at the margins has been thoroughly theorized by Chris Atton as alternative media.[18] Atton explores this type of cultural margin, a space where, for example, young women produce their own 'zines to nourish and defend alternative identities against the social and cultural expectations of their social milieu; here, the medium plays the role of a life raft, used by young women to survive in a sea of mainstream narratives with limited options.

Instead of debating what term is a stronger theoretical descriptor for these types of media, I believe we need to maintain a healthy multiplicity. If there were enough scholars and plenty of research done about media at the margins, we could see that citizens' media are different from social movement media, and both are distinct from alternative, counter-cultural media; there are also, for sure, many more types of media at the margins. If we took the study of media at the margins seriously, it would be clear that each of these media is a different creature. In each case, technology is used to address very different communication and information needs and the potential and the weaknesses of each technology only become apparent in interaction with local conditions. Specific uses of technology are determined by local conditions and the always-idiosyncratic communication needs of local communities.

2. Embracing complexity

At the margins, the interaction between media and people is highly complex. In some cases, such as EAIBA, understanding the media produced, in this case video narratives, requires making sense of a complex mesh of interactions between hegemonic and counter hegemonic narratives and notions of self and place, access, appropriation of audiovisual technologies, media pedagogies, and historical dynamics of silencing and empowerment. Understanding EAIBA requires in-depth analysis of complex cultural and social processes that frame the use of media technologies.[19] And yet, the media ecology of EAIBA is quite simple; they use video cameras, computers, and YouTube. Research on EAIBA may focus exclusively on the use of video, problematizing what some scholars have called "the one-medium bias" understood as "prioritizing the analysis of one medium or platform over others."[20]

In other cases, media ecologies can be highly complex, including a variety of technologies, platforms, commercial media, and alternative media—a complexity not accessible to analyses that prioritize one medium or platform. Only research models that embrace complexity will be able to make sense of multi-faceted and polyvocal media at the margins. In her research on the Tunisian uprising after the Bouazizi immolation in 2010, Merlyna Lim uses the concept of "a hybrid network" to make sense of the events that spiraled into the Tunisian uprisings, which in turn gave rise to the Arab Spring.[21]

Her analysis illustrates several different nodes, hubs, and media working in unison. She relates that Bouazizi's uncle called independent journalist Zouhayr Makhlouf; after the call, Makhlouf spread information and photos of Bouazizi's immolation via Facebook and emailed and called other journalists, including his contact at Al Jazeera's office in Qatar;[22] although Al Jazeera was banned in Tunisia and could not send reporters to the area, it used its Sharek citizen journalism portal, first used during the Gaza war in 2008, to receive and redistribute footage, images, and news from the events around Bouazizi. Over five days this hybrid network grew increasingly resilient. A local web-based community radio called SBZone picked up the news, maintained coverage of the Sidi Bouzid events, and called various other independent journalists. Although most Tunisians do not have access to the internet on their own phones (only 2% of all phones in Tunisia are smartphones), they used cell phones to call others, send photos, and even transmit live; the hybrid network included social media, community media, and mainstream media.

Sidi Bouzid, Tahrir Square, Zuccotti Park: each marginal situation exists as a unique media ecology in which activists perform information and communication processes that embolden their political agency. In their comparative study of protest camps, Feigenbaum, Frenzel, and McCurdy explain the complexity of media ecologies:

> We pay attention to the ways in which protesters' strategies are entwined with each other, as well as with their material environments. From concerns about internet and mobile phone connections to undercover reporters infiltrating action planning meetings, the human and non-human elements that make up protest camp life affect the media and communication practices of protesters. While some media strategies deployed by protesters are planned and based on long histories of social movement campaigning (e.g. spokespersons, media liaisons, camp-based newsletters), others emerge spontaneously or are improvisational as protesters make do with available resources. In some cases, protesters monitor the media and file complaints against slanderous coverage. Engaging a range of strategies, media teams at protest camps figure out how to find, protect, and generate the resources needed to both make their own media and respond to mainstream media reports. At Occupy Wall Street, the campers needed electricity for their communications and therefore devised a system for bringing generators into the park. In Tahrir Square, protesters rewired street lamps to get electricity to run computers and charge mobile phones. In Oaxaca, women took over existing infrastructure, occupying a broadcast television station to film and air their own programming.[23]

One of the daunting challenges of media at the margins is that they exist as a mesh, a chaotic tangle of different actors using various technologies in unpredictable ways. Many scholars seem to be articulating a notion of "media ecology" as they try to make sense of this chaos. In the same vein, some scholars talk about a "media environment,"[24] others talk about "the communication ecology,"[25] "communication culture(s),"[26] or "transmedia mobilization."[27] Drawing from Tarrow's "repertoire of contention," Alice Mattoni coins the term "repertoire of communication";[28] Teune uses a similar term, "communication repertoire."[29] Some, like Sasha Costanza-Chock, are coming up with very interesting ways to capture this complexity in language: Costanza-Chock writes about the "media bridging" that is happening more and more in an environment that is increasingly "fragmented across the hypersegmented and multimodal mediascape."[30]

Lim's hybrid networks in Tunisia and Feigenbaum, Frenzel and McCurdy's emphasis on the importance of micro-structures, spontaneous processes of "making do with what you have," and the serpentine ways in which communication know-how travels from one social movement to another, suggest that social movements' media ecologies could be understood as "communication rhizospheres." The notion of mediascape or media ecology seems too stable and focused on macro-structures. Rhizosphere, on the other hand, captures micro-structures and processes that breed media uses and communication processes within social movements. To think of communication and media uses as rhizosphere shifts our attention to individual and collective processes by which activists share their experiences and acquire new skills, hybridize media platforms, adapt communication strategies from one context to another, creatively solve communication and technical problems (using what Feigenbaum, Frenzel, and McCurdy call "tactical knowledge"[31]), respond to challenges, bypass restrictions, use media to overcome interpersonal communication problems, and use face-to-face communication to overcome technology challenges.

Trying to classify what activists and grassroots communicators do with media, scholars come up with new terms and a long inventory of categories. For example, *activist media practice* is split into the categories of media knowledges practice and relational media practice;[32] Kavada splits activist uses of media into strategic, organizing, and decision-making dimensions. "Communication culture" is also split into several dimensions including content, form, objectives, infrastructure, content production, content consumption, distribution, communication flow, and social relations.[33] Similarly, scholars try to categorize different types of media used at the margins: digital mainstream media, non-digital mainstream media, non-digital alternative media, and digital alternative media.[34] Others talk about "communication horizontals" and "communication verticals,"[35] and still others talk about old media and new media or participatory media and strategic media.[36] Mattoni and Treré propose their own classification of social movements' interactions with media objects and media subjects.[37]

3. From media to communication needs

I would like to suggest we move away from naming and classifying technologies and platforms, types of actions, and modes of communication. If the reality we are trying to comprehend is complex, capricious, and always changing, I'd like to think we can find theoretical and methodological ways to accompany and embrace such fluidity without having to cut it into little pieces. One of the ways I learned to do this is by shifting my perspective to focus on subjects and their actions rather than focusing on media technologies. Instead of looking at technologies and actions, what if we explore media at the margins in terms of how media technologies are used to meet always changing, historical, localized, information and communication needs?

For example, during my fieldwork I studied Santa Rosa Estéreo, a community radio station in the region known as Magdalena Medio, one of the most violent regions in Colombia, where right-wing paramilitary groups (sometimes in alliance with the army) fought left-wing guerrillas, trapping civilian communities in the crossfire. José Botello, the director of the radio station and a highly esteemed community leader, was kidnapped by a local guerrilla. Immediately, the community communicators at the radio station made the decision to use the station to respond to the kidnapping. Their idea was to make the kidnapping a public event, something that had an impact on the entire community, not just Botello's family. They announced the kidnapping and asked the guerrilla to respect Botello's rights as a civilian. Letters and messages of support began pouring in. The station decided to read them all on air. The guerrilla called the station with a challenge: if it was true that Botello had so many friends, why didn't they come to get him? The station made this challenge public to listeners. The response was immediate and dozens of people volunteered to go wherever was necessary to rescue Botello. The station began organizing the rescue mission. Six hours later, a caravan of fifty buses, cars, and trucks carrying 480 men and women snaked up the Andean mountains to the guerrilla camp. They forced their way into the camp and demanded the release of their leader. They held their ground and finally, three days later, the guerrilla gave up and released Botello. In this case, the communication and information needs were very specific. The armed group victimized a civilian. The potential to resist such victimization existed in community, but it was scattered. It was up to the radio producers at the community radio station to use communication to galvanize this potential into a collective voice capable of resisting the guerrilla's violent intrusions in the community. These community communicators had to step very carefully because they knew that any wrong move could put Botello's life at risk, but they were so deeply embedded in their local context that they knew how far they could push, how far the guerrilla was willing to go before the political cost of a violent act became too high. In a series of impromptu decisions, they re-directed the radio station, turning it into a hub of communication and information processes between members of the community, from the community to Botello, from the community to the guerrilla group, and from the community to the Colombian government.

If we shift perspectives and focus on the communicator trying to figure out how to use media, what becomes clear is that, at the margins, grassroots communicators exist in a media ecology or communication rhizosphere that offers different potentialities in each historical situation. What determines media use is not whether the technology is old or new, digital or not digital; what determines media use is a flux of historical information and communication needs and how embedded community communicators employ available technologies to address these needs. Gómez García and Treré propose a similar model based on affordances on one side, and uses, appropriations, and domestication of technologies on the other.[38] For community communicators to be able to detect and understand local information and communication needs, they have to be deeply embedded in the social, cultural, and political fabric of their communities. On this basis, I question the many C4D initiatives based on exporting or replicating formulas from one context to another.

Thus, when it comes to media at the margins, the level of expertise, skill, and technological know-how of community communicators is key. Re-inventing, hybridizing, converging, and bridging technologies from one platform to another are dependent on the skills of local communicators. I cannot stress enough the importance of training, cross-fertilization, and the sharing of lessons learned among local grassroots communicators. In my view, this is much more urgent than access or connectivity.

Long-term studies are necessary to understand the complexity of how technological expertise develops in specific contexts. Mattoni and Treré propose a model for studying social movements and media that includes three different temporalities: a short-term temporality of punctuated events; a middle-term temporality of cycles, tides, or waves; and a long-term temporality of cultural epochs of contention.[39] A good example of this type of longitudinal study is Sterpka's ethnography of transnational activist communication networks from the Asia-Africa Conference held in Bandung, Indonesia, in 1955 to the post-Zapatista People's Global Action (PGA) and World Social Forum in the late 1990s.[40] According to Sterpka, "Networks incorporate out of diversity to assemble and form part of a larger trajectory. The history of social struggle is similarly diverse and borrowed from preceding movements, fashioned from the cherished heirlooms of resistance and spun out of a cross-fertilization of activities, ideas, and strategies."[41]

I cannot emphasize enough the crucial importance of ethnographic methods as excellent methodological strategies for studying the multiple complexities and layers activated when local communicators detect information and communication needs and figure out how to tap into the potential of their own communication and media rhizospheres. In the words of Juris and Khasnabish:

> Ethnography, and its attention to everyday life realities, is thus an indispensable tool for exploring transnational activism as well as the more general search for and articulation of new practices of knowledge production capable of generating democratic, liberatory, and just social futures.[42]

In conclusion, understanding media at the margins is about embracing complexity, maintaining the notion of media ecologies and communication rhizospheres, focusing on how local community communicators and activists, deeply embedded in the social and cultural fabric, detect local information and communication needs, and wedge appropriated and domesticated media technologies into place to meet these needs.

Notes

1 Nick Couldry, *The Place of Media Power. Pilgrims and Witnesses in the Media Age* (London: Routledge, 2000).
2 Clemencia Rodríguez, *Citizens' Media Against Armed Conflict. Disrupting Violence in Colombia* (Minneapolis: University of Minnesota Press, 2011).
3 Clemencia Rodríguez, "From Alternative Media to 'Citizen's' Media" in *Fissures in the Mediascape: An International Study of Citizens' Media*, Ed. Clemencia Rodríguez (Cresskill, NJ: Hampton Press, 2001), 1–23.
4 Chantal Mouffe, "Hegemony and New Political Subjects: Towards a New Conception of Democracy," in *Marxism and the Interpretation of Culture*, Eds. Larry Grossberg and Cary Nelson (Urbana and Chicago: University of Illinois Press, 1988), 89–102; Chantal Mouffe, "Democratic Citizenship and the Political Community," *Dimensions of Radical Democracy: Pluralism, Citizenship, Community*, Ed. Chantal Mouffe (London: Verso, 1992), 225–239.
5 Jesús Martín-Barbero. "Identities: Traditions and New Communities," *Media Culture and Society* 24, no. 5 (2002): 621–641.
6 Clemencia Rodríguez, "Citizens' Media," in *The Encyclopedia of Social Movement Media*, Ed. John Downing (Thousand Oaks, CA: Sage, 2011), 98–103.
7 Camilo Pérez Quintero, *Images to Disarm Minds: An Examination of the "Pasolini in Medellín" Experience in Colombia*, M.A. Thesis, Communication and Development, Ohio University (2013), 58.
8 Quintero, *Images to Disarm Minds*, 104.
9 Quintero, *Images to Disarm Minds*, 104.
10 Lilian Radovac, "Mic Check: Occupy Wall Street and the Space of Audition," *Communication and Critical Cultural Studies* 11, no. 1 (2014): 35.
11 Radovac, "Mic Check," 36.
12 Radovac, "Mic Check," 34.
13 Michael Nardone, "Repetition and Difference: On the Human Microphone as Interventionist Form," *The Human Microphone*, 25 April 2012, http://thehumanmicrophone.blogspot.ca/2012/04/repetition-and-difference-on-human_25.html
14 Anna Feigenbaum, Fabian Frenzel, and Patrick McCurdy, *Protest Camps* (New York: Zed Books, 2013), 64.

15 Ruth Milkman, Stephanie Luce, and Penny Lewis, "Changing the Subject. A Bottom-Up Account of Occupy Wall Street in New York City," *City University of New York, The Murphy Institute*, 2013, http://sps.cuny.edu/filestore/1/5/7/1_a05051d2117901d/1571_92f562221b8041e.pdf; Radovac, "Mic Check."
16 Feigenbaum, Frenzel, and McCurdy, *Protest Camps*, 61.
17 Alice Mattoni and Emiliano Treré, "Media Practices, Mediation Processes, and Mediatization in the Study of Social Movements," *Communication Theory* 24 (2014): 255.
18 Chris Atton, "Popular Music Fanzines. Genre, Aesthetics, and the Democratic Conversation," *Popular Music and Society* 33, no. 4 (2010): 517–531; Chris Atton, *Alternative Media* (London: Sage, 2002).
19 Clemencia, Rodríguez, Benjamin Ferron, and Kristin Shamas, "Four Challenges in the Field of Alternative, Radical and Citizens' Media Research," *Media, Culture and Society* 36, no. 2 (2014): 150–166.
20 Alice Mattoni and Emiliano Treré, "Media Practices, Mediation Processes and Mediatization in the Study of Social Movements," *Communication Theory* 24, no. 3 (2014): 254.
21 Merlyna Lim, "Framing Bouazizi: 'White lies', hybrid network, and collective/connective action in the 2010–11 Tunisian uprising," *Journalism* 14, no. 7 (2013): 1–21.
22 Lim, "Framing Bouazizi: 'White lies', hybrid network, and collective/connective action in the 2010–11 Tunisian uprising," 9–11.
23 Feigenbaum, Frenzel, and McCurdy, *Protest Camps*, 70–71.
24 Patrick McCurdy, "Mediation, Practice and Lay Theories of News Media," in *Mediation and Protest Movements*, Eds. Bart Cammaerts, Alice Mattoni, and Patrick McCurdy (Bristol, UK and Chicago, US: Intellect, 2013), 57–74.
25 Anastasia Kavada, "Internet Cultures and Protest Movements: The Cultural Links Between Strategy, Organizing and Online Communication," in *Mediation and Protest Movements*, Eds. Bart Cammaerts, Alice Mattoni, and Patrick McCurdy (Bristol, UK and Chicago, US: Intellect, 2013), 75–94.
26 Defined as "the diverse values that influence the activists' engagement with the communication ecology," in Kavada, "Internet Cultures and Protest Movements," 77.
27 Defined as "the process whereby a social movement narrative is dispersed systematically across multiple media platforms, creating a distributive and participatory social movement 'world', with multiple entry points for organizing, for the purpose of strengthening movement identity and outcomes," in Sasha Costanza-Chock, "Transmedia Mobilization in the Popular Association of the Oaxacan Peoples, Los Angeles," in *Mediation and Protest Movements*, Eds. Bart Cammaerts, Alice Mattoni, and Patrick McCurdy (Bristol, UK and Chicago, US: Intellect, 2013), 100.
28 Defined as an "entire set of activist media practices that social movement actors might conceive as possible and then develop in both the latent and visible stages of mobilization, to reach social actors positioned both within and beyond the social movement milieu"; Alice Mattoni, "Repertoires of Communication in Social Movement Processes," in *Mediation and Protest Movements*, Eds. Bart Cammaerts, Alice Mattoni, and Patrick McCurdy (Bristol, UK and Chicago, US: Intellect, 2013), 47.
29 Defined as "the variety of communication strategies and tactics that social movement actors employ to sustain interactions with broader political arenas"; Mattoni, "Repertoires of Communication in Social Movement Processes," 46.
30 Costanza-Chock, "Transmedia Mobilization in the Popular Association of the Oaxacan Peoples, Los Angeles," 111.
31 Feigenbaum, Frenzel, and McCurdy, *Protest Camps*, 105.

32 Mattoni, "Repertoires of Communication in Social Movement Processes," 39–56.
33 Kavada, "Internet Cultures and Protest Movements," 82.
34 Mattoni, "Repertoires of Communication in Social Movement Processes," 43.
35 Kavada, "Internet Cultures and Protest Movements," 83–87.
36 Costanza-Chock, "Transmedia Mobilization in the Popular Association of the Oaxacan Peoples, Los Angeles."
37 Mattoni and Treré, "Media Practices, Mediation Processes, and Mediatization in the Study of Social Movements," 259–260.
38 Rodrigo Gómez García and Emiliano Treré, "The #YoSoy132 movement and the struggle for media democratization in Mexico," *Convergence: The International Journal of Research into New Media Technologies* (2014): 1–15.
39 Mattoni and Treré, "Media Practices, Mediation Processes, and Mediatization in the Study of Social Movements," 256–257.
40 M.K. Sterpka, "The Transnational Struggle for Information Freedom," in *Insurgent Encounters. Transnational Activism, Ethnography and the Political*, Eds. Jeffrey S. Juris and Alex Khasnabish (Durham, NC: Duke University Press, 2013), 295–317.
41 Sterpka, "The Transnational Struggle for Information Freedom," 300.
42 Jeffrey S. Juris and Alex Khasnabish, "Introduction," in *Insurgent Encounters: Transnational Activism, Ethnography and the Political*, Eds. Jeffrey S. Juris and Alex Khasnabish (Durham, NC: Duke University Press, 2013), 1–8.

Chapter 4

The online translation activism of bridge bloggers, feminists, and cyber-nationalists in China

Guobin Yang

An important part of media activism in the contemporary world happens in the networked spaces of digital media. Such digital or online activism depends centrally on language or discourse. Yet although the discursive character of online activism has attracted considerable attention, the full spectrum of the power of language in online activism remains elusive. By studying online translation activism in China, this chapter aims to contribute to a broader understanding of the diverse forms of online activism as well as the multiple ways in which languages and their translations and interpretations are mobilized for political struggle.

Online translation activism refers to the use of translation for activist purposes in online spaces.[1] It is mainly conducted online and thus mediated by internet networks. And then translation is itself a form of mediation—it mediates social interactions and cultural and political encounters. Online translation activism is thus a doubly mediated form of activism.

Practices of translation are always political and deeply tied to projects of colonization, religious proselytization, as well as modern revolutions and nation building.[2] As forms of activism, however, they have begun to attract scholarly attention only in the last decade. Sherry Simon writes in her introduction to a special issue on "Translation and Social Activism" for the journal *TTR: Traduction, terminologie, rédaction* that "Translations are a form of engagement when the necessary partiality of translation becomes partisan, when translators adopt advocacy roles in situations of sociocultural inequalities."[3] The articles in that special issue range from studies of the role of interpreters in health care services and HIV/AIDs prevention discourse to translations of literary texts from vernacular languages into English, anthropological translations of aboriginal narratives, the translation practices of missionaries, and activist translations in immigration legal practices. Conny Roggeband focuses on the reception process in the translation of social movement repertoires.[4] Mona Baker's studies of professional translators highlight their ability to produce alternative narratives that challenge dominant institutions of society and to forge their own narrative communities. In her most recent work, Baker argues that translation, interpreting, subtitling, and other forms of mediation "must be brought to the centre of the political arena and conceptualized as integral elements of the revolutionary project."[5]

"Translation may be conceptualized narrowly as the rendering of texts from one language to another, or broadly as the communication of expressive forms and experiences from one context into another—the latter is sometimes called cultural translation."[6] In this narrow sense of translation, translation activism refers to the use of linguistic translation, or translingual practices,[7] for activist purposes. Although this chapter is mainly concerned with translation in the narrow sense of the word, such an analysis cannot be entirely separated from translation in its broader sense, because, as a particular form of narrative, translation is embedded in broader processes and politics of intercultural communication.

Because translations are typically used to reach constituencies in a foreign language, translation activism often has a transnational character. It is most common in global and cross-border advocacy and social movements. As part of the broader landscape of online activism in China, translation activism comprises several varieties. Inside China, civil society groups, cyber-nationalists, human rights advocates, and dissidents are engaged in translation activism.[8] Outside of China, civil society groups and dissident communities use translation to shape public opinion about China. Some of these translation projects have a clear advocacy orientation.

This chapter studies three types of online translation activism related to China. The first type is the translation activism of bridge blogs, which engage in English-Chinese and Chinese-English translations of news, blogs, and other content of contemporary interest. The second type is the activism of a feminist subtitle translation group in China. The third type is the translation activism of cyber-nationalists. I will argue that in each case, translation serves the larger goals of the activist group. These goals include 1) the provision of information; 2) the narration of alternative identities and communities; 3) the performance of protest strategies; and/or 4) a mixture of these. In other words, online translation activism is engaged in the politics of information, identity, and performance. In these politics, questions of objectivity and fidelity in translation become secondary. The process of translation, such as the selection and deployment of translated content, becomes as important as its semantics. And it is as a process that translation activities serve as sites of identity and community as well as means of resistance and protest.

The politics of Chinese-English two-way translations

The global internet is linguistically divided and stratified. Communication across linguistic and cultural boundaries in the global blogosphere remains difficult without the support of translation and translators. In the global blogosphere related to China, two-way translations between Chinese and

English are becoming increasingly common. Online translation communities, which produce almost real-time translations of popular television and film subtitles, enjoy great popularity among Chinese internet users.[9] Major news media like the *New York Times* and the *Wall Street Journal* run news websites in Chinese, in addition to their regular English editions. Some of these news institutions maintain an active presence on Chinese social media platforms. The *Wall Street Journal*, for example, tweets frequently in Chinese on China's major microblog platform Weibo.

A neglected but important type of online translation practices about China is what I call online activist translations, a form of translation activism that is conducted and circulated mostly through online networks. Translated by organized groups as well as unorganized individual internet users, bloggers, and activists, they are published in online platforms and disseminated through diverse digital networks, including email lists, Twitter, Sina Weibo, wechat, and online video-sharing sites such as the popular bilibili.com. They include translations of Chinese content into English and English into Chinese. The content being translated encompasses a great variety, ranging from news and videos to documents or slogans of protest. Taken as a whole, it constitutes a new form of political action aimed at constructing or challenging realities.

The translators who are engaged in these activities occupy a liminal space not just between two worlds, but among multiple worlds. Some are professional journalists. Others are activists and dissidents. Still others are NGOs. Many more are just regular internet users who are proud of their linguistic skills.

World-wide, NGOs are among the most actively engaged in translation activism. Thus human rights organizations, such as the New York-based Human Rights in China, are engaged in numerous translation projects. Many NGOs in China interact with their international counterparts or global media and thus often engage in translation activism. Environmental NGOs routinely translate foreign language sources into Chinese and Chinese sources into English. Green Earth Volunteers, for example, publishes an English-language online newsletter about environmental issues in China. Friends of Nature publishes an annual yearbook on environmental issues in China that is then translated into English by volunteers and published by Brill, thus making civil society perspectives on China's environmental issues available to an international audience.[10] In the broader sense of translation, Chinese environmental NGOs translate the discourses and organizational forms of global environmentalism into their own cultural context.[11]

One of the burgeoning areas of volunteer translation is in online subtitle communities. Although the translation work done in many of these communities is for entertainment, some is in the area of open course materials. Such translation may be viewed as a form of civic participation.[12]

Dissidents and dissident communities in China often rely on translation to bring their causes to the attention of global media and gain international support. Some, like the artist-activist Ai Weiwei, are fluent in English and can communicate easily on the global stage. Others rely on translators and translations. On May 29, 2012, the well-known activist lawyer Xu Zhiyong published an essay about China's new citizen movement on his blog. It was instantly translated into English. Soon afterwards, on June 7, 2012, Xu was taken away by public security authorities for questioning. Afterwards, he wrote an account about his disappearance, which was soon translated into English and published overseas.[13]

Finally, citizen translation happens in times of protest. A street protest in China may be reported in English on Twitter in order to attract international media attention. A petition campaign launched by Chinese activists may issue open petition letters in both Chinese and English, again to grab international attention. During the protest surrounding the censorship of the *Southern Weekend* magazine in January 2013, there were numerous tweets on Twitter in both Chinese and English about the protest. Many of these came from activists in China while some were picked up or quoted by Western mainstream media.[14]

Another case was the environmental protest in Ningbo in November 2012. According to *China Digital Times*, most Chinese media kept silent on the protest, but the foreign journalists at the scene helped to break the news:

> Angus Walker, the China correspondent for British ITV, has especially stood out. His on-the-spot tweets (@anguswalkeritv) were translated by netizens and posted to major Chinese social networking sites and forums. An ITV cameraman at the scene with Walker was hoisted up by protesters so he could film over the crowds.[15]

Translation renders information available and meaningful to an international audience. In cases where the information is hidden or suppressed, making it public is a powerful form of political challenge (e.g. in the exposure of human rights abuses). Here translation is the crux of an information politics.

But information politics is only one of many goals of a translation. The *process* of translation, a process of participation and solidarity building, is integral to translation activism. The product of translation, while delivering information, takes on other functions in the process of its reception and dissemination. It can be constitutive of new identities, communities, and public spaces. In addition, activist translations have a performative function. The act of publishing the translations is itself a public statement and a political intervention. As Baker puts it, translation "does not reproduce texts but constructs cultural realities, and it does so by intervening in the processes of narration and renarration that constitute all encounters, and that essentially construct the world for us."[16]

These three types of politics are not mutually exclusive; they may be mingled in any particular protest event or activist project. Nor is online translation activism in China limited to these three types. This chapter highlights these three types, however, because they are among the most common varieties and because each type exemplifies a particular way of mobilizing translation for political action.

The information politics of bridge blogs

The idea of bridge blogs is popularized in the works of Zuckerman and MacKinnon.[17] Zuckerman defines bridge blogs as "weblogs that reach across gaps of language, culture and nationality to enable interpersonal communication."[18] Many of these blogs are informational and cover news and current affairs. Zheng and Reese's study of Chinese bridge blogs similarly treats bridge bloggers as foreign news providers, arguing that "bridge blogs serve as the 'weak ties', linking cultural spheres formed by the 'strong ties' among traditional national media."[19]

The most influential bridge blogs related to China are advocacy blogs. Two examples are *Global Voices* and *China Digital Times*, where translation is central to an information politics in their transnational advocacy work. *Global Voices* describes its mission as the following: "We work to find the most compelling and important stories coming from marginalized and misrepresented communities. We speak out against online censorship and support new ways for people to gain access to the Internet."[20] One of its main activities is translation and, according to its website, many of its stories are translated into more than 35 languages.

Launched in 2003 as a blog and now a comprehensive website with translations of news, commentaries, and archives, *China Digital Times* describes itself as "an independent, bilingual media organization that brings uncensored news and online voices from China to the world."[21] It does so through, among other things, "amplifying the voices of Chinese citizens through translation" and "revealing the hidden mechanisms of state censorship by collecting and translating filtered keywords, propaganda directives, and official rhetoric."[22]

Over the years, *China Digital Times* has built a resourceful and influential project through its work of selecting, translating, archiving, and compiling English translations of Chinese news and blog postings with a focus on internet censorship and resistance. Internal censorship policies issued by Chinese authorities are sometimes obtained by *China Digital Times* and posted in English translations. A form of information politics, these expose the specifics of how the censorship apparatus works. Its website features "Netizen Voices," which are English translations of Chinese blogs complete with the original Chinese versions and editorial commentaries. In June 2010, it launched a participatory Web 2.0 initiative called the "Grass-Mud Horse Lexicon," an online glossary of English translations of terms created by Chinese netizens. According to its editor, the aim of the project is to vividly illustrate the increasingly dynamic and sometimes surprising presence of an alternative political discourse: images, frames, metaphors and narratives that have been generated from Internet memes. This "resistance discourse" steadily undermines the values and ideology that reproduce compliance with the Chinese Communist Party's authoritarian regime, and, as such, force an opening for free expression and civil society in China.[23]

The significance of the project is two-fold. On the one hand, it introduces the new language of Chinese digital dissent to Western audiences and shows its creative and subversive character. This is a language of humor, puns, and allusions. On the other hand, by systematically collecting, documenting, archiving, translating, and disseminating this oppositional language, the project helps to build, transmit, and sustain Chinese digital dissent outside China. The very existence of the "Grass-Mud Horse Lexicon" has a performative function, serving as an international voice of protest against censorship.

In contrast to the translation activism of *China Digital Times*, which is oppositional to the Chinese regime, other translation activists are critical of mainstream Western media's coverage of China. They position themselves as both advocates and intercultural communicators using translation to add more diverse perspectives about China. This is also a form of information politics.

One example is *ChinaHush*, a bridge blog that publishes both English translations and original English postings on current affairs in China. According its editor, *ChinaHush* was created out of dissatisfaction with how mainstream Western media cover China:

> *ChinaHush* is created first and mostly for personal reasons, as a way to record what I have been learning about China, and to share this knowledge with those who also have an interest in China. I think the Western media does not do a good job of presenting China to the western world. We hope we present another perspective, so that friends who have this common interest will learn more about Chinese cultures, lifestyles, trends, what Chinese people are talking about, and the latest memes in China.[24]

Another bridge blog site with a similar politics is *Hidden Harmonies*, which describes its mission as follows:

> The mission of *Hidden Harmonies* is to articulate and seek out Chinese perspectives, smart perspectives, and translations of Chinese perspectives from around world. It is run by people who love China. It is about fostering a community of intellectual and influential citizens from around the world interested in China to comment, discuss, praise or critique (as the case may be) a world that is fast-changing.[25]

Compared with *ChinaHush*, *Hidden Harmonies* has more of an activist edge and its postings are more unapologetically positive toward China. *ChinaHush* and *Hidden Harmonies* are little known, however, and much less influential than *Global Voices* and *China Digital Times*.

The identity politics of an online feminist subtitle group

The editor and authors of *Spaces of Their Own: Women's Public Sphere in Transnational China* explore the emergence of a transnational women's public sphere at the end of the twentieth century through studies of a women's museum, a telephone hotline in Beijing, the films of a Hong Kong filmmaker, the transnational contacts of a Taiwanese feminist organization, the diaspora of mainland women writers, and so forth.[26] This was at a time when the internet was still in its infant stage of development in China. Yet even in that early stage of internet development, feminist activists in China were already employing the new networked spaces to advance their causes, such as the establishment in 2000 of the anti-domestic violence network in Beijing.[27] Today, Chinese feminist activism is highly visible in both cyberspace and in the streets and theaters.[28] All these forms of feminist activism have expanded the "spaces of their own."

Importantly, translation is a crucial aspect of these various forms. The anti-domestic violence network which was set up in 2000, for example, strove to translate, both literally and culturally, the global discourses of gender equality and human rights advocacy into the Chinese social context.[29] The performances in China of such popular American feminist plays as *The Vagina Monologues* similarly involved translation work both in the linguistic sense and as a practice of cultural translation.[30]

Translating subtitles of feminist videos in the English language for the popular video-sharing website bilibili is a new way of expanding feminist spaces in China. Unlike other video-sharing sites, bilibili allows viewers to add real-time running comments, called bullet subtitles (弹幕), which appear on the streaming video screens together with the subtitles and their Chinese translations. Obviously, the Chinese translations of the subtitles make the videos legible to Chinese viewers. But their function is more than translation: they are an essential element for online interactions. The interactions are not limited to the real-time comments. As on YouTube sites, viewers can interact by leaving comments in the comment space below the video window.

It is on this website that a feminist subtitle group called Join-FeministSubtitleGroup posts English-language feminist videos with Chinese subtitle translations. One of the items posted on the site is a YouTube video called "When You Are a Girl Questioning Your Sexuality." As of this writing, the subtitled video posted on bilibili has 245 running comments that show up on the video screen and 196 comments in the comment section on the website. These comments are mostly short personal thoughts and questions about personal identities and sexual orientations. Some are reflections on one's own or one's friend's sexual orientations. One comment posted on July 15, 2016 goes as follows: "There is pressure. The reason for lingering here may be due to some pressure from the environment. Some who are opposed to homosexuality [out there] can be sarcastic. We really need to respect one another. Respect every person's choice."[31]

Here feminist subtitle translation becomes a way of creating an interactive online space for openly discussing sexual orientations and identity anxieties. In this sense, the translation activism exemplified by JoinFeminismSubtitleGroup is oriented to personal expression, identity explorations, and the building of alternative communities.

The information and performative politics of cyber-nationalists

Cyber-nationalism in China originated in the very early days of the internet, but took on global prominence in 2008, the year of the Beijing Olympics.[32] Qiu finds that while earlier cases of Chinese cyber-nationalism depended on textual communication in bulletin-board forums, the expansion of internet bandwidth makes it possible for speedy posting of images, thus giving cyber-nationalism an image-driven character.[33] This image-driven feature became even more prominent in the cyber "expedition" of nationalistic youth to bombard the Facebook page of Taiwan's newly elected president Tsai Ing-wen in January 2016, when dramatic and sensationalizing emoticons and images of slogans became weapons of the "expedition".

Images have the advantage of overcoming language barriers in cross-cultural communication, at least to certain extent. Yet images are themselves translations of ideas and therefore may present similar problems of translation for viewers unfamiliar with the cultural context in which the images are produced. As Guyer shows in his study of Egyptian political cartoons, images—in this case cartoons—require translation just as language does in international communication.[34] Images with local contexts and histories may not speak directly to audiences in other contexts or histories.

Even when images saturate contemporary political arenas, however, language still matters. Underhill's study of Egyptian diaspora's protest in London to support the revolutionary movement in their homeland finds that the use of Arabic slogans and banners was a way of foregrounding an Egyptian identity.[35] But at the same time, the Egyptian diaspora used banners in English to communicate to the mainstream media in the UK.

In China, translation and language became a notable aspect of cyber-nationalism in 2008, when youth in China and the Chinese diaspora protested against Western media coverage of China's hosting of the Beijing Olympics. On March 18, 2008, Rao Jin, a graduate of the prestigious Tsinghua University, registered the anti-cnn.com domain name. Rao Jin set up the website in direct response to what he perceived as biased Western media depictions of China in the days and months leading up to the Olympics.[36] The website caught on quickly, reaching over 100,000 subscribed members within two months according to the site's own description. As an online community of cyber-nationalism, the website puts together a team of translators and researchers. According to an online recruitment notice issued on the website's first anniversary, the job of the translation team is to 1) gather information, 2) translate simple news headlines and subtitles if the translator's language skill is at the beginner's level; 3) translate things about foreign culture, religion, society, literature, and so forth if the person is not interested in news and current affairs; 4) translate research reports of foreign think tanks; 5) translate TV programs, interviews, documentary films about current affairs; and 6) translate stories from foreign news and blog sites.[37]

This job description suggests that in its first two years, the translation activism of anti-cnn.com was primarily an information politics. It entailed translating English-language sources into Chinese to better inform Chinese users about Western depictions of China. In 2010, the website changed its name to m4.cn, m4 meaning the month of April—China's young nationalists had by then attained the nickname of "April youth." Besides expanding into a portal site of news and current affairs, m4.cn opened an English website called 4th Media (www.4thmedia.org/), which describes its mission as follows:

> Our platform translates relevant information, news analyses from both mainstream and progressive independent foreign media outlets to the Chinese speaking audience and vice-versa.
> In order to give a true and more objective picture of the world, we also package hot issues in current affairs, arguments, media critiques, celebrity news, youth topics and literary communication, etc. We do news, audio and video editing.[38]

If the translation activism of m4.cn is mainly informational, the new wave of cyber-nationalism in 2016 was more performative. This new wave was inaugurated by the "Diba Expedition" (thereafter "Expedition") to the Facebook page of newly elected Taiwanese president Tsai Ing-wen. Diba, or King Ba, is the nickname of the most popular online message board run by Baidu, with a membership in the tens of millions. The "Expedition" was launched on January 20, 2016 from the "Diba" message board. The most striking feature of this "Expedition," in comparison with earlier cyber-nationalistic protest, was not that it must have had some kind of covert official endorsement, because otherwise it would have been impossible for large numbers of users to access Facebook from inside China where it is blocked. It is not even the mass participation of the post-90s cohort. What was most striking was the form of participation, namely, posting large numbers of emojis, called "emoji packs" (biaoqing bao), on Tsai's Facebook page. These emoji packs attacked pro-Taiwanese independence positions and expressed pride for mainland China, including even its cuisines, which are also shown in emoji packs. Some of these emoji packs are ridiculously silly; others are plain texts like "Taiwan belongs to my country." Still others are humorous. But they are all emotional expressions in eye-catching images.

The importance of translation in this "Expedition" is evidenced in the fact that the organizers of this protest, like their "April youth" predecessors in 2008–2010, set up a translation team. Some slogans were translated into English and displayed in both Chinese and English. A popular song called "Missing Home" ("xiang chou"), with lyrics like "My wandering son, do you still remember the sweetness of our land," was rendered into multiple languages. An official Chinese slogan about socialist morality called "eight honorable things and eight shameful things" was translated into English and bilingual versions of it were posted on Tsai Ing-wen's Facebook page.[39] The first of these "eight things" reads like: "Honor to those who love the motherland, shame on those who harm the motherland." This was used to shame their target.

But translation was only partly about information. It was also a performative act, a statement that the cross-border and transnational character of the "expedition" might just need to have translations and that the participants in the "expedition" were cosmopolitans, and not narrow nationalists. Never mind that some translations do not make sense—a Confucian phrase which means "Develop morality first, and then one turns into a person" was rendered into the nonsensical "First into Germany, then adults"—a transformation of which only Google Translate is capable.

Yet despite such nonsensical translations, perhaps even partly because of the additional publicity they attracted, the "Diba Expedition" was a huge success in terms of the domestic and international media coverage it generated.

Conclusions

The analysis of online translation activism in this chapter leads to several tentative conclusions. First is the importance of new communication technologies to what I have called online translation activism in China. The three types of online translation activism studied here are all embedded in online networks. The translations are conducted and disseminated online. The translators are individuals or groups connected through online networks. It is hard to imagine that any of the three groups would even exist without the internet.

Second is the variety of digital platforms used by online translation activists. These differences suggest that the locations of the activist-translators, their resources, and the issues of interest to them may shape the processes and strategies of their translation activism. They also suggest that online translation activism, like many other forms of online activism in China or elsewhere, is not only embedded in online networks, but is also embedded in online communities, activist networks, or protest campaigns. It is part of, not separate from, the broader contexts or situations.

The main platform of *China Digital Times* is its own website, which functions as both a publishing platform and an online archive of its growing amount of translated material. In addition, it maintains an active presence on Twitter, where it disseminates its information. In the case of the JoinFeministSubtitleGroup, its main platform is the video-sharing site bilibili.com, while it also maintains an account on the microblogging platform Sina Weibo. The choice of bilibili.com as a main platform suggests that this group is targeting the youth population, probably the post-1990s among whom the rather recent fad of bullet subtitling is especially popular. Such an open platform requires few resources. The cyber-nationalist protests were organized by internet users in large online communities in China. Their target was Western media in the 2008 case and, in the 2016 case, the newly elected Taiwanese president Tsai Ing-wen. The media platforms in the 2016 case were particularly interesting, because cyber-nationalists in online fandom communities in the People's Republic "jumped" the Great Firewall in order to access Tsai's Facebook page. Since Facebook is blocked in China, it is hard to imagine that an army of cyber-nationalists could bypass the firewall without some sort of covert official support.

Third, my analysis shows that in translation activism, the selection of source texts is highly political; it is related to the goals and tactics of the specific case of activism. *China Digital Times* selects sources from the Chinese blogosphere to track and expose practices of censorship and resistance. This is consistent with its mission. Its "Grass-Mud Lexicon" project is the result of its cumulative work in this area over many years. The source videos selected by the JoinFeministSubtitleGroup to translate are available on YouTube. Similar videos are not available on Chinese video sites. The cyber-nationalist "Expedition" in 2016 is the most interesting and revealing case. Many of the emoji packs are re-creations of things and images in the popular internet culture, but some of them, such as the official slogan about socialist morality, come from official political culture. This shows that the source texts of cyber-nationalists, their weapons of protest, are derived from what they are familiar with, which includes hackneyed vocabularies in Chinese official discourse.

Fourth, while the informational value of translation is important in online translation activism, information is mixed with other political functions. Translation can be a form of identity politics, performance politics, as well as information politics. In the case of the feminist subtitling group, translation serves as an occasion for generating paratexts such as viewer comments and responses. Once paratexts appear, viewer interactions may take their own path, leading away from the translated texts to interpersonal interactions. In this way, translation enables explorations of personal identities, sexual orientations, and alternative communities. In the case of the cyber-nationalistic "Expedition," translation is itself a statement about the nature of the protest. The information conveyed through the translation seems to be of secondary importance. What matters is the act of translation, itself part of the package of protest. In this sense, the act of translation, more than its content, is the message.

Finally, it bears emphasizing that although online translation activism has its own distinct features, it is not isolated from, but forms an integral part of, online activism in the contemporary world. The networked nature of contemporary activism often gives it a transnational and intercultural character; it often involves the participation of diaspora and migrant communities. And it targets audiences beyond the immediate locales of protest. In other words, translation is an increasingly important way of performing politics and identities in global networked politics.

Notes

1 For studies of translation activism, see among others, Lui Pérez-González, "Ad-hocracies of Translation Activism in the Blogosphere: A Genealogical Case Study," in *Text and Context: Essays on Translation and Interpreting in Honour of Ian Mason*, Eds. Mona Baker, Maeve Olohan, and María Calzada Pérez (Manchester: St. Jerome, 2010): 259–287; Mona Baker, "Translation and Activism: Emerging Patterns of Narrative Community," in *Translation, Resistance, Activism*, Ed. Maria Tymoczko (Amherst and Boston: University of Massachusetts Press, 2010): 23–41.
2 Maria Tymoczko, "The Space and Time of Activist Translation," in *Translation, Resistance, Activism*, Ed. Maria Tymoczko (Amherst and Boston: University of Massachusetts Press, 2010), 227–254.
3 Sherry Simon, "Presentation," in *Traduction engagée/Translation and Social Activism*, Ed. Sherry Simon *TTR: Traduction, terminologie, rédaction* XVIII, no. 2 (2005): 11.
4 Conny Roggeband, "Translators and Transformers: International Inspiration and Exchange in Social Movements," *Social Movement Studies* 6, no. 3 (2007): 245–259.
5 Mona Baker, ed., *Translating Dissent: Voices From and With the Egyptian Revolution* (London: Routledge, 2015). For Baker's earlier studies of translation activism, see Mona Baker, "Translation and Activism," and Mona Baker, "Translation as an Alternative Space for Political Action," *Social Movement Studies: Journal of Social, Cultural and Political Protest* 12, no. 1 (2013): 23–47.
6 Leah Lievrouw, *Alternative and Activist New Media* (Cambridge, UK and Malden, MA: Polity Press, 2011), 59; Sally Engle Merry, "Transnational Human Rights and Local Activism: Mapping the Middle," *American Anthropologist* 108, no. 1 (2006): 38–51; Guobin Yang, "Civic Environmentalism," in *Reclaiming Chinese Society: The New Social Activism*, Eds. You-tien Hsing and Ching Kwan Lee (London: Routledge, 2010): 119–139.
7 Lydia Liu, *Translingual Practice: Literature, National Culture, and Translated Modernity—China, 1900–1937* (Stanford: Stanford University Press, 1995).

8 Jian Xu, *Media Events in Web 2.0 China: Interventions of Online Activism* (Brighton: Sussex Academic Press, 2016); Guobin Yang, *The Power of the Internet in China: Citizen Activism Online* (New York: Columbia University Press, 2009).
9 Weiyu Zhang and Chengting Mao, "Fan Activism Sustained and Challenged: Participatory Culture in Chinese Online Translation Communities," *Chinese Journal of Communication* 6, no. 1 (2013): 45–61.
10 For full disclosure, this author is on Brill's international advisory board of the English editions of these publications.
11 Yang, "Civic Activism."
12 Zhang and Mao, "Fan Activism Sustained and Challenged."
13 The translation is prefaced by the following:

> Dr Xu Zhiyong is a lecturer of law at Beijing University of Posts and Telecommunications, and one of the founders of Open Constitution Initiative (公盟) that offers legal assistance to petitioners and rights defenders, and has been repeatedly harassed, shut down and persecuted. In 2010 it changed its name to simply "Citizen". Just weeks ago on May 29, Dr Xu posted a blog post titled China's New Civil Movement to renew his call for a "new civic movement are a free China with democracy and the rule of law, a civil society of justice and happiness, and a new national spirit of freedom, fairness and love." The post has since been deleted by the authorities, and he himself was taken away by security police to answer questions. With Dr Xu's permission, Yaxue translated his account of the recent disappearance.
> Source: https://chinachange.org/tag/open-constitution-initiative/page/2/, accessed 8/15/16.

14 Jonathan Kaiman, "China Anti-censorship Protest Attracts Support Across Country," *The Guardian*, 7 January 2013. Retrieved from www.theguardian.com/world/2013/jan/07 /china-anti-censorship-protest-support
15 http://chinadigitaltimes.net/2012/11/netizen-voices-foreign-journalists-at-ningbo-protests/, accessed 10/16/16.
16 Baker, "Translation as an Alternative Space for Political Action": 23–24.
17 Ethan Zuckerman, "Meet the Bridgebloggers," *Public Choice* 134, nos. 1–2 (2008): 47–65. Rebecca MacKinnon, "Blogs and China Correspondence: Lessons about Global Information Flows," *Chinese Journal of Communication* 1, no. 2 (2008): 242–257.
18 Zuckerman, "Meet the Bridgebloggers," 48.
19 Nan Zheng and Stephen D. Reese, "Emerging Networks in the Global News Arena: Theorizing the Structural Role of Chinese Bridge Blogs," *Journalism* (2016): 1, http://doi.org/10.1177/1464884916643681
20 https://globalvoices.org/about/, accessed 8/12/2016.
21 http://chinadigitaltimes.net/about/, accessed 8/12/2016.
22 http://chinadigitaltimes.net/about/, accessed 8/12/2016.
23 http://chinadigitaltimes.net/space/Introduction_to_the_Grass-Mud_Horse_Lexicon, accessed 11/20/12.
24 www.chinahush.com/about/, accessed 8/12/2016.
25 http://blog.hiddenharmonies.org/about/, accessed 8/12/2016.
26 Mayfair Yang, ed., *Spaces Of Their Own: Women's Public Sphere in Transnational China* (Minneapolis: University Of Minnesota Press, 1999).
27 Cecilia Milwertz and Wei Bu, "Non-governmental Organizing for Gender Equality in China—Joining a Global Emancipatory Epistemic Community," *The International Journal of Human Rights* 11, nos. 1–2 (2007): 131–149.

28 Jinyan Zeng, "The Politics of Emotion in Grassroots Feminist Protests," *Georgetown Journal of International Affairs* 15 (2014): 41–52; Wei Wei, "Street, Behavior, Art: Advocating Gender Rights and the Innovation of a Social Movement Repertoire," *Chinese Journal of Sociology* 1, no. 2 (June 1, 2015): 279–304.
29 Milwertz and Bu, "Non-governmental Organizing for Gender Equality in China"; Lu Zhang, "Domestic Violence Network in China: Translating the Transnational Concept of Violence against Women into Local Action," *Women's Studies International Forum* 32, no. 3 (2009): 227–239.
30 Zhongli Yu, *Translating Feminism in China: Gender, Sexuality and Censorship* (London: Routledge, 2015).
31 Source omitted to protect anonymity.
32 Jack Qiu, "The changing web of Chinese nationalism," *Global Media and Communication* 2, no. 1 (1996): 125–128, http://doi.org/10.1177/1742766506061846; Xu Wu, *Chinese Cyber Nationalism: Evolution, Characteristics, and Implications* (Lanham, MD.: Lexington Books, 2007); Lijun Yang and Yongnian Zheng, "Fen Qings (Angry Youth) in Contemporary China," *Journal of Contemporary China* 21, no. 76 (2012): 637–653, http://doi.org/10.1080/10670564.2012.666834
33 Jack Qiu, "Go Baobao! Image-Driven Nationalism, Generation Post-1980s, and Mainland Students in Hong Kong," *Positions* 23, no. 1 (2015): 145–165, http://doi.org/10.1215/10679847-2870546
34 Jonathan Guyer, "Translating Egypt's Political Cartoons," in *Translating Dissent: Voices From and With the Egyptian Revolution*, Ed. Mona Baker (New York: Routledge, 2016), 208–220.
35 Helen Underhill, "Translation and Diaspora Politics: Narrating the Struggle at Home and Abroad," in *Translating Dissent: Voices From and With the Egyptian Revolution*, Ed. Mona Baker (London: Routledge, 2016), 45–59.
36 www.m4.cn/about/m4history.shtml, accessed 8/10/2016.
37 http://bbs.m4.cn/forum.php?mod=viewthread&tid=150492#pid2128707, accessed 8/10/16.
38 www.4thmedia.org/aboutus/, accessed 8/10/16.
39 http://news.sina.com.cn/c/zg/2016-01-21/doc-ifxnuvxe8316358.shtml, accessed 8/10/16.

Section II
Policy interventions

Introduction

Timothy Libert

Social movements often function outside of dominant political hierarchies, and are primarily concerned with promoting agendas ignored by the "mainstream." This is particularly true in the realm of media activism where the term "mainstream media" has itself become shorthand for the systemic exclusion of diverse voices in public discourse. And while many movements may seek to establish alternative media structures, just as many, if not more, seek to gain entrance to the "MSM" in order to give voice to those who have been voiceless. Alternative media strategies have an important place in activism, especially in the age of the Internet, but access to traditional media is still of vital necessity for many forms of structural change. Quite often the key to opening doors of traditional power hierarchies is policy advocacy.

However, scholars often place less emphasis on what the goals of policy reform should be than the nature of the movements themselves. Therefore, we must ask ourselves, how may activists advance their missions through policy advocacy? What are the institutional dynamics that activists must cope with as they seek to advance representation for minorities and women? What opposing powers must they face? How have policy battles been shaped (and stacked) historically? How should scholars fit media policy into existing conceptual frames and scholarship? All of the authors in the following chapters provide essential guidance and insights into these questions.

Before we may advance the cause of including diverse voices in the mainstream media, we need solid data that allows us to see who is excluded, to what degree, and to what effect. Mark Lloyd gives us valuable insight into how these issues have been approached at the US Federal Communications Commission. Lloyd first points out that while women make up slightly over 50 percent of the population, their participation in decision-making for full power television stations is only 6.3 percent. Likewise, while non-Hispanic whites make up 63 percent of the population, they control 94 percent of television stations. However, more fine-grained information is surprisingly hard to come by. As Lloyd documents, efforts at the FCC to study the issue in greater depth have been derailed by political battles for years. Entrenched powers appear so threatened by the very idea of data being collected and analyzed that they have put up a significant fight to stop legitimate research activities in the public interest. Likewise, when the FCC has sought to explore the topic of critical information needs—namely how communities learn about topics such as public safety, consumer welfare, transportation, health care, education, jobs, the environment, and civic participation—broadcasting associations have questioned the constitutionality of mere information gathering. Lloyd demonstrates that even revealing deficiencies in the distribution of media power, let alone challenging them, is a task to be met with real political and economic force. In sum, Lloyd shows us that the first step in getting more diverse voices into mainstream media—collecting and analyzing basic data—is itself a challenge, but one we must champion to achieve meaningful social change.

Carolyn Byerly focuses on another area where there is a disturbing lack of equality in media power which has deep effects on half the population: namely, the participation of women in media governance. Like Lloyd, Byerly cites data that show very low rates of participation in traditional media governance among women. She takes this analysis a step further and points out that new media and technology companies do quite a bit better in gender representation—but the bar for women's participation in media governance is so low that a mere 19 percent of women on technology boards qualifies as a significant improvement over other sectors of the economy where their representation is closer to 10 percent. Furthermore, this situation is not new, systemic exclusion in media governance has been the norm since the early days of radio licensing, which has been exacerbated by media consolidation. Quite often, media conglomerates concentrate more power into the hands of the few elite, strongly disadvantaging women. Despite these unsettling trends, there is a paucity of research on women's control of media institutions, a fact which underscores both the value and timeliness of Byerly's chapter. Using a theoretical framework of feminist political economy and women's media activism, Byerly sheds light on the reasons why present injustices have come to be. An additional contribution of Byerly is to highlight the fact that while media institutions have given some focus to minorities groups, they have done very little to directly advocate or research the role of women in media. Byerly highlights an area of acute need for reform and gives the reader valuable tools to conceptualize the structural discrimination faced by women in the media.

While Lloyd and Byerly attempt to situate the missing figures in media policy, Des Freedman seeks to address why media policy battles are often left out of critical scholarship. Freedman finds that the role of media within social movements has been historically ignored, or treated as just one variable among many rather than a focal point itself. This is a puzzling situation as the ability for nearly all contemporary social movements to achieve success is tied up in their media strategies—be they pursued via traditional channels, or through new media opportunities. Even when newer scholarship does address issues of media use by social movements directly, it is often to focus on the exciting possibilities of alternative media strategies, and attempts by insurgents to remake the media system anew. Yet it remains traditional publishing and broadcast outlets which have the largest concentrated audience and—as shown by Lloyd—are often protected by powerful corporate interests. Thus, Freedman suggests scholars and activists should expand their media strategies to include "amelioration"—the pursuit of improving existing media systems. Despite the fact that true wonks may disagree, Freedman advances the idea that part of the reason reform efforts are often given short shrift is that they tend to be boring when compared to other aspects of social and media movements. Nonetheless, Freedman's approach is in harmony with that of Lloyd and Byerly: in addition to focusing on the sexier aspects of activism, strong efforts must be made to expand broad-platform media to incorporate the voices of the underserved and underrepresented.

While Freedman may have a point that policy battles may be less interesting than other aspects of social movements, Lloyd and Byerly tell us that this is partially because policy reform is a long, slow, intergenerational process. True revolutions are rare, and often fail to achieve their goals, but nonetheless garner vastly more attention than staid policy battles. However, it is often the day-to-day grind of gradual advances in media policy that has long-term benefits for the rights of all peoples in media systems. This observation is not a call to embrace undue patience for vital change or acceptance for unequal representation; rather we should highlight the true determination of those activists whose battles and victories often occur far away from the limelight. The following chapters highlight the work that has been done, the work left to do, and the reasons for committing to the long slog that is social justice.

Chapter 5

The battle over diversity at the FCC

Mark Lloyd

The Federal Communications Commission has found itself in an odd and unfortunate maze, constructed of legislative mandates, appellate court demands, constitutional considerations, our pathetic public discourse about communication policy, and, of course, the FCC's own shifting regulatory rulings and interpretations. This quandary is: what to do about the obvious lack of gender and racial diversity among those licensed by the government to operate over the public airwaves while adhering to equal protection law.

It is long established that our republic requires, and that the First Amendment conveys to the public, a right to "the widest possible dissemination of information from diverse and antagonistic sources."[1] The public discussion about how to advance this constitutional right to free speech is too often drowned out by the broadcasters' cries about government intrusion of a separate and distinct right enumerated in the First Amendment—a free press. Nonetheless, the Supreme Court has consistently found that when there is a conflict with the broadcasters' free-press rights, the public's free-speech rights are paramount. And, in the words of the court, "safeguarding the public's right to receive a diversity of views and information over the airwaves is ... an integral component of the FCC's mission."[2] When the Commission fails to properly balance the conflicting rights of the public and the press, it is failing a constitutional obligation.

Compounding the FCC's difficulty protecting the free-speech rights of the public against the free-press claims of the broadcasters is the Commission's duty to respect the boundaries of equal protection law.

Even into the twenty-first century the US remains mired in a fierce fight over how to address the ongoing legacy of government-sanctioned racism and gender discrimination—a debilitating legacy now embedded in the status quo preserved by FCC regulation. The goal of encouraging greater women and minority participation in the communications industry is understandably seen as one aspect of the battle over "civil rights"—the reach toward equal protection under the law for all Americans. But the battle over the public's right to diverse sources of information and the battle over establishing greater political equality are both power struggles over the same terrain—the structure of our national conversation. The right to contribute to and access the diversity of our national conversation is one of our civil rights.

The timid steps taken by the FCC toward improving the participation of traditionally marginalized groups are sometimes distorted as intrusive government bureaucracy; sometimes they are framed as affirmative action run amok. This distortion about the rules regarding who gets a federal license to broadcast (to speak most powerfully in a local community) is possible, at least in part, because it is a debate that takes place over a battleground largely controlled by media.

What is offered here is not an analysis of jurisprudence, or a comparison of competing normative visions, but a case study of an independent agency seeking a careful path between free speech and equal protection while confronting real-world hardball politics. This is a case study of the impact on the FCC of what Kathleen Hall Jamieson calls the conservative echo chamber.[3] In order to understand the importance of what has happened, we must first navigate the maze in which the FCC, and thus the public, is stuck.

Conflicting responsibilities

While the First Amendment goal of public access to diverse and antagonistic sources was established in the earliest days of broadcast regulation, the Commission did not begin to consider women and minority participation, or rather the lack thereof, until after the civil rights and women's movements of the 1950s and 60s. In May 1978, the FCC issued a "Statement of Policy on Minority Ownership of Broadcasting Facilities," noting that its efforts in the late 1960s to expand broadcast diversity through equal employment opportunity rules were not increasing viewpoint diversity:

> [W]e are compelled to observe that the views of racial minorities continue to be inadequately represented in the broadcast media. This situation is detrimental not only to the minority audience, but to all of the viewing and listening public. Adequate representation of minority viewpoints in programming serves not only the needs and interests of the minority community but also enriches and educates the non-minority audience. It enhances the diversified programming which is a key objective not only of the Communications Act of 1934 but also of the First Amendment.[4]

As a result of this finding the FCC established policies to promote greater broadcasting participation among women and minorities. This link between increasing the participation of groups long under-represented among federal licensees and the idea that policies that promote a more inclusive participation in the communications industry advances the First Amendment goal of viewpoint diversity was affirmed by the Supreme Court in the 1990 *Metro Broadcasting* decision.[5] But five years later, a different Supreme Court altered the standard used to determine whether federal race-conscious programs are constitutional, thus overturning the ruling in *Metro Broadcasting*.[6]

In brief, *Adarand v. Pena* requires federal agencies to establish a compelling governmental interest and to narrowly tailor its policies to address that interest when race-conscious measures are at issue. *Adarand* was a case about regulations set by the Department of Transportation, but the new conservative court majority (a dissenting minority in *Metro Broadcasting*) took special pains to discuss and reverse the *Metro Broadcasting* standard of intermediate scrutiny. While some contemporary critics of the ruling described it as part of the Reagan-era backlash (or correction, if you like) in response to affirmative action,[7] it is worth noting that the court took exception to "the notion that strict scrutiny is 'strict in theory, but fatal in fact.'" The court added: "The unhappy persistence of both the practice and the lingering effects of racial discrimination against minority groups in this country is an unfortunate reality, and government is not disqualified from acting in response to it."[8]

And while the judicial standard of strict scrutiny also applies when First Amendment issues are at stake,[9] the Supreme Court in *Adarand* did not address the First Amendment issues raised in *Metro Broadcasting* or how to balance them against equal protection law.

And what about women? Applying intermediate scrutiny, the DC Circuit overturned the FCC's policies promoting women ownership in *Lamprecht v. FCC*.[10] The court concluded that while *Metro Broadcasting* established broadcast diversity as an important government objective, thus meeting the first prong of intermediate scrutiny, the study the FCC relied upon to support its gender-based policy was the Congressional Research Service report, *Minority Broadcast Station Ownership and Broadcast Programming: Is There a Nexus?*,[11] and this failed to establish a statistically meaningful link between ownership by women and programming of any particular kind.[12] In other words, the FCC could not demonstrate that its policies were *substantially related* to an important government objective, thus failing the second prong of intermediate scrutiny.

At present the FCC continues to profess an interest in promoting greater communications industry participation by women and minorities. But as the Commission has argued in court, it views its "power to address race-conscious measures ... a matter of considerable constitutional doubt after the *Adarand* case."[13] As far as the FCC has been concerned, strict scrutiny *is* fatal in fact.

In 2003, the Commission announced an extensive revision of its broadcast ownership rules, while ignoring proposals to advance the First Amendment goal of diversity.[14] In 2004, the Third Circuit Court of Appeals remanded much of the FCC's work.[15] The Third Circuit largely repeated this rejection in 2011, and admonished the Commission for citing the "difficulties" presented by the Supreme Court's decision in *Adarand* as a rationale for failing to consider proposals to improve greater ownership among women and minorities. In the words of the court:

> The FCC's own failure to collect or analyze data, and lay other necessary groundwork, may help to explain, but does not excuse, its failure to consider the proposals presented over many years. If the Commission requires more and better data to complete the necessary *Adarand* studies, it must get the data and conduct up-to-date studies, as it began to do in 2000 before largely abandoning the endeavor.[16]

The FCC has made some progress on gathering data. In 2014, the Commission reported that women, a little more than 50 percent of the US population, held a majority of the voting interests in 6.3 percent of the full-power television stations and 6.7 percent of the commercial FM radio stations. Hispanic/Latino persons, approximately 17 percent of the US total population, held a majority of the voting interests in 3.0 percent of the full-power commercial television stations and 3.2 percent of the commercial FM radio stations. Racial minorities (including all African-Americans, Asian-Americans, and Native Americans combined), approximately 20 percent of the population, held a majority of the voting interests in 3.0 percent of the full-power commercial television stations and 3.0 percent of the commercial FM radio stations.[17] The numbers get a little better with less powerful media (low-power TV, for example), but the numbers do not begin to approach parity with the population of women or the growing numbers of either Latinos or other so-called racial minorities in the United States.

Is this a Fair Slice of the Pie?

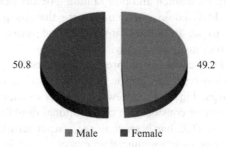

Figure 5.1 US Gender 2010 Census

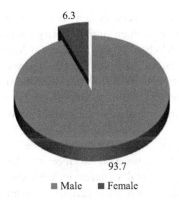

Figure 5.2 Full-power TV ownership by Gender 2014

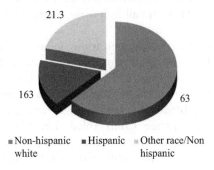

Figure 5.3 US population by race/ethnicity 2014 Census

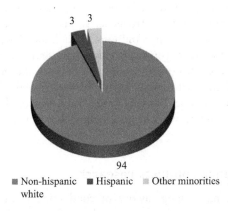

Figure 5.4 Full-power TV ownership by Hispanic Demo 2014 Census

The 2014 FCC report on ownership is a small advance over the paucity of hard, reliable data about women and minority ownership available in the years the Republicans Michael Powell and Kevin Martin directed the Commission.[18] But simply citing these raw numbers does not meet either intermediate scrutiny or strict scrutiny. While the apparent disparity suggests something is out of kilter, the numbers alone do not establish either a compelling governmental interest, or help the Commission narrowly tailor policy.

Does the race or gender of a broadcast licensee matter? Aren't the licensees just going to do what is necessary to meet the demands of the audience? Does ownership have any real connection with content? Does ownership have any real connection with who actually operates the station? And if women and minorities were more interested in purchasing a broadcast property and getting a broadcast license, what is stopping them? Have the developments of new communications technologies lessened the importance of broadcast licenses? These are all legitimate questions. The answers are not settled.

While the media and telecommunications industries have never stopped questioning the right of the federal government to insist that they operate in the public interest, the challenge to FCC authority has long been settled. In short, the Federal Communications Commission is a legitimate government institution overseeing broadcasters. In an 8-0 decision, *Red Lion Broadcasting v. FCC*, the Supreme Court ruled that when the rights of the broadcasters conflict with the speech rights of the public, including the right to access diverse speech over the public airwaves, the rights of the public are paramount.[19]

The supposed declining authority of *Red Lion* because of the purported irrelevance of the "scarcity rationale" is a too-widespread confusion.[20] There remains a scarcity in government licenses to operate exclusively over designated electromagnetic spectrum frequencies. This frequency license scarcity is why spectrum auctions raise millions of dollars. There are still more people who want these government licenses than there are licenses available. Again, despite the confusion, the question of why the government has a right to be concerned with the behavior of government licensees is not a particularly interesting one. But there are, again, unsettled issues and unanswered questions; and as we will note below, some would rather the FCC not seek answers.

An expert agency conducts research

The Commission has a long history of conducting research to determine whether its regulations or the entities it licenses are furthering the "public interest, convenience and necessity."[21] After all what good is an expert agency if it is not able to conduct research and maintain its expertise? What good is a regulatory agency if the only information it has to rely upon comes from the corporations it is supposed to regulate?

A good deal of the Commission's research is focused on engineering questions—such as determining whether there is frequency interference between different licensed services. Much of the research is economic analysis—for example, game theory studies regarding the best way to conduct spectrum auctions. Some of this economic work occurs when the FCC has to determine whether to approve a proposed merger, some of this mirrors the work of the antitrust division of the Justice Department. Much of the FCC's research is creating form questionnaires posed to FCC-regulated media and telecommunications industries and tallying up the replies. But upon too rare an occasion the Commission actually seeks information about how its "public interest" policies and various licensees actually serve the public.

Sometimes this research into whether the public interest is being met is *ad hoc*, sometimes it is done with limited public engagement. This was the case with the research that supported the controversial and quickly abandoned report and order regarding the "Public Service Responsibility of Broadcast Licensees"—notoriously known as the "Blue Book."[22]

Another example of how not to do it occurred in 2003 when FCC Chairman Powell offered a reward to the first FCC economist who would create "an objective scientific formula that will accurately measure the diversity of media voices in a local market."[23] Once he found the formula he liked, he dubbed it the Diversity Index.

Powell's Diversity Index took into account *all* available media voices in a local market, including legacy media such as newspapers, and emerging media such as Internet web sites ... not just broadcasting. Powell pointed to the abundance of media sources on the Internet as a rationale to promulgate a set of policies to allow greater broadcast media concentration.

While the broadcast industry applauded the results, Congress turned back Powell's effort.[24] And in *Prometheus v. FCC*, the Third Circuit rejected not only Powell's new media ownership rules, it also made a special point of rejecting the conclusions he drew from this Diversity Index:

> We do not object in principle to the Commission's reliance on the Department of Justice and Federal Trade Commission's antitrust formula, the Herfindahl-Hirschmann Index ("HHI"), as its starting point for measuring diversity in local markets. In converting the HHI to a measure for diversity in local markets, however, the Commission gave too much weight to the Internet as a media outlet, irrationally assigned outlets of the same media type equal market shares, and inconsistently derived the Cross-Media Limits from its Diversity Index results.[25]

The public and potentially contrarian peer experts had little input into Powell's Diversity Index.

The FCC's attempt to identify market entry barriers to participate in the communications industry, and in the process to identify a compelling governmental interest that might justify regulations to address these barriers, was not *ad hoc*, and it was not conducted in secret.

The rationale for this research was based on sound precedent; it was the same rationale used prior to 2000. And the proposed research was explicitly neither race nor gender focused. Like the Powell Diversity Index, the proposed research was acutely aware of the rapidly changing media and telecommunications industries the FCC is mandated to regulate. Unlike the Powell Diversity Index, the 2012 work on market entry barriers was also aware of the dynamic complexities of the diverse American public. And, unlike the Powell Index, the FCC's work toward a barrier study reached for expertise beyond FCC staff and sought public input before it moved forward.[26]

A barrier study

On February 6, 2012, the Commission asked for bids from the public—issued a Request for Quotation (RFQ) in government-speak—to conduct a "Barrier Study" described as a "Review of the Literature Regarding Critical Information Needs of the American Public." In the solicitation, the Commission noted that Section 257 of the Communications Act of 1934, as amended (Communications Act),

> mandates that, every three years, the Commission review and report to Congress on identifying and eliminating, by regulations pursuant to its authority under this chapter (other than this section), market entry barriers for entrepreneurs and other small businesses in the provision and ownership of telecommunications services and information services.[27]

The solicitation also noted that in order to

> develop policy that would advance the goal of diversity, including the promotion of greater women and minority participation in media, the Commission needs to conduct or commission research that illuminates the diversity of views available to local communities, the diversity of sources in local markets, and the diversity of critical information needs of the American public, including women and minorities.[28]

This view was consistent with the "National Policy" set out in Section 257(b): "To promote the policies and purposes of this [Communications] Act favoring a diversity of media voices, vigorous economic competition, technological advancement, and promotion of the public interest, convenience, and necessity."[29] Indeed, the legislative history cited by the

Commission in its initial 1996 Notice of Inquiry on the first 257 report, noted a specific concern about the "under-representation" of women and minorities in the telecommunications industry,[30] quoting Rep. Cardiss Collins (D-IL):

> [W]e cannot disregard the lessons of the past and the hurdles we still face in making certain that everyone in America benefits equally from our country's maiden voyage into cyberspace. I refer to the well-documented fact that minority and women-owned small businesses continue to be extremely under represented in the telecommunications field ... Underlying [Section 257] is the obvious fact that diversity of ownership remains a key to the competitiveness of the U.S. communications marketplace.[31]

In the late 1990s the FCC commissioned several *Adarand* studies in response to Section 257.[32] While the Commission followed the precedent set by the FCC under Chairman William Kennard in citing Section 257 as the rationale for the solicitation, the Commission could also call on Section 309 (j)[33] as it did in 1996, and if absolutely necessary, it could rely upon Section 202(h),[34] which mandates that the Commission review its ownership rules every four years and determine whether they are in the public interest as the result of competition.

But the citation to either 257 or to multiple statutes was not necessary, particularly not at such a preliminary stage. The FCC was not setting policy, it was not asking for comments about proposed policy, it was not even requiring forms to be filled out by regulated industries. The Commission was trying to understand how it might meet both its statutory obligations and its constitutional obligations. It was trying to understand how it might *begin* conducting research to advance the First Amendment goal of diversity while searching for information that might guide it to stay within the bounds of equal protection law.

The FCC was attempting to take the requirements of strict scrutiny head on. Was there a compelling governmental interest? What research would be sufficiently robust to help the FCC narrowly tailor policy to address a compelling governmental interest? Quoting from the solicitation:

> In order to assess *whether government action is needed* to ensure that the information needs of *all Americans* are being addressed, to determine the relationship, if any, between meeting critical information needs, and the available opportunities for *all Americans* to participate in the communications industries, it is first necessary to examine what prior research has been conducted with regard to how the public acquires *critical information*, how the media ecosystem operates to provide critical information, and what barriers exist to participation.[35]
>
> (Emphasis added)

The research requested was not to focus narrowly on gender and/or race/ethnicity, and it was not meant to identify information needs in general, but *critical information needs* (CIN). Information needs, that might, in other words, justify governmental action.[36]

Several respondents submitted proposals, and after careful consideration, on April 16, 2012, the Commission awarded a contract to a team of researchers led by the University of Southern California's Annenberg School for Communication and Journalism. On June 26, 2012, the FCC's Office of Communications Business Opportunities hosted a public meeting to review a draft report by the awardees, who named themselves the Communications Policy Research Network (CPRN). Peer scholars, unaffiliated with the CPRN, were given a draft of the literature review, and participated in the open meeting along with interested members of the public. And on July 16, a final 90-page report and a bibliography of over 500 reports covering a wide range of areas related to the critical information needs of the American public was submitted to the Commission.

The CPRN literature review reported "clear and significant information needs of Americans at the individual and community level." Based upon a careful review of hundreds of studies from a variety of disciplines, the CPRN concluded that "many of these needs are not being met" and that "[e]xclusion from the networked benefits of participation in an information society are not simply additive, but they may be exponential, with long term consequences for minorities, non-English speakers, those with low-income, and the disabled." The CPRN recommended that "the FCC conduct serious, rigorous, research into whether and how these needs are being met." It recommended:

> modeling *community communication ecologies* that can investigate whether and how local information needs are met is a critical first step to understanding how markets, government policies and individual and group actions can work together to meet the information needs of their communities.

The CPRN insisted that in order to develop relevant public policy the FCC could no longer look at media in silos, but that it must look at the information and operations of entire local media ecologies. And the CPRN argued that the FCC needed to draw on multiple social science disciplines in addition to economics. The public peer-review panel was glowing in its praise of the report.

The FCC then contracted with Social Solutions International, Inc. (SSI), an 8(a) certified and Small Disadvantaged Business, Hispanic and woman-owned firm with experience in both social science research and government contracts and procedures, to hold a research design conference with a multi-disciplinary group of media scholars using the findings of the CPRN's literature review as a foundation. That meeting was held on September 13 and 14, 2012. SSI was contracted to report on that meeting and construct a practicable research plan that would be made available for public comment.

And then the Chairman of the FCC put it all on hold.

Perhaps it was the lack of funding. The "Tea Party" takeover of the Republican Party ushered in a time of budget gridlock, "fiscal cliffs," seemingly perpetual short-term continuing resolutions, and across the board cuts that affected nearly all government operations.[37] There may have been a few other considerations, but let's just say the project did not have the support of the FCC Chairman, Julius Genachowski.

Competing studies

Chairman Genachowski did, however, put his full support behind a research plan announced by a media brokerage firm and council of industry attorneys led by David Honig. Honig's group occasionally gathers signatures from various groups which claim to represent "minorities" and so he calls it the Minority Media and Telecommunications Council.[38]

In the late fall of 2012, Genachowski was eager to move forward on a proposal to relax the ownership rules that limited joint ownership of broadcast and newspaper operations in the same market, also known as media cross-ownership rules.[39] After considerable criticism that these rules may impact media diversity,[40] Genachowski put on hold a vote on his media ownership rules and issued the following statement:

> Yesterday, the Minority Media and Telecommunications Council informed the Commission that it will conduct a focused, independent study on the effects of cross-ownership rules on minority ownership and newsgathering, in order to enhance the record in the Commission's proceeding. The study is expected to take several weeks and will be filed with the Commission, after which MMTC suggests that the agency solicit public input, to be followed by a Commission vote. In this heavily-litigated area where a strong record is particularly important, I believe this is a sensible approach to moving forward and resolving the issues raised in this proceeding.[41]

A month later, Genachowski announced he was leaving office.[42]

The Honig study, which also had the support of the National Association of Broadcasters, was conducted by the research firm of BIA/Kelsey. It was an eight-question, online survey of 14 broadcast owners. The Honig study was released on May 30, 2013, and like Honig and Genachowski, the study seemed to support the relaxation of the media cross-ownership rules. "We are struck by the lack of any large concern by almost all of the respondents to these cross-media operations," wrote Mark Fratrik, BIA/Kelsey's vice president and chief economist.[43] Though Honig claimed his study was subject to peer-review, he has blocked all attempts by the public to access the comments of the reviewers.

While the National Association of Broadcasters and a few corporate interests were pleased to cite the Honig study as support for their arguments to relax media ownership rules, even a cursory examination of the study revealed major problems. On July 22, S. Derek Turner, Research Director for the group Free Press, captured many of the concerns of the public-interest community:

- The study fails to examine the perceived impact of cross-ownership on broadcast radio-station owners separately from the impact on broadcast television station owners. The study also fails to distinguish between the impact on female owners and the impact on minority owners.
- The study's reliance on online survey responses is not appropriate for a study that claims to employ an "unaided recall methodology."
- The study identifies owners who perceive cross-ownership as negatively impacting their businesses, but concludes that cross-ownership has "no material impact."
- MMTC claims the study was peer-reviewed, yet it failed to submit any written reviews or provide any indication of the reviewers' opinions of the study.[44]

On May 20, 2013, FCC Commissioner Mignon Clyburn was appointed by President Barack Obama to serve as Acting Chairwoman of the Federal Communications Commission. Clyburn was a staunch supporter of the critical information needs work.[45] And on May 28, the Commission made public the SSI-proposed research design and asked for comment.[46]

Based upon the CPRN literature review, the public comments regarding that work, the work of the research design group, and input from the FCC, SSI proposed a combined study of a "media market census" and a "community ecology study" to be conducted in six markets. The core goal of the proposed study was to determine "the access (or potential barriers) to CINs as identified by the FCC."

As noted in the SSI-proposed research design, the FCC identified two primary areas of critical information needs: that information necessary for the public to live safe and healthy lives; and that information necessary to participate fully in the civic and economic life of their communities should they choose. And borrowing from the CPRN literature review, the congressional mandate to the FCC to establish a national broadband plan, and public comments the FCC determined that in order to meet these two core needs, local media ecologies should provide in a timely manner, in an accessible form (language and dis/ability appropriate) via media that are reasonably accessible, the following critical information needs:

1) Public safety information (information related to severe weather, accidental disasters, national security or health-related alerts)
2) Consumer welfare information (including information about nutrition and harmful products)
3) Transportation information
4) Health care delivery information
5) Education information (including school choice and performance, and adult education)
6) Economic information (including employee training, investment opportunity, and jobs)
7) Information about energy and the environment
8) Information about civic and political participation.

The media market census would analyze the media content for broadcast news, newspapers, and local Internet news, and would conduct a voluntary survey of media providers focusing on ownership characteristics, employment, and barriers to entry. The community ecology study would be a general population survey of the actual and perceived critical information needs of the designated market and in-depth neighborhood interviews to capture "neighborhood effects." Comments regarding the SSI research design were submitted to the Commission by a variety of groups, including the National Association of Broadcasters (against) and the Communications Policy Research Network (in favor).

The NAB argued that the Commission "is not primarily a research institution; rather, it directly regulates some of the speakers to be analyzed in the CIN Study. That raises some constitutional concerns." NAB questioned the critical information needs categories as unrelated to consumer needs and not relevant to how news broadcasters operate. More pointedly, NAB argued that "the Commission should decline to direct its researchers to probe into either the news judgment of professional journalists or their personal demographics such as race, ethnicity, or gender. These questions raise constitutional implications."[47]

The CPRN defended the CIN categories as supported by its literature review of hundreds of relevant scholarly reports, and argued that whether the "CIN categories fit 'actual consumer needs or interests' is, of course, an empirical question; it is precisely what the proposed SSI research is designed to address." The CPRN argued that "research into the decision-makers and decision-making process of media operations seems to us to be limited in scope and necessary to determine whether newsroom employment and practice has any impact on the provision of local critical information needs." And more pointedly: "The underlying assumption of the NAB seems to be that the Commission is somehow constitutionally bound to remain ignorant of conditions, behaviors, and practices that reside outside of their authority to regulate directly." The CPRN noted minor "quibbles" with the study design, but argued that it was a good test of the fundamental concept it suggested months earlier and urged the Commission to move forward.[48]

The right-wing echo chamber attacks the critical information needs study

On October 30, conservative talker/blogger Tucker Carlson's media operation, *The Daily Caller*, published an article quoting from the NAB's critique, with the headline: "FCC to police news media, question reporters in wide-ranging content survey."[49] Two days later, on November 1, 2013, the FCC announced a planned test of the critical information needs research design in one market, Columbia, South Carolina.

Tom Wheeler was sworn in as Chairman of the Federal Communications Commission on November 4, 2013. The champion of the CIN work, Mignon Clyburn, returned to her position as Commissioner.

On December 10, 2013, the Republican leadership of the House committee with oversight of the FCC sent a letter to the new FCC chairman entitled, "Committee Leaders Urge FCC to Suspend Work on 'Fairness Doctrine 2.0.'" The letter borrowed heavily from both the NAB critique of the test pilot of the CIN research design and some of the cruder right-wing blogs.[50]

After the Christmas break, when Congress was back on watch on February 10, 2014, the FCC Commissioner Ajit Pai (one of the two Republican Commissioners), published a commentary in the Wall Street Journal criticizing the FCC's plan to test the critical information needs study design. His commentary was titled, "The FCC Wades Into the Newsroom: Why is the Agency Studying 'Perceived Station Bias' and Asking About Coverage Choices?"[51] Pai's commentary borrowed heavily from the NAB comments, the right-wing blogs, and the letter from the House Republicans.

Soon scores of conservative radio hosts and other right-wing bloggers were spreading the word that the White House was ordering the FCC to police newsrooms and that this amounted to a return of the Fairness Doctrine.[52] Some of these false reports targeted SSI and the different academic institutions with professors who were involved in the CPRN. This resulted in a barrage of threatening calls and emails from angry citizens upset about a return to the Fairness Doctrine. On February 20, the right-wing cable television network Fox News devoted a segment on their prime-time program to what they called the FCC's supposed plan to police newsrooms.

On February 21, the new FCC Chairman Wheeler issued a statement indicating that the proposed questions to journalists would be dropped from the draft study, but that the planned pilot would proceed.[53]

The drumbeat from the right-wing blogs continued, as did the threatening calls. The mainstream media largely ignored the story, though the Columbia Journalism Review ran an article with the news that "stations in [the] South

Carolina test market [are] still waiting to hear from federal government" about the "FCC's Study of Newsrooms."[54] The mainstream media never mentioned the support given to the study by the nation's premier free-speech advocate, the American Civil Liberties Union.[55] And while one of the contributors to the literature review posted an article defending the critical information needs work in a *Washington Post* blog, media scholars were largely silent in the face of the right-wing attacks.[56]

On May 16, Wheeler announced he was bringing the plans for the test pilot of the critical information needs study to an end.[57]

Conclusion

The Federal Communications Commission is an independent agency, but it remains a political body limited by the politics of its time. The Commission must negotiate not only the conflicts between sometimes ambiguous statutory mandates, but it must address the conflicts that arise from the work of radically different prior Commissions, while keeping in line with evolving constitutional doctrines. And, of course, this does not mention the fact that the FCC regulates the communications industry that, while licensed to serve ever-changing notions of the public interest, dominates the national debate about the rules governing the communications industry.

In beginning the process of research into whether local media ecologies were meeting the critical information needs of diverse populations, the Commission was seeking guidance as to whether there was a compelling governmental interest in advancing the public's right to access the widest possible dissemination of antagonistic sources of information and how best to narrowly tailor policy to address its First Amendment obligation. A proposed test pilot of a research design to determine whether local media was serving the critical needs of local communities was distorted and stopped by the right-wing media, and the Republicans in Congress and at the FCC, screaming "Fairness Doctrine 2.0!" and "FCC Polices Newsrooms!"

In the absence of relevant research into how its regulations or its licensees serve the public, the FCC is left without a clue as to how best to establish the widest possible dissemination of diverse and antagonistic sources of information. This is a testament to the power of the right wing, and it is a testament to the weakness of those who profess to believe in the importance of a political voice for *all* Americans.

Notes

1 *Associated Press v. United States*, 326 US 1, 20 (1945).
2 *Metro Broadcasting v. FCC*, 497 US 547 (1990) at 567.
3 Kathleen Hall Jamieson and Joseph N. Cappella, *Echo Chamber: Rush Limbaugh and the Conservative Media Establishment* (New York, NY: Oxford University Press, 2008).

4 "Statement of Policy on Minority Ownership of Broadcasting Facilities," 68 FCC.2d 979 (1978).
5 *Metro Broadcasting*, 497 US 547 (1990) at 567; *FCC v. National Citizens Committee for Broadcasting*, 436 US 775, 795 (1978); *Red Lion Broadcasting Co. v. FCC*, 395 US 367, 409 (1969).
6 *Adarand v. Pena*, 515 US 200 (1995).
7 Tamar Lewin, "5–4 Decision Buoys Some, for Others, it's a Setback," *The New York Times*, 13 June 1995, www.nytimes.com/1995/06/13/us/the-supreme-court-reaction-5-4-decision-buoys-some-for-others-it-s-a-setback.html; see also David Kairys, "Unexplainable on Grounds Other Than Race." *Am. UL Rev.* 45 (1995): 729, www.wcl.american.edu/journal/lawrev/45/kairys.pdf
8 *Adarand* op. cit., citing *Fullilove v. Klutznick*, 448 US 448 (1980) at 519 (Marshall, J. concurring in judgment).
9 *Denver Area Educ. Telecomm. Consortium, Inc. v. FCC*, 518 US 727, 741 (1996); see also Adam Winkler, "Fatal in Theory and Strict in Fact: An Empirical Analysis of Strict Scrutiny in the Federal Courts," *Vanderbilt Law Review*, Vol. 59, 793 (2006), http://ssrn.com/abstract=897360
10 *Lamprecht v. FCC*, 958 F.2d 382 (1992). This policy was not before the Court in *Metro Broadcasting*, 497 US at 558, n. 7.
11 Ibid. at 396–398. The D.C. Circuit also noted that the CRS report was methodologically flawed in that it "does not define terms such as 'women's programming' (or 'minority programming,' for that matter), but rather, relied on the reporting stations to characterize themselves." Ibid. at 397, n. 8. The Supreme Court relied in part on the CRS report in *Metro Broadcasting*, 497 US at 583, n. 31.
12 *Lamprecht*, 958 F.2d at 395. The court questioned whether such a thing as "women's programming" exists and, if so, whether it is underrepresented. Ibid.
13 Jacob Lewis, FCC Deputy General Counsel, Oral Argument, *Prometheus Radio Project v. FCC* (2011).
14 See Report and Order and Notice of Proposed Rulemaking, 18 FCCR 13, 620 (2003).
15 *Prometheus Radio Project v. FCC*, 373 F.3d 372 (3d Cir. 2004) (Prometheus I).
16 *Prometheus Radio Project v. FCC*, 652 F.3d 431 (3d Cir. 2011).
17 FCC, "Report on Ownership of Commercial Broadcast Stations," 2014, www.fcc.gov/document/report-ownership-commercial-broadcast-stations-0
18 Christopher Terry, "Minority Ownership: An Undeniable Failure of FCC Media Ownership Policy," *Widener JL Econ. & Race* 5 (2013): 18, http://blogs.law.widener.edu/wjler/files/2014/01/6Terry.pdf
19 *Red Lion Broadcasting Co. v. FCC*, 395 US 367, 390 (1969).
20 Mark Lloyd, "Red Lion Confusions," *Administrative Law Review*, Washington College of Law/American University, Washington, DC, 60 (2009).
21 The Communications Act of 1934, 47 USC § 151 et seq.
22 Victor Pickard, "The Battle over the FCC Blue Book: Determining the Role of Broadcast Media in a Democratic Society, 1945–8," *Media, Culture & Society* 33, no. 2 (2011): 171–191, http://mcs.sagepub.com/content/33/2/171.full.pdf+html
23 Edmund Sanders, "FCC Eyes an Index for Media Mergers," *Los Angeles Times*, 10 February 2003, http://articles.latimes.com/2003/feb/10/business/fi-formula10
24 Stephen Labaton, "Senators Move to Restore F.C.C. Limits on the Media," *New York Times*, 5 June 2003, www.nytimes.com/2003/06/05/business/senators-move-to-restore-fcc-limits-on-the-media.html
25 *Prometheus Radio Project v. FCC*, 373 F.3d 372 (3d Cir. 2004) (Prometheus I).
26 A number of well-meaning public interest and civil rights advocates suggest, with the Third Circuit, that the Commission simply conducts up-to-date *Adarand*

The battle over diversity at the FCC   97

studies. The critical information needs work may be characterized as an *Adarand* study appropriate to the dynamic industry regulated by the FCC. But if the suggestion is to conduct the disparity studies that have been used to determine the constitutionality of race-based set-asides or incentives for government contracts such as those offered by other agencies, that approach is far too limited to guide the Commission in establishing narrowly tailored regulations appropriate to the First Amendment concerns of a dynamic communications industry. Such a limited, race-based approach would be an invitation to Court rejection.

27 47 USC § 257. Congress added Section 257 to the Communications Act through the Telecommunications Act of 1996, Public Law No. 104–104, 110 Stat. 56 (1996) (Telecommunications Act of 1996). 47 USC § 257 (c). Subsection (c) requires periodic review and reporting by the Commission every three years. The Commission's last report covered years 2006 through 2009, and was adopted and released in March, 2011. See Section 257 Triennial Report to Congress, Identifying and Eliminating Market Entry Barriers for Entrepreneurs and Other Small Businesses, 26 FCC Rcd 2909 (2011).
28 Ibid.
29 47 USC § 257(b).
30 Identifying and Eliminating Market Entry Barriers for Small Businesses, Federal Communications Commission, 47 CFR Chapter I, General Docket No 96–113; FCC 96–216at Fed Reg. 33066, 61, no. 124, 26 June 1996, www.gpo.gov/fdsys/pkg/FR-1996-06-26/pdf/96-16259.pdf
31 142 Cong. Rec. H1141 at H1176-77 (daily ed. February 1, 1996) (statement of Rep. Collins).
32 "Studies Indicate Need to Promote Wireless and Broadcast License Ownership by Small, Women-, and Minority-Owned Businesses," Statement of FCC Chairman William Kennard, December 12, 2000. It is worth noting that in the 2004 and 2007 Section 257 reports, the Commission, without explanation, ignored its 2000 interpretation of Section 257 and submitted a "[r]eport that details our regulatory activity in these areas and that identifies statutory barriers to entry for entrepreneurs and other small businesses." This willful misinterpretation of a statute entitled "Market Entry Barriers" to limit the Commission's focus to statutory barriers has been embraced by a few critics of the critical information needs work. For example, one blogger, a communications attorney at a DC law firm, asserted "Section 257's narrow focus [is] on identifying and removing governmental barriers." Harry Cole, "R.I.P.: Critical Information Needs Study," *CommLawBlog*, Fletcher Heald and Hildreth, 3 March 2014, www.commlawblog.com/2014/03/articles/broadcast/r-i-p-critical-information-needs-study/. This is clearly not what the statute states.
33 47 USC 309(j)(4)(D) provides that the Commission shall "consider the use of tax certificates, bidding preferences, and other procedures" to "ensure that small businesses, rural telephone companies, and businesses owned by members of minority groups and women are given the opportunity to participate in the provision of spectrum-based services."
34 Andrew Jay Schwartzman, Harold Feld and Parul Desai, "Section 202(h) of the Telecommunications Act of 1996: Beware of Intended Consequences," *Federal Communications Law Journal* 58, no 3 (2006): Article 17, www.repository.law.indiana.edu/fclj/vol58/iss3/17
35 Ibid.
36 See Barrier Studies, Solicitation Number: FCC12Q0009, www.fbo.gov/index?s=opportunity&mode=form&tab=core&id=fbc47f717812c2c9efd450d07e0 b4565&_cview=0

37 Robert Pear, "Budget Stalemate Leaves Chaos at Many Agencies," *New York Times*, 14 March 2011, www.nytimes.com/2011/03/15/us/15spend.html
38 Jason McLure, "Civil Rights Group's FCC Positions Reflect Industry Funding, Critics Say," *The Center for Public Integrity*, 6 June 2013, updated: 13 May 2014, www.publicintegrity.org/2013/06/06/12769/civil-rights-groups-fcc-positions-reflect-industry-funding-critics-say
39 Edward Wyatt, "F.C.C. Takes On Cross-Ownership," *New York Times*, 14 November 2012, www.nytimes.com/2012/11/15/business/media/fcc-is-again-examining-looser-cross-ownership-rules.html
40 "Congress Tells FCC to Preserve Local News in Media Ownership Rules," *Mike Doyle Media Center*, 6 December 2011, http://doyle.house.gov/press-release/congress-tells-fcc-preserve-local-news-media-ownership-rules
41 FCC, "Chairman's Statement on the Status of Media Ownership Proceeding," 26 February 2013, www.fcc.gov/document/chairmans-statement-status-media-ownership-proceeding
42 Cecilia Kang, "FCC Chairman Announces Resignation," *Washington Post*, 22 March 2013, www.washingtonpost.com/business/technology/fcc-chairman-announces-resignation/2013/03/22/c748f8a0-92f3-11e2-ba5b-550c7abf6384_story.html
43 Katy Bachman, "Study: Cross-Ownership of Media Doesn't Impact Minorities, Critics Cry Foul over this Next Step in the FCC's Process of Reviewing Rules," *AdWeek*, 30 May 2013, www.adweek.com/news/television/study-cross-ownership-media-doesnt-impact-minorities-149895
44 In the Matter of 2010 Quadrennial Review: Free Press, *Comments of Free Press*, 22 July 2013, www.freepress.net/sites/default/files/resources/Free_Press_MMTC_Study_Comments.pdf
45 FCC, "Statement of Acting Chairwoman Mignon Clyburn," 24 May 2013, www.fcc.gov/document/acting-chairwoman-clyburn-ocbos-critical-needs-research-design
46 FCC, "Research Design for the Multi-Market Study of Critical Information Needs," www.fcc.gov/encyclopedia/research-design-multi-market-study-critical-information-needs
47 Comments, "In the Matter of Research Design for the Multi-Market Study of Critical Information Needs," *National Association of Broadcasters*, 23 July 2013.
48 "Letter to FCC Chairwoman, Mignon Clyburn," *Communications Policy Research Network*, 16 September 2013.
49 Tim Cavanaugh, "FCC to Police News Media, Question Reporters in Wide-ranging Content Survey," *Daily Caller*, 30 October 2013, http://dailycaller.com/2013/10/30/fcc-to-police-news-media-question-reporters-in-wide-ranging-content-survey/
50 The Energy and Commerce Committee, "Committee Leaders Urge FCC to Suspend Work on 'Fairness Doctrine 2.0'," 10 December 2013, https://energycommerce.house.gov/news-center/press-releases/committee-leaders-urge-fcc-suspend-work-fairness-doctrine-20
51 Ajit Pai, "The FCC Wades into the Newsroom," *Wall Street Journal*, 10 February 2014, http://online.wsj.com/news/articles/SB10001424052702304680904579366903828260732
52 American Center for Law and Justice, "Why is the Obama Administration Putting Government Monitors in Newsrooms?," 2015, http://aclj.org/free-speech-2/why-is-obama-administration-putting-government-monitors-in-newsrooms; Jordan Sekulow and Matthew Clark, "FCC Backpedals on Wrongheaded Newsroom-monitoring Plan," *Washington Times*, 21 February 2014, www.washingtontimes.com/news/2014/feb/21/sekulow-a-tone-deaf-fcc-hears-a-retort-loud-and-cl/#ixzz3Gp8jRaId; "Gov't Monitors in Newsrooms? FCC to Look into Media Decision-Making," *Fox News*, 19 February 2014, http://insider.foxnews.com/2014/02/19/

govt-monitors-newsrooms-fcc-look-media-decision-making; Glenn Beck, "Is Freedom of the Press Dead? FCC to Monitor Newsrooms Around the Country," 20 February 2014, www.glennbeck.com/2014/02/20/is-freedom-of-the-press-dead-fcc-to-monitor-newsrooms-around-the-country/

53 FCC, "Setting the Record Straight About the Draft Study," Office of the Chairman, FCC, 21 February 2014, www.fcc.gov/document/setting-record-straight-about-draft-study

54 Corey Hutchins, "FCC Revamps Controversial Study of TV Newsrooms," *Columbia Journalism Review*, 17 February 2014, www.cjr.org/united_states_project/fcc_revamps_controversial_study_of_tv_newsrooms.php?page=all

55 Gabe Rottman, "Relax, It's Not the Thought Police," *American Civil Liberties Union*, 21 February 2014, www.aclu.org/blog/free-speech/relax-its-not-thought-police

56 Lewis Friedland, "The Real Story Behind the FCC's Study of Newsrooms," *Washington Post*, 28 February 2014, www.washingtonpost.com/blogs/monkey-cage/wp/2014/02/28/the-real-story-behind-the-fccs-study-of-newsrooms/

57 FCC, "Chairman Wheeler's Response Regarding Critical Information Needs Study," Office of the Chairman, FCC, 16 May 2014, www.fcc.gov/article/doc-327310a2

Chapter 6

Feminist activism and US communications policy

Carolyn M. Byerly

> Exploitive capitalist business models, embedded in a white supremacist patriarchal culture, have shaped representations of marginalized groups for centuries. Media representations are thus related to the legal and social structures that have oppressed people of color, women, gays and lesbians.[1]
> Catherine R. Squires, reflecting on bell hooks' critique of media

In its broader sense, this chapter concerns the communications policy structure that has oppressed and continues to oppress people of color, women, and others in the United States, blocking their access to decision-making and ownership levels in media companies and thereby limiting their voices in public arenas where issues are addressed and political strategies are formulated and pursued. In its more focused sense, the chapter is concerned with how women have—and have not—responded to the deeply gendered flaws in national communications policy. There has been substantially less academic attention paid to gender in communications policy and to feminist activism related to policy than there has been to race and activism by racial minorities, particularly African-Americans.[2] African-Americans and other people of color have had a longer history of challenging regulatory discrimination, and therefore currently have a stronger apparatus in place than do women. In problematizing communications policy with respect to gender, and in scrutinizing women's behavior in addressing it, this chapter seeks to extend the literature on women and the inequities of communications policy, and to shed greater light on women's active efforts to engage the problems and reshape policy to better serve their interests.

Access issues: Women's media ownership

Levels of women's media ownership have been low throughout American history, and the implications of this have long been recognized. The situation motivated nineteenth-century suffrage leader Susan B. Anthony to observe that as long as men owned the newspapers, women's views would never be heard.[3] As Anthony and other early women's rights leaders led campaigns to gain women's suffrage and other civil liberties, they established their own magazines and newspapers to provide a public sphere of their own. Some also allied with Black newspapers of the day, like abolitionist leader Frederick Douglass' *North Star*, in seeking venues to publish their views and activities.

Women's access to the mainstream channels of communication has improved only minimally in our modern era. Though women represent more than half the population and have moved forcefully into all sectors of the economy and social institutions since the second wave feminist movement of the 1970s, they continue to lag behind in their advancement into ownership of both traditional media (e.g. newspapers, magazines, television, and radio), and new communication technologies. The power to control major decisions about investment, corporate structure, and policy in media industries is located at the macro-level of the industries, i.e. in ownership, on boards of directors, and in top management—places where women are in short supply.

A gender-and-race analysis of today's ownership of radio and television stations shows gross inequalities. The most recent ownership figures published by the Federal Communications Commission (Table 6.1) reveal that in 2013, both women and minority ownership were in the single digits for full-power radio and television stations. Women's ownership of radio appears to have increased a tiny amount in full-power AM radio (from 7.8% to 8.3%) and FM radio (5.8% to 8.6%) between 2011 and 2013, but dropped in full-power television in the same years (from 7.8% to 6.3%). In low-power television station ownership—something women helped to lobby for more than a decade ago—female ownership is slightly higher, but the audiences are very small, given the low signal and reach. In all cases, whether full power or low power, women own broadcast companies in percentages that say they are not significant players in today's communication landscape and that their voices are largely silenced in mainstream discourse. In the US, where racial inequality has also historically shaped the national media landscape, today's broadcast ownership figures are also abysmally low for minority owners. The FCC's longstanding policy has held that increased diversity of viewpoints in broadcast programming is in the public interest, and the courts have reinforced this assumption with their rulings through the years.[4] And yet, the FCC's own data demonstrate lack of access for women (and minorities) and a corresponding lack of equality in today's airwaves.

Nor do women have access to corporate decision-making—the meso-level of the industries. A gender analysis of corporate boards of the nation's largest media conglomerates reveals women's lack of access to the governance structures, as represented by boards of directors (Table 6.2). Women occupy only between 8 and 30 percent of the seats in these media conglomerates, which own the vast majority of broadcast, cable, magazine, book publishing, and other communications companies.

Table 6.1 Comparative broadcast ownership data*

Ownership	FPAM 2011	FPAM 2013	FPFM 2011	FPFM 2013	Class A TV 2011	Class A TV 2013	FPTV 2011	FPTV 2013	LPTV 2011	LPTV 2013
Women	300/ 7.8%	310/ 8.3%	323/ 5.8%	383/ 6.7%	35/8.6%	30/7.6%	91/6.8%	87/6.3%	185/ 14.8%	217/ 13.1%
Black/African American	106/ 2.8%	93/2.5%	93/1.7%	73/1.3%	6/1.5%	8/2.0%	10/0.7%	9/0.6%	16/1.3%	16/1.3%
Hisp/Latino	172/ 4.5%	194/ 5.2%	151/ 2.7%	180/ 3.2%	31/7.6%	29/7.4%	39/2.9%	42/3%	120/ 9.6%	126/ 10.0%
Asian	100/ 2.6%	104/ 2.8%	45/0.8%	41/0.7%	8/2.0%	6/1.5%	6/0.5%	19/1.4%	28/2.2%	14/1.1%
American Indian	16/0.4%	12/0.3%	28/0.5%	23/0.4%	4/1.0%	2/0.5%	12/0.9%	11/0.8%	4/0.3%	1/0.1%
Native Hawaiian	6/0.2%	9/0.2%	28/0.5%	26/0.5%	0	0	1	1	2/0.2%	0
Multiple race	9/0.2%	7/0.2%	8/0.1%	6/0.1%	8/2.0%	7/1.8%	1	1	20/1.6	10/0.8%

*In 2011, there were 1,348 full-power TV stations, 1,662 low-power (Class A) TV stations, 3,830 full-power AM stations, and 5,611 full-power FM stations.
*In 2013, there were 1,386 full-power TV stations, 1,651 low-power (Class A) TV stations; 3,737 full-power AM stations; and 5,714 full-power FM stations.

Table 6.2 Gender representation on the boards of the largest diversified media companies in the US

Company	Total	Men	Women	% Women
CBS	14	12	2	14
Comcast	12	11	1	8
Disney	10	7	3	30
General Electric	17	12	5	29
News Corp	12	9	3	25
Time Warner Cable	12	10	2	17
Viacom	13	9	4	31
TOTAL	90	70	20	22

Source: Company websites October 2014.

A comparative analysis of the boards of high-tech companies (Table 6.3) reveals similar findings, with women representing between 8 and 27 percent of telecommunication industries that include social media. Some of these companies would seem to have made greater progress in their gender representation. After all, isn't a company governed by boards where women are something above 25 percent showing some effort? Statistically, yes. In fact, according to *Forbes Magazine*, the watchdog of the business sector, media companies overall have among the highest numbers of women in US corporations where board composition is typically 90 percent male.[5]

Our discussion will turn to women's activism as regards corporate board representation shortly. However, at this point the data compel us to emphasize that under-representation at the top of media corporations suggests serious, even profound in some cases, gender marginalization in industries that today represent the public sphere. Feminist theorists have recognized the dominant public sphere created by mainstream media industries as a male-dominated space and identified feminist media activism as an essential component of democratizing the public sphere for women's full social participation.[6]

The situation of women in ownership and decision-making within the United States is considerably direr than for women in European nations. A recent comprehensive study of gender equality in decision-making within media companies in 29 nations of Europe, commissioned by the European Institute for Gender Equality (2013), found women accounted for only 16 percent of those in CEO roles, but the percentage was slightly higher on boards of directors (25%), and for heads of departments (32%). Even so, the trend across developed nations is for women to be greatly under-represented in the controlling layers of media industries. As the EIGE study noted, "the influential nature of the media industry informing public opinion underlines the

Table 6.3 Gender representation on boards of technology companies

Company	Total	Men	Women	% Women
Amazon	10	8	2	20%
Apple	8	6	2	25
Chegg	7	6	1	14
Cisco	11	8	3	27
eBay	12	11	1	8
Facebook	9	7	2	22
Google	11	8	3	27
Groupon	8	7	1	13
Hewlett-Packard	12	9	3	25
Intel	10	8	2	20
Intuit	9	7	2	22
LinkedIn	7	6	1	14
Microsoft	10	8	2	20
Nvidia	10	9	1	10
Oracle	11	9	2	18
Pandora	8	7	1	13
Salesforce	10	9	1	10
Twitter	8	7	1	13
YELP	9	7	2	22
Yahoo	9	6	3	33
TOTAL	189	153	36	19%

Source: Rainbow PUSH press release, October 2014 (www.rainbowpush.org)

need to address the representation of women in high-profile decision making posts"[7]—and, we would add, that includes ownership.

Regulation: Imbedded gender biases

Whereas print media have not been regulated in their ownership in US history, the same has not been true for electronic media. Such regulation dates from the early years of radio technology. The Radio Act of 1912, the first comprehensive law to provide government oversight of broadcasting, required wireless operators to be licensed and established some minimal regulations for frequency modulation.[8] Between this time and the passage of the Radio Act of 1927, Marie Zimmerman, the first woman known to own a radio station, became the owner and operator of WIAE-AM, in Vinton, Iowa, from 1922 to 1923. Zimmerman allegedly carried her microphone and makeshift equipment around with her in her car and broadcast local events and political speeches in her rural community. Her ownership was short lived, as she apparently decided not to renew her license.[9] Ida McNeil also owned and operated a one-woman station, KGFX-AM, in Pierre, South Dakota, in the 1920s and 1930s.[10] Women did make their way onto the air from the 1920s onward, but they did not similarly advance into ownership or management.

From the earliest years of regulation, financial status, technical ability, and broadcaster experience were the major criteria used to grant radio licenses.[11] Although the Federal Communications Commission (FCC)—the federal agency created by the Communications Act of 1934, and made responsible for licensing broadcast stations and otherwise regulating telecommunications—had no written policy excluding women and racial minorities from media ownership, such was the practice until the 1960s. Honig[12] recounts vividly how the commission systematically and intentionally excluded African-Americans from owning radio and television stations until the United Church of Christ's Office of Communications sued the FCC in the groundbreaking *Lamar Broadcasting Company v. FCC cases* (1965, 1969) in the 1960s. In the early 1970s, the FCC began to grant certain preferences for racial minorities in comparative hearings for licensure, and in 1978, the FCC extended these preferences to female license applicants, though women would never gain the same weight as race-based preferences.

The passage of the Radio Act of 1927 established a five-member Federal Radio Commission and authorized that commission to regulate station licensing, among other things. The members of the FRC possessed considerable discretion to decide questions of law and policy.[13] That power would expand when Congress passed the Communications Act of 1934, consolidating federal powers under one agency called the Federal Communications Commission (FCC), and establishing the radio spectrum as a public resource that should serve the public interest. By the 1960s, details as to how the public interest would be served had begun to slip into place, including the requirement that broadcasters determine the "tastes, needs and desires" of their audiences through local area surveys known as "community ascertainment."[14] The "1960 Programming Policy Statement" adopted by the FCC listed 14 major elements broadcasters were to follow in serving the public interest. These included the opportunity for local self-expression, development, and the use of local talent; programs for children; religious, educational, and public affairs programs; editorials by licensees; political broadcasts; agricultural programs; news, weather, and market reports; sports; service to minority groups; and entertainment.[15]

However, broadcasters became increasingly resistant to caring about the needs of their local audiences as conglomeration became rampant. With the advent of neoliberal (i.e. pro-corporate) policies in the federal government in the 1970s, these 14 elements were gradually eroded, and in 1981, the FCC ended the use of rules and policies requiring stations to keep program logs, commercial time limits, ascertainment of community problems, and other standards previously used to ensure the public interest would be served.[16] As large financially powerful media companies bought out weaker ones, localism and public interest went by the wayside. The Telecommunications Act of 1996, which was written by attorneys for the telecommunications companies and passed easily through Congress with barely any public comment, enabled the FCC to deregulate media ownership. In a short amount of time, that commission would allow a single corporation to own almost unlimited numbers of individual companies.[17]

A second impact of conglomeration was the erosion of women's majority ownership in broadcast companies. The FCC considers a woman-owned company to be one in which women control more than half of the voting rights. Research shows that women had entered broadcast ownership in greater numbers after 1978 when the FCC placed emphasis on diversifying gender and race in ownership as a means of diversifying the range of perspectives.[18] It was race and gender preferences that allowed Cathy Hughes to build her Radio One empire, the largest African-American female-owned radio conglomerate in the US, beginning in 1980.[19] However, those policy strategies to increase female and minority ownership began to unravel in the 1990s. By 1997, the FCC had shifted its methods of awarding licenses—from competitive bidding to the present system of lottery and auction—something that meant wealthy (male-dominated) conglomerates would thereafter have the advantage.

Neither were the courts helpful to women in these years. Though the FCC tried to argue that gender preferences in the sale of stations should be allowed because they contributed to greater diversity in content, the US Court of Appeals in the DC Circuit disagreed in *Lamprecht v. the FCC* (1992). The judgment that women did not constitute a minority was reinforced a year later with the Supreme Court's 1993 decision in *Bechtel v. the FCC*, which ruled that there is no empirical basis for giving women preferences in the sale of stations. These cases assured that the most valuable stations thereafter would be owned by men. Add to these events the hostile regulatory environment for women created by the Telecommunications Act of 1996. One expert—quoted in research among women broadcast owners by Byerly—said deregulation "changed everything—the big groups are able to outbid you and women lose out."[20]

Literature review: Women, policy, and activism

There is a limited amount of research on women's relationship to media at the macro- and meso-levels, particularly with regard to communications policy. Virtually none of it seems to have been done by male (and, in some cases, female) critical scholars who research and write about media policy and media ownership as if gender (and, of course, race) were not deeply imbedded in both of these. It is therefore useful to highlight the few analyses of gender politics in policy making that have been published. Gallagher provides an important global view, accurately characterizing women's efforts to enter the policy realm as "struggling for space."[21] She chronicles feminists' work at the global level since the 1970s, first as they tried to participate in the New World Information and Communication Order (NWICO) debates and more recently when they tried to gain attention for women's interests in the World Summit on the Information Society (WSIS) forums. In both instances, women and their global policy-related concerns were marginalized, pushed out of the process by powerful male leaders with their own agendas. Feminists' own meetings, such as the UNESCO-sponsored event that spawned the Beijing Platform for Action that included a section on bringing women in to full participation in media industries, have never had any specific agendas or methods of implementation. She also notes women's difficulties in their respective nations when trying to influence media policy, though she cites hope in examples like Gender Links' work in the Southern Africa region, which she says is a model of "potential partnerships between governments and civil society."[22]

Katharine Sarikakis and Leslie Regan Shade's book *Feminist Interventions in International Communication* contains a few chapters with substantive discussions of women-and-media policy making and/or ownership.[23] Among these are Barbara Crow and Kim Sawchuk's chapter on gender and policy governing mobile communication technologies,[24] Valentina Marinescu's chapter on women,[25] economics and media policy in Eastern Europe, and Gallagher's chapter on media policy and other global issues related to women.[26]

My own work has been critical of feminist scholarship's neglect of media policy, saying that feminist media scholars have "barely paid attention to the macro-level aspects of the media that form the structures within which media operate and content is produced" and criticized feminists' greater attention to analyses of women's representations to the exclusion of concern about the structures that create such content as having created a literature that is "partial, incomplete, and, some might argue, flawed."[27] Recent work by Byerly[28] shows the low rates of women in media governance and management; and identifies the ways that neoliberal policies have prevented women from entering "fully into the media macro-level in finance, policy-making, or ownership."[29]

Feminists had begun to show concern for media policies' impact on women by the 1970s. Beasley and Gibbons noted that feminist leaders challenged the media for sexist stereotypes, staging a sit-in at the *Ladies' Home Journal* magazine offices in 1970, for example, to protest such depictions.[30] Media monitoring at the national level also focused on sexist content in broadcast (particularly television) by the late 1970s, with feminists protesting misrepresentations of women in television programming and the omission of women from serious news of the day. They charged that the problem lay in men's control of content, demonstrated in things like female characters that were created by male producers and writers.[31] Activists of the period recognized that bias in television depictions also extended to race, with more minority representations (including by Black women) but no programs that tackled issues of prejudice.[32] After passage of Title VII (of the US Civil Rights Act of 1964), which outlawed discrimination in the workplace and institutions on the basis of gender, race, national origin, and other characteristics, the exclusion and marginalization of women in media professions was challenged legally. Beginning in the 1970s, the National Organization for Women's (NOW) legal team filed discrimination lawsuits on behalf of women journalists at a number of prominent news organizations, saying the companies had treated women unfairly in hiring and promotion. Women filed similar lawsuits against the *New York Times*, *Washington Post*, Associated Press, and other companies, winning cases that slowly opened the doors to women's employment in news.

In spite of these important gains, the current research continues to show that few women have advanced into top management of news companies or onto boards of directors in the United States. Feminist economist Donna Allen, who founded the Women's Institute for Freedom of the Press in the 1960s, was among the earliest to point to women's exclusion at ownership and management levels as something that would worsen under the male authority that came with conglomerated media industries.[33] Leslie Regan Shade examines the gender dynamics at work in Canadian and United States movements for media reform.[34] She cites the work of Women in Media and News,[35] which formed in 2001, as a media analysis, education, and advocacy group to increase women's presence in the policy realm (among other things), and the work of Free Press which has conducted research on the levels of women's and minorities' ownership in media. However, her discussion misses a fuller discussion of the ways that women have tried to intervene in media policy, or any assessment of that activism's impact.

Carolyn M. Byerly and Karen Ross' analysis of women's media activism in both developed and developing nations is aimed at describing the different kinds of activism over a 40-year period, as well as theorizing how such activism serves to advance women's rights campaigns.[36] In spite of its contributions to theory, which inform the theoretical framework for the present study, this book includes only a few examples of the vast numbers of activism that feminists have engaged in internationally since global feminism made its appearance as a universal movement in the 1970s.

Theoretical framework

The analytical framework for the remaining discussion is informed by theories of feminist political economy and women's media activism. Feminist political economy, as defined by Riordan, is concerned with the meso- and macro-levels of capitalism as they shape women's day-to-day interactions, and the routine ways that social institutions within capitalist society naturalize male bias.[37] Feminist political economy theory incorporates a commitment to praxis, or changing the situation causing women's oppression under capitalism.[38] Meehan and Riordan were among the first to provide a theoretical connection between women's oppression under capitalism and the long-standing male domination within media industries.[39] In this paper, feminist political economy will be useful to examining US federal communication policy, which has favored men's ownership and control of commercial media industries, particularly in the years under neoliberalism since the late 1970s.

A theory of women's media activism, which embodies the praxis that Meehan and Riordan refer to, can be found in Byerly and Ross' formulation of the model of women's media action.[40] Byerly and Ross' model provides categories (or forms) of women's media activism that they call "paths," and they show the way that such activism functions within women's liberation movements. One path they define is the "advocate change agent." Women who are advocate change agents use a range of strategies to expand women's communicative structures and infrastructures. They typically carry on their work through organizations with specific goals of pressuring the media to disseminate information from a feminist perspective or to expand access for women.[41] This path will be useful to the present study in considering ways that feminist attorneys, scholars, and grassroots activists have contested sexist practices in media policies, particularly since 2003 with the rise of a national media-reform movement. In addition, the model will help to formulate additional ways feminists might expand their organizing to address the structural inequalities in communications policies that inhibit women's ability to own, manage, and enter into decision-making roles within media companies.

Neoliberalism, women, and media

Women's rights and civil rights movements of the twentieth century brought laws against discrimination in the workplace, but deeply imbedded misogynistic practices continue to impose a glass ceiling on women's advancement into decision-making layers of organizations. These practices include excluding women from men's activities where many decisions are made informally (i.e. "the old boy's network"), denial of promotions, lack of mentorship/ sponsorship, and dismissal of women's skills as equal to those of men.[42] Ironically, companies benefit financially from having more women in top roles. After studying 2,400 companies around the world, one Swiss research group found that companies with at least one woman on their boards delivered higher than average returns on equity and better average growth.[43] Even though women's board representation is higher in the US-based telecommunications sector than most other sectors, and their presence may indeed be an advantage to their companies' revenues, they are still unable to influence corporate policies and practices in the same way they would if their numbers were closer to parity. Few women actually own broadcast media companies in the US today, as shown earlier, and this is particularly pronounced in broadcast (radio and television) stations, which are still the mainstay of mass communication.[44]

Women's greatest barrier is typically their inability to acquire the financial backing needed to purchase stations. Those who do own tend to come into their ownership through inheritance or transfer from a family member, or through a combination of transfer and purchase, rather than through purchase at auction.[45] Investors reject women seeking loans large enough to purchase stations, even if they can demonstrate the necessary experience to run them, because they doubt women's ability to perform successfully or they have other unstated reasons.[46]

In addition, the larger, macro-level environment within which media companies operate has been increasingly hostile to women since neoliberalism asserted itself in the late 1970s. Robin Mansell has observed that economic and political forces contribute to the dynamics of social exclusion.[47] And, neoliberalism has been that force for women in relation to gaining greater control within media industries. Neoliberalism is seen clearly in public policy that emphasizes free market capitalism, as well as reductions in public expenditures, tax reform to benefit the private (corporate) sector, privatization of public services and assets, and the marginalization of organized labor.[48] Neoliberalism and its twin, the globalization of capitalism, have served to consolidate and strengthen men's economic power and control over resources and policy making at every level (international, national, state, and institutional). Women have suffered disproportionately the world over under neoliberalism, but pertinent to the present discussion is how that has occurred within the media sector, where women have not been able to advance into either policy making or ownership. Congress, the national bicameral legislature, is still only 17 percent female. Additionally, there is no evidence that the two women among the FCC's five members have been able to exert any influence on women's behalf.[49] In fact, the commission, the majority of whose members (of both parties) have been pro big business for three decades, has engaged in systematic discrimination against both women and racial minorities in its policies of deregulation.

Feminist media activism

Feminists in the US began to stand up to this situation in the 1990s, first in lobbying for the establishment of low-power FM radio (which was finally passed by Congress in 2000) and in helping to organize the Independent Media Center in 1999, through which young, progressive reporters covered events like the massive popular protests against the World Trade

Organization meeting in Seattle that same year.[50] However, feminists organized around FCC policies specifically in 2002 to challenge what they saw as threats to the public's right to a "free, independent and critical press."[51] The organization Women in Media & News (WIMN),[52] which had formed in 2001 to increase women's presence in public media debates including media reform, helped to rally women to a demonstration in front of the FCC headquarters in March 2002, in Washington, DC, to protest proposed rule changes that would further deregulate media ownership. At that event, WIMN's executive director and founder, Jennifer Pozner, engaged in a satirical presentation she called "Calling All Billionaires for More Media Mergers."[53] Pozner has played an instrumental role in raising awareness about women-and-media policy issues through her popular website, which features a "WIMN's Voices Blog" to which nearly 50 feminists of varied backgrounds contribute, a *Resource Guide for Media Activists*, links to many other grassroots groups, and numerous other resources.

Feminists have also benefited from other grassroots efforts in media reform, particularly from organizations they helped to establish and lead. In 2003, as the FCC was poised to severely relax ownership limits, media activists were watching the potential outcome and plotting strategies to intervene. If limits were lifted, as it appeared might happen, the effects would have fallen heaviest in local markets[54]—the markets where women have always been most likely to own stations in the few numbers their ownership history had shown.[55] Hannah Sassaman was director of the Prometheus Radio Project, a low-power FM advocacy group based in Philadelphia, in 2003, as those FCC plans came into public view. Sassaman and her young activist colleagues were launched into the national spotlight for their resistance to the FCC's proposed deregulation when their legal petition to halt FCC's proceedings was selected for hearing in September by the US Third Circuit Court in Philadelphia. Attorneys for the Media Access Project representing the Prometheus group argued successfully that the proposed media ownership rule violated federal statutes, and the court's ruling in *Prometheus Radio Project v. the FCC*—what has become known as the Prometheus I decision—stands as the first major legal landmark in the media-reform movement. Sassaman's work in community radio is extensive, including serving as the campaign director for the Local Community Radio Act, which was passed by Congress in 2010 and signed into law by President Obama a year later.[56] That law expanded the number of LPFM stations and increased the strength of signal frequencies. Low-power stations are community-based, non-commercial radio stations that operate at 100 watts or less and reach a radius of three to seven miles.[57] Prometheus Radio Project had used the potential benefits to women in their campaign, saying:

> LPFM stations offer an opportunity for women to enter the debate and engage on their own terms, creating content that better serves their

needs. Women's rights organizations and women-led social justice groups could use LPFM stations to discuss, debate and organize around issues related to women's and girls' social, political, economic and physical equality and security.[58]

The FCC has released two reports on ownership to date, one in 2012, the other in 2014. Neither report shows ownership data for LPFM; however, these reports did contain data for low-power TV stations, including Class A stations. Class A stations are a low-power station category that Congress created in 1999 which have been given special benefits, including the ability to transition early to digital.[59] And, the benefits to women to date have been measurable, as seen in Table 6.1. Women today own more LPTV and Class A TV stations than they do full-power AM, FM, or TV commercial TV stations. Such ownership levels suggest that women have similarly benefited in LPFM, though such data have yet to be reported.[60]

While feminist advocacy for media reform has been extensive, it has been largely unmentioned by critical scholars who have chronicled the media-reform movement, and largely unexamined by feminist media researchers.[61] In addition to Pozner and Sassaman, the leadership of at least two others who have specifically tried to shape FCC policies with the interests of women in mind should be noted here.[62]

Angela Campbell, co-director of the Institute for Public Representation (IPR) and professor of law, Georgetown University Law Center, Washington, DC, played a major role in developing the legal arguments for what became the *Prometheus Radio Project v. FCC* case. Campbell worked in alliance with Andrew Schwartzman of the Media Access Project to represent the Prometheus group, as well as the National Organization for Women, the

Table 6.4 Female ownership by media format*

Women's ownership	2010	2011	2013	% of US Population
% Full-power commercial TV stations	5.5	6.8	6.3	50.8
% Class A TV stations	8.3	8.6	7.6	50.8
% Low-power TV stations	15.1	14.8	14.9	50.8
% Commercial FM radio	6.2	5.8	6.7	50.8
% Commercial AM radio	7.0	7.8	8.3	50.8

Source: Institute for Public Representation, Georgetown Law Center, Washington, DC, 2014.

*In 2011, there were 1,348 full-power TV stations; 1,662 low-power (Class A) TV stations; 3,830 full-power AM stations; and 5,611 full-power FM stations.

*In 2013, there were 1,386 full-power TV stations; 1,651 low-power (Class A) TV stations; 3,737 full-power AM stations; and 5,714 full-power FM stations.

Consumer Federation of America, the United Church of Christ, and the Media Alliance to demand blockage of the FCC's new ownership rules, as outlined in the FCC's 2003 Report and Order. Their rationale was that the FCC had failed to consider how raising the limits of cross-ownership of media would impact female and minority ownership of broadcast stations. The court agreed with them in a two-to-one vote, remanding the matter of cross-ownership rules back to the FCC and stating that the commission must consider female and minority ownership before further loosening ownership limits.[63] Aware that the FCC had made no effort to establish ways of measuring such impacts or otherwise addressing potential harm to female and minority broadcast ownership years after the Prometheus ruling, Campbell and her law students at the IPR acted again in 2009 to ask the Third Circuit Court to intervene and require the FCC to consider such measures. In what would be called Prometheus II, the court ruled in July 2011 to dismiss the FCC rules that would have allowed one company to own a newspaper and broadcast stations in the same market, upheld the FCC's decision to retain its other local broadcast ownership restrictions, and instructed the FCC to better consider and address how its rules would affect and might promote ownership by women and people of color in its 2010 Quadrennial Review.[64] Campbell was recognized for her front-line legal work on behalf of women and minorities in 2005 when she received the Everett C. Parker award at the annual Parker Lecture sponsored by the Office of Communications, United Church of Christ.[65] It bears noting, however, that the FCC has to this day not responded to either the Prometheus I or II rulings requiring ownership levels by women and racial minorities to be addressed through policy, as they were mandated to do.

Malkia Cyril, founder and executive director of the Center for Media Justice in Oakland, California, in 2002, has been at the forefront of the media justice movement, a sister movement to the media reform movement. Cyril has received numerous awards for her work, which envisions communications policy as part of a broader plan for a democratic society. Her work is said to be premised on Article 19 of the UN Declaration of Human Rights, which defines the right to communicate as a human right. The agenda she articulates, however, places media concerns within a wide spectrum of variables in the struggle for social justice that includes racial and economic justice. Media and media policy are "the terrain we have chosen for struggle," she has said, because media are "just a vehicle, a means to change, not the change itself."[66] Cyril's work, which recognizes the media's messages have much to do with how problems and issues are understood, and how people in marginalized communities are perceived, has expanded the numbers of women of color and young people in media-reform work. Additionally, her savvy field organizing has built the national "Media Action Grassroots Network" (MAG-Net), now with more than 175 community organizational members. The MAG-Net played a major role in successfully advocating for a new FCC policy, which the commission adopted in 2013. That policy lowers phone rates for those in prison, dropping costs from $1 per minute to between 10 and 30 cents a minute.[67] Though she routinely says "it's not about me" and "this award could have been given to anyone in this room," it has been her loud, thoughtful voice that has most often helped to lead racially diverse views on open Internet policies, low-power (community) radio, lower phone rates for those in prison, and the rights of workers who would be laid off by media mergers, among other things.[68] Cyril was honored with a Donald H. McGannon award in 2013 for "advancing the roles of women and persons of color in the media and in the media-reform movement."[69]

Limits of space prevent a fuller examination of these activists' efforts on behalf of women and racial minorities, or of identifying additional ones. Their work is meant to be indicative of feminist media activism, not wholly representative of all such activism taking place.

Conclusion

What should emerge from the foregoing discussion are both the seriousness of women's marginalization in media ownership and management, and the ways that public policy and court action contribute to that marginalization. In spite of some efforts by the FCC to extend preferences to women in the 1970s and 1980s, those efforts unraveled as the commission became guided by neoliberal laws (like the Telecomm Act of 1996), and courts issued conservative (pro-corporate, anti-gender equality) decisions. While feminist leaders have emerged to challenge the current gender disparity in media ownership and seek greater access to decision-making levels, there has never been an articulated, unified feminist agenda, or strategy for change. In spite of the fact that the National Organization for Women is represented before the FCC by Angela Campbell and her team of lawyers and law students from Georgetown University Law Center's Institute for Public Representation, NOW has no apparent ongoing program to address women's inequality in media or media policy. Its most recent conference had not a single session on the topic.[70] Feminist activism following the "advocate change agency" path would seem to be woefully unfilled as regards women's marginalization in media policy and representation in decision-making.

Nor has there been any apparent forum within the media reform or media justice movements to formulate a feminist strategy. In response to feminist media activists' criticism that women's voices were marginalized at the National Media Reform Conferences sponsored biannually by the advocacy group Free Press, the group publicized its April 2013 event as one that would put women "front and center" and where women would "rock the house at the National Conference for Media Reform."[71] However, none of the feminist-oriented sessions at that conference focused on structural issues that lessen women's access and control in media companies. Even the session titled "Building the Future: Women, Code and Inclusion" was concerned with examining "the ways women programmers are finding a place within the male-dominated world of the tech industry"[72] rather than with changing the conditions that discriminate against women in that industry.

There is nonetheless the need for feminists to develop a road map through the legislative, policy, and political mazes that presently block women's ability to enter into the world of media ownership and greater control over employment, content, and other decisions. The role for feminist media scholars in this process should be, at a minimum, to expand the present minimal literature on women's ownership; the impact of laws, policies, and court decisions on women's media ownership; and the relationship between ownership and media content; among other things. There will also be merit in conducting case studies of women-owned media companies in which female proprietorship has influenced programming or other content. The collaboration between feminist scholars and public interest attorneys and media activists is one whose synergy is likely to move the present stalemate forward.

Notes

1 Catherine R. Squires, *bell hooks: A Critical Introduction to Media and Communication Theory* (New York: Peter Lang, 2013), 51–52.
2 Carolyn M. Byerly, "The Geography of Women and Media Scholarship," *The Handbook of Gender, Sex and the Media*, Ed. Karen Ross (Malden, MA: Wiley Blackwell, 2012), 3–19.
3 Lynn Sherr, *Failure is Impossible: Susan B. Anthony in Her Own Words* (New York: Times Books [Random House], 1996), 203–204.
4 Bruce R. Wilde, "FCC Tax Certificates for Minority Ownership of Broadcast Facilities: A Critical Re-Examination of Policy," *University of Pennsylvania Law Review* 138 (1990): 980.
5 Liyan Chen, "Not Just Google and Facebook: America's Boardrooms Are Still Woefully Bereft of Women," *Forbes Magazine* (online), 9 July 2014, www.forbes.com/sites/liyanchen/2014/07/09/not-just-google-and-facebook-americas-boardrooms-are-still-woefully-bereft-of-women/
6 Carolyn M. Byerly and Karen Ross, *Women and Media: A Critical Introduction* (Malden, MA: Blackwell Publishing, 2006).
7 European Institute for Gender Equality, *Advancing Gender Equality in Decision-making in Media Organizations* (report) (Luxembourg: European Union, 2013), 26.
8 Fritz Messere, "Regulation," *Encyclopedia of Radio*, www.oswego.edu/~messere/RadioReg.pdf; Nicholas Johnson, "A Hasty History of US Broadcast Regulation" [Seminar on Proposed Broadcast Legislation, Tbilisi, Georgia], 27 February 1998.
9 "Marie Zimmerman—Broadcasting's First Female Owner," www.oldradio.com/archives/people/zimmerman.htm
10 Donna L. Halper, "Remembering the Ladies—A Salute to the Women of Early Radio. From *Popular Communications*," *Popular Communications*, January 1999, www.distinguishedwomen.com/biographies/remembering.html

11 Messere, "Regulation," 8.
12 David Honig, "How the FCC Helped Exclude Minorities from Ownership of the Airwaves," Fordham University, McGannon Lecture on Communications Practices and Ethics, 5 October 2006, http://apps.fcc.gov/ecfs/document/view?id=7521829795
13 Messere, "Regulation," 3.
14 Messere, "Regulation," 8.
15 *Report and Statement of Policy*, 25 *Federal Regist*er 7291 (Washington, DC: Federal Communications Commission, 1960).
16 Carolyn M. Byerly, Yong Jin Park, and Reginald D. Miles, "Race-and Gender-Conscious Policies: Toward a More Egalitarian Communications Future," *Journal of Information Policy* 1 (2011): 425–440.
17 Robert W. McChesney, *The Problem of the Media: US Communication Politics in the 21st Century* (New York: Monthly Review Press, 2004).
18 ERLA Group, Inc., *Female Ownership of Broadcast Stations* (East Lansing, MI, and San Francisco: ERLA Group, Inc., 1982).
19 Janean Chun, "Cathy Hughes, Radio One: From Teen Mom to Media Mogul," *Huffington Post*, 26 September 2012, www.huffingtonpost.com/2012/08/17/catherine-hughes-radio-one_n_1798129.html
20 Carolyn M. Byerly, "Behind the Scenes of Women's Broadcast Ownership," *Howard Journal of Communication* 22, no.1 (2011): 37.
21 Margaret Gallagher, "Gender and Communication Policy," in *The Handbook of Global Media and Communication Policy*, Eds. Robin Mansell and Marc Raboy (Malden, MA: Wiley Blackwell, 2014), 451–461.
22 Gallagher, "Gender and Communication Policy," 460.
23 Katharine Sarikakis and Leslie Regan Shade, Eds., *Feminist Interventions in International Communication* (Lanham, MD: Rowman & Littlefield, 2008).
24 Barbara Crow and Kim Sawchuk, "The Spectral Politics of Mobile Communication Technologies: Gender, Infrastructure, and International Policy," in *Feminist Interventions in International Communication*, Eds. Katharine Sarikakis and Leslie Regan Shade (Lanham, MD: Rowman & Littlefield, 2008), 90–105.
25 Valentina Marinescu, "Communication and Women in Eastern Europe: Challenges in Reshaping the Democratic Sphere," in *Feminist Interventions in International Communication*, Eds. Katharine Sarikakis and Leslie Regan Shade (Lanham, MD: Rowman & Littlefield, 2008), 276–290.
26 Margaret Gallagher, "Feminist Issues and the Global Media System," in *Feminist Interventions in International Communication*, Eds. Katharine Sarikakis and Leslie Regan Shade (Lanham, MD: Rowman & Littlefield, 2008), 17–32.
27 Carolyn M. Byerly, "The Geography of Women and Media Scholarship," in *The Handbook of Gender, Sex and the Media,* Ed. Karen Ross (Malden, MA: Wiley Blackwell, 2012), 14.
28 Carolyn M. Byerly, *Global Report on the Status of Women in News Media* (Washington, DC: International Women's Media Foundation, 2011); Carolyn M. Byerly, "Factors Affecting the Status of Women Journalists: A Structural Analysis," in *The Palgrave Handbook of Women and Journalism,* Ed. Carolyn M. Byerly (Basingstoke, UK: Palgrave Macmillan, 2013), 11–26.
29 Carolyn M. Byerly, "Women and Media Control: Feminist Interrogations at the Macro-level," in *The Routledge Companion to Gender and Media*, Eds. Cynthia Carter, Linda Steiner, and Lisa McLaughlin (London, UK: Routledge Taylor & Francis, 2014), 113.
30 Maurine H. Beasley, M. H. and Sheila Gibbons, *Taking their Place: A Documentary History of Women and Journalism*, 2nd ed. (State College, PA: Strata Publications, 2003), 296.

31 Ibid., 203.
32 Ibid.
33 Maurine H. Beasley, "Donna Allen and the Women's Institute: A Feminist Perspective on the First Amendment," *American Journalism* 9, nos. 3–4 (1992): 154–166.
34 Leslie Regan Shade, "Media Reform in the United States and Canada: Activism and Advocacy for Media Policies in the Public Interest," in *The Handbook of Global Media and Communication Policy*, Eds. Robin Mansell and Marc Raboy (Malden, MA: Wiley Blackwell, 2014), 147–165.
35 *Women in Media & News*, www.wimnonline.org
36 Byerly and Ross, *Women and Media*.
37 Ellen Riordan, "Intersections and New Directions: On Feminism and Political Economy," in *Sex & Money: Feminism and Political Economy in the Media*, Eds. Eileen R. Meehan and Ellen Riordan (Minneapolis, MN: University of Minnesota Press, 2003), 6–7.
38 Ellen Riordan, "Intersections and New Directions," 11.
39 Eileen R. Meehan and Ellen Riordan, Eds., *Sex & Money: Feminism and Political Economy in the Media* (Minneapolis, MN: University of Minnesota Press, 2003).
40 Byerly and Ross, *Women and Media*.
41 Ibid., 187.
42 Carolyn M. Byerly, "Behind the Scenes of Women's Broadcast Ownership."
43 Credit Suisse, *Gender Diversity and Corporate Performance* (Zurich, Switzerland: Credit Suisse Research Institute, 2012).
44 Minority Media and Telecom Council, *On the Path to the Digital Beloved Community: A Civil Rights Agenda for the Technological Age* (Washington, DC: MMTC, 2012).
45 Byerly, "Behind the Scenes of Women's Broadcast Ownership."
46 Ibid., 37.
47 Robin Mansell and Mark Raboy, "Introduction: Foundations of the Theory and Practice of Global Media and Communication Policy," in *The Handbook of Global Media and Communication Policy* (Malden, MA: Wiley Blackwell, 2014): 1–20.
48 Nick Couldry, *Why Voice Matters: Culture and Politics After Neoliberalism* (Los Angeles, CA: Sage Publications, 2010); David Harvey, *A Brief History of Neoliberalism* (Oxford, UK: Oxford University Press, 2005).
49 The members of the FCC are appointed by the President of the United States, and two of the three members will be of the same political party as the president. At this writing, the FCC's two female members are Mignon Clyburn and Jessica Rosenworcel, both Democrats. The chairman is Tom Wheeler, also a Democrat. The two Republican members are Ajit Pai and Michael O'Rielly.
50 The Indymedia Center is today a global network with centers in most major cities around the world. The organization provides audio and print news feeds and a vibrant website crowded with activist social and political events and issues related to overcoming various forms of oppression. The Indymedia Center is an alternative to corporate media and was formed specifically to protest media conglomeration. There is no central coordination for the several hundred journalists that contribute, and, as a result, the organization has come under criticism for some of its news, particularly about Jews. (For a synopsis of the organization, its formation, and both its contributions and problems, see Wikipedia entry "Independent Media Center," en.wikipedia.org/wiki/Independent_Media_Center.)
51 *Women in Media & News*, www.wimnonline.org
52 Ibid.
53 "Calling All Billionaires for More Media Mergers," *Women in Media & News*, www.wimnonline.org/Billionaires-Heart-FCC.html#CallingBillionaires

54 McChesney, *The Problem of the Media*, 272.
55 Byerly, "Behind the Scenes of Women's Broadcast Ownership."
56 Prometheus Radio Project, *Local Community Radio Act* (Philadelphia, PA: Prometheus Radio Project), www.prometheusradio.org/LCRA
57 Ibid.
58 Ibid.
59 David Oxenford, "Category Archives: Low Power Television/Class A TV," *Broadcast Law Blog*, Washington, DC: Wilkinson Barke Knauer, LLP, www.broadcastlawblog.com/articles/low-power-televisionclass-a-tv/
60 The FCC began to collect ownership data by race and gender—after extensive lobbying by the civil rights and feminist communities in the 1990s—by requiring owners to report demographics in their biannual Form 323 statements. Commissioners made the raw data available for public consumption in 2003 and 2006, but these reports were grossly incomplete and unreliable; see C. M. Byerly, "Questioning Media Access: Analysis of FCC Women and Minority Ownership Data," in *Does Bigger Media Equal Better Media?* (Report) Social Science Research Council and Benton Foundation, 2006, www.ssrc.org/programs/media. They only began to publish the results of their data gathering from Form 323 in 2012 after another round of pressure by advocacy groups, particularly Professor Angela Campbell, co-director of the Institute for Public Representation, Georgetown Law Center. To obtain data on LPFM ownership would require laborious, time-consuming research using the Commission's CDBS data base, which contains station-by-station information. No one to date has undertaken this research. There are grounds here for feminists and other advocacy groups to lobby for the ownership of LPFM stations to be included in their biennial reports.
61 Such examination is now emerging, e.g. Aitza Haddad and Carolyn M. Byerly presented a paper, "Epistemic Communities and FCC Policy: Case Study of African-American and Feminist Activism," at the Institute for Information Policy Seminar, Penn State University, held at New American Foundation Washington, DC, September 29 to October 1, 2013.
62 My own work has figured into this feminist activism since 2004 through my research on women's and minorities' media issues, and in my faculty role with the Howard Media Group, an activist faculty-graduate student collaborative at Howard University, Washington, DC. Research, such as that illustrated in the present chapter, is one example of my activist scholarship. Other activities include speaking at National Media Reform Conferences, meeting with FCC commissioners and their staffs, testifying at FCC-sponsored panels and hearings, submitting numerous comments to the FCC on proposed rulemaking, and establishing the HMG website. See the Howard Media Group's website, www.howardmedia.group
63 See *Prometheus vs. the FCC*, www.prometheusradio.org/prp_vs_the_fcc
64 Ibid.
65 "Past Parker Lecturers and Honorees," OC, Inc., United Church of Christ, https://org2.salsalabs.com/o/6587/content_item/pasthonorees
66 "Oakland Rising Honors Malkia Cyril," *Oakland Rising*, 16 February 2012, www.oaklandrising.org/blog/oakland-rising-honors-malkia-cyril; Malkia Cyril, "Malkia Cyril, The Center for Media Justice," 6 June 2008, www.youtube.com/watch?v=WftYx1vKmbE
67 Malkia Cyril, "FCC Chairman Puts End to Ten Years of Sky-high Prison Phone Rates," *The Hill*, 15 August 2013, http://thehill.com/blogs/congress-blog/civil-rights/317101-fcc-chairman-puts-end-to-10-years-of-sky-high-prison-phone-rates

68 "Shelton, Kramer, Cyril Honored at 31st Annual Everett C. Parker Lecture," Benton Foundation, 1 October 2013, http://uccmediajustice.org/p/salsa/web/common/public/content?content_item_KEY=11503
69 "2013 Everett C. Parker Lecture," *OCC, Inc.*, 2013, http://uccmediajustice.org/content_item/parkerlecture2013
70 NOW, "Agenda," National Organization for Women (NOW) Conference, 27 June 2014, http://now.org/about/conference/agenda/
71 Free Press, "Women will Rock the House at the National Conference for Media Reform," 29 March 2013, http://conference.freepress.net/blog/2013/03/29/women-will-rock-house-national-conference-media-reform
72 Ibid.

Chapter 7

A return to prime-time activism: Social movement theory and the media

Des Freedman

Introduction

There is a hierarchy within social movement theory related to media activism where some methods, objectives, and priorities appear to carry more weight and are more passionately pursued than others.

Let us consider this claim in the light of the very comprehensive definition of media activism provided by Hoynes that sees activism as composed of interlocking fields:

> Media activists seek to change both the structure and content of mainstream media, and they use a wide variety of tactics to alternately woo and pressure journalists, call public attention to the failures of mainstream media, build public support for policies aimed at promoting diversity in media ownership and content, and support alternative media across the range of media platforms.[1]

How does this relate to the practices of media activists on the ground? Activists are increasingly focused on developing targeted media strategies and thinking about how best to relate to journalists and news routines in order to secure coverage of their activities.[2] They are also energetically committed to exposing the limitations of the mainstream media and to pointing out how their own perspectives are largely marginalized by corporate actors—witness the media monitoring work of groups like Fairness and Accuracy in Reporting, and Media Lens together with critiques of mainstream media performance, the most famous of which remains Herman and Chomsky's propaganda model.[3] Activists have long been committed to creating their own channels of communication via radical media and distributed technologies to promote their own viewpoints and to mobilize publics in search of social justice.[4] For example, only recently a Greenpeace campaign aimed at persuading Lego to cut its links with energy giant Shell produced a video viewed more than six million times in turn generating substantial media coverage.[5]

Activists have been, however, perhaps less successful in mobilizing citizens to tackle existing media institutions and to press for progressive media policies such as those that will challenge existing patterns of media concentration, foster new voices through the creation of more equitable systems of production and distribution, and provide the basis for a more representative media system at all levels (i.e. one staffed by diverse communities and that caters to the whole of the population and not just the most privileged audiences). And even where citizens have organized in support of structural changes to existing communication systems—for example in defense of Net Neutrality or democratic internet governance—it is very rare for campaigners' objectives to be realized in durable and significant media reforms.

Yet this unevenness is especially exaggerated within social movement *theory* and it is on this latter point—that there is a hierarchy of interest within the theory of activism in relation to communications—that I want to focus. This paper reflects on how we might challenge social movement theory to engage more productively in media policy battles and to make sure that policy activism is not an adjunct to but a central part of media activism more broadly. Activists seem to be prepared to apply the spirit of social change to most public institutions with the exception of core constituents of the state such as the police, the army, and the security services. Yet there is also a reluctance to apply democratic pressure to mainstream media institutions because they appear—at least from the perspective of increasing numbers of activists—to be irreconcilably tied to vested interests and therefore incapable of radical change. Better to sidestep existing institutions or to play them at their own game by providing relevant content and seeking source status than it is to confront fully the dynamics of existing media structures.

Social movement theory has an important role to play in both galvanizing and strengthening media activism and yet it appears to have little to say about how activists should relate to *mainstream* media and how best to engage in projects that are aimed at reforming and democratizing some of our most popular media outlets. How do we explain the reluctance to embrace a media policy focus within social movement theory and why is this element of media activism often absent from the political and intellectual agendas of many left-leaning academics and activists?

Social movement theory and the media

Despite contemporary trends concerning mediatization and the centrality of information to contemporary power relations,[6] there is still a strong perception that social movement theory has not yet grasped the scale and significance of the role of media and communications in processes of social change. Todd Gitlin may have observed that in a "floodlit society, it becomes increasingly difficult, perhaps unimaginable, for an opposition movement to define itself and its world view … outside the dominant culture,"[7] but disciplines like sociology, politics, and international relations "largely ignore the relationships between activism and media."[8] In a recent review of the literature on the relationship between social movements and the media, the Italian theorist Lorenzo Mosca argues that "only recently have scholars of unconventional collective action begun to consider communication as worthy of analysis in its own right."[9] Even now, it is still considered to be "a dependent variable of limited importance." In contrast to examinations of organizational structures, targets pursued, and strategies adopted, media and communication therefore appear to be of secondary importance. As John Downing argues: "It is on the edge of being weird that there is so little systematic analysis of communication or media in the social movement literature."[10]

However, let us not exaggerate the problem nor insist that the media matters *have* to be the first item on the social movement agenda. The fact is that increasing numbers of media theorists are being heard outside of their own discipline and that more social movement theorists are, in turn, reflecting on issues of communication. For example, della Porta and Diani note in their textbook introduction to the topic that social movements "depend on the mass media to get their message across."[11] Social movements need to pose a challenge to the media's symbolic power, in particular by developing their own autonomous channels of communication via counter-public spheres, counter information, alternative, and radical media. Many social movement theorists acknowledge the media to be crucial sites of negotiation and transmission with Melucci, as another example, regularly invoking the significance of the "power of information" in the construction of collective action and arguing that movements have shifted from being conceived as "organizational or political actors to movements as *media*."[12] But while he recognizes that the "'power of the media' is not the power of a monolithic and treacherous Goliath," his attention is focused more on discursive rather than material battles within the media environment. Movements need to take part in a battle over "the power of naming" in order to "expand the intimations of public discourse into an authentic public space."[13]

Indeed, where it is discussed in the literature, the focus is concerned not so much with democratizing existing structures than with developing appropriate media strategies for resource-poor groups (which is why we are seeing a growth industry in media handbooks for grassroots campaigners to which I referred earlier). So despite some fundamental critiques of the mainstream media as hostile to social movement goals, movements themselves increasingly relate to these institutions as a "political opportunity structure."[14] As the sociologist Harvey Molotch argues in relation to social movements, "the mass media represent a potential mechanism for utilizing an establishment institution to fulfill nonestablishment goals: communicating with movement followers, reaching out to potential recruits, neutralizing would-be opponents, and confusing or otherwise immobilizing committed opponents."[15] Gamson, in his pioneering study of *The Strategy of Social*

Protest, focuses on strategies used by "challenger groups" to secure favorable coverage and the kinds of activities designed to attract media attention in the first place.[16] According to Hoynes, the relationship between media and social movements is more about issues of framing and about how to correct the low status of activist groups as desirable sources although, in general, "the work of scholars and activists remains largely in separate domains."[17]

Even one of the very few books that takes seriously both the possibilities and limitations of mainstream media foregrounds media strategies over policy activism. Charlotte Ryan's wonderful *Prime Time Activism* provides a comprehensive and subtle critique of the media that seeks to avoid both "underdetermination" and "overdetermination," i.e. "overemphasizing constraints and underestimating possibilities for action," and "underestimating the constraints and overestimating the possibilities for organizing."[18] Yet, above all, the book sets out to equip grassroots activists with a detailed knowledge of news routines such as gatekeeping, framing, and agenda-setting in order to most effectively win coverage of their struggles. She provides a salutary warning about using the mainstream media as a shortcut for other campaign strategies, arguing that an emphasis on the mainstream media "seduces us into thinking in terms of American individualism"[19] and insists that activists need to recognize media as only one particular channel of mobilization. Yet, the title is effectively a handbook for activists to secure maximum column inches and airtime for social justice campaigns in the light of the very real structural constraints that Ryan painstakingly details.

Of course much has changed in the last 25 years and the participatory possibilities of communication technologies originally identified by Brecht and Enzensberger[20] have been enormously expanded by digital developments such that social movements are increasingly able to take advantage of distributed technologies for their own purposes. Spurred on by the role of social media platforms in the Arab Spring, the Occupy movement, and anti-austerity movements, theorists are now highlighting the significance of "networked protest"[21] and "emancipatory communication activism" described by Stefania Milan as "ways of social organizing to create alternatives to existing media and communication infrastructure."[22]

This is, of course, where most of the (practical and theoretical) action is today: in possibilities for meaningful protest inspired, powered, or at least organized by digital technologies. As Cammaerts puts it:

> Most recent empirical studies on activism within Media and Communication Studies focus foremost on the opportunities and constraints the Internet provides in organizing movements, "networking," mobilizing online, as well as offline, and/or strengthening the public sphere by facilitating discussion and the development of counter-hegemonic discourses.[23]

It is a vital area of research and praxis, not least because of some of the exaggerations made about the power of "networked protest."[24] But the one thing that is frequently pushed to the side is what is sometimes seen as the banal and pedantic legislative sphere of "media reform."

It is worth noting straight away that this is *not* the case with all areas of media policy activism. As has been well documented, there is certainly quite a vigorous movement in the sphere of internet governance and communication rights, which combines governments, NGOs, academics, and social movements in trying to democratize the networks on which our movements increasingly depend.[25] Clearly, there are prospects for similar sorts of campaigns in opposition to state surveillance where national security agencies and private companies are complicit in their campaigns to monitor our communications activity. But this is mostly because these are emerging systems and platforms where there is not yet a consensus on how best to construct stable regimes both of oversight and control.

With this obviously very important exception, the idea of media *policy* activism is often absent from much of the literature on media and social movements. It barely features in some of the classic social movement texts to which I have already referred. To be more precise, it is sometimes hinted at but rarely followed up. Della Porta and Diani, for example, argue that the "more autonomous and pluralistic the media structure, the greater the possibility of access for challengers."[26] In other words, it matters to the movements themselves—to their opportunities to speak and be heard—about what kind of media system it is. It makes a difference whether it is a state-controlled authoritarian system, a highly commercial model that presents different forms of controls, a public service system with a mandated yet very elitist system of pluralism, or one with a strong community and nonprofit core. So della Porta and Diani are quite right to raise this but it is not something to which they return.

Even from within media and communications theory, John Downing's majestic overview of "rebellious communication and social movements" neglects discussions of policy action in favor of an emphasis on communication forms, aesthetics, and politics. Significantly, however, he attempts to correct this in his conclusion: "I find it hard to discount the importance of trying to make a dent in media and communication policies that otherwise are the happy hunting ground of corporate leaders who draft legislation for our supposed political representatives."[27]

Similarly, in a recent, and I think important, collection on the relationship between mediation and "contentious politics"[28] there is also barely a mention of media policy activism. In a particularly interesting chapter, Dieter Rucht talks about four reactions on the part of protest movements to the mainstream media: the four "A's."[29]

- *Abstention* which arises out of the indifference or outright hostility of the media toward protest.

- *Attack* on mainstream media, which can be written, verbal, or, in some cases, physical.
- *Adaptation*, where campaigners comply with mainstream agendas and routines in order to stand the best chance of securing sympathetic, or perhaps any, coverage.
- *Alternative* media where the movement makes its own media.

This is a very helpful typology of media/movement relations but it is nevertheless very revealing that Rucht chooses *not* to address a further "A"—what I, in the absence of any better word that starts with A, call "amelioration," in other words, reform: campaigns to change the failing institutions that make up the media. None of the examples discussed above are accidental or the result of neglect on the part of the authors. Instead, they reflect some fundamental reasons why media policy activism has a relatively low profile within social movement literature.

The first part of the explanation is that an orientation on policy is often perceived to be a compromised political project in that it is reformist in spirit and incomplete (or worse) in practice. Calabrese distinguishes between media reform and media justice where the former is intimately tied to "liberal" conceptions of communication rights and where "liberal reforms can be viewed as enabling the persistence of fundamental injustices by failing to address, and even naturalizing, their root causes."[30] This also feeds into Silverstone's critique of state regulation as being more concerned with procedural questions—about providing enabling structures—than with fundamental questions of justice and the ability to speak freely and respectfully. He argues that "regulation is like grammar. It addresses the rules of language, not how that language is spoken or what it said."[31]

For many social movement activists, this type of media reform—of trying to democratize the media—is seen as potentially counter-productive in that activists are likely either to be incorporated into official channels or to tailor their demands to meet the values and demands of vested interests. De Jong, Shaw, and Stammers are right to suggest that many social movements are non-institutionally oriented and largely anti-institutional[32] and therefore likely to doubt the need to engage with formal processes and "official" channels. Thinking in particular of the US media-reform group Free Press, Mickey Huff of *Project Censored* warns of the dangers of "working through the system" and of attempting merely to fix, rather than to replace, a social system that has been found to be demonstrably unfair and unequal. This lends itself to reformist illusions both that the system can indeed be repaired and that, even if we do fix media institutions, they will ever deliver social justice within the existing frame of capitalism. As Huff argues, we need to "[b]e the Media in word and deed … not lobby those in power to reform their own current establishment megaphones for their own power elite agendas, as that will not happen, and indeed, has not, for the most part, in the past."[33]

Social movement theory's failure to engage with the policy sphere of media activism isn't due to absent-mindedness or prevarication. It is more deliberate and purposeful and based on a perception that, because established media structures are unrepresentative, unaccountable, and ideologically committed to a neoliberal consensus, why bother to focus on efforts to reform failed institutions? Why waste energy on spending time on something as anodyne and moderate as campaigns for an ethical press, or more democratic media ownership, or for the survival of local news—when these institutions have long been part of the problem in undermining democracy, stifling prospects for social and political equality, and indeed in marginalizing social movements themselves?

Of course, this is not a problem solely to do with the limitations of media policy questions but also reflects the highly ambiguous position and politics of civil society groups themselves. Trapped within a Foucauldian nightmare of incorporation and reinforcement, one critic argues that "civil society associations and organisations help to stabilise and normalise conditions that are seen as threats or disturbances to the welfare of human populations, *but not to alter the structural conditions responsible for those threats and disturbances.*"[34] The result of this is in that relation to child poverty, environmental disaster, or media power, civil society action that is focused on "improvement" simply runs the risk of reproducing the social relations of neoliberalism.

Second, media policy is far from a space that social movements control. This reflects a crucial argument about the most efficient use of movement resources and our ability to shape public debate and foster public action. Why prioritize an environment that is fundamentally hostile to our interests when we have the ability to produce our own materials that we can disseminate through our own networks? If you agree with Cammaerts that activism is concerned with "the ability to act and make or change history,"[35] in other words with the changeability and "makeability" of society, than why choose a series of institutions that have proved to be so resistant to change? Of course, this is not simply a matter of efficiency but pragmatism as movements are likely to grow in confidence and impact if they are able to express themselves in their own terms and not only to pander to the frames, vocabularies, and agendas of others.

In the knowledge, therefore, that we cannot rely on the mainstream media to cover our struggles, indeed to represent our lives as they are lived, we are forced to make our own media. Both the theory and practice of alternative media draws on participatory accounts of democracy to produce media that better reflect the diversity of the population and that more productively fit the needs of our movements. Social movement theory has a particular role to play here in considering the communicative competences, performances, and structures that are necessary to publicize, organize, and galvanize movements for social justice. We have a whole host of platforms, technologies, and practices in place—from "hacktivism" to citizen journalism, and from "culture jamming" to community media—that both challenge the agendas and narratives of mainstream media and allow "ordinary" media users to take control of the technologies.

This relates to a third problem with media policy activism: that it lacks the participatory, grassroots structures that populate alternative media environments, and that it reflects the hierarchical, exclusive, and "insider" character of the administrative processes that account for formal policy making and regulatory environments. In other words, policy activism too often looks like the structures it aims to contest: depoliticized, top-down, and unequal, as well as white, male, and middle class. This takes us in a different direction to the objectives of the media justice movement that seeks to "build meaningful participation from communities of color and indigenous communities to take back this important right [to a free media], to take back our airways, networks, and cultural spaces."[36] Traditional approaches to media policy activism therefore are seen not only to marginalize certain groups of people and issues but also—to put it very crudely—to lack the excitement and passion of more grassroots movements. In a nutshell, media policy activism is kind of boring. Is this an accurate representation?

Features of a radical media policy activism

Joe Karaganis distinguishes between two "geographies of activism": a more civil and polite "consumer-rights-based model of policy advocacy" encapsulated in media reform strategies, and more militant demands for media justice that emerge from "predominantly civil-rights-informed concerns with accountability, representation and voice in the media."[37] To what extent is it possible to imagine the concerns of media justice campaigners applied to the objectives of media reformers committed to transforming the policy environment and is Karaganis right to assert—despite the reservations outlined earlier—that "systemic change requires a social movement capable of linking policy agendas with grassroots activism?"[38]

Media policy activism ought not to be seen as separate to other stands of media activism. It builds on a critique of the limitations of the mainstream media and is buoyed by efforts to communicate movement ideas and actions in our own terms but it focuses on efforts to democratize actually existing media through initiatives like diversifying media ownership, opening up the media policy process, campaigning for new forms of funding for marginalized content, opposing surveillance, challenging existing copyright regimes, and pressing for more ethical forms of journalism. This often requires an engagement with official structures—with formal legislative processes, with parliaments and policy makers, with lobbyists and lawyers—in order words, with the very constituents of the system that are responsible for a diminished and degraded media culture. As I have just explained, it is hardly surprising that it is this dimension of media activism that is most noticeably absent from social movement theory in relation to the media.

Let us examine these debates—whether we should attempt to work through the system or not—and investigate this particular strand of media activism in relation to a major debate in the UK since 2011: efforts to produce a more responsible and ethical press in the light of the phone hacking crisis, and, in particular, the legacy and implications of the Leveson Inquiry into press standards and the practices that followed it.

The reaction to the whole Leveson process from many social movement activists—in particular those who are most concerned with the media—was that Leveson was about "ruling class recuperation" in which one faction of the state sought to discipline and humble the "unruly elements" of the Murdoch empire.[39] A focus on challenging just one element of private power, it was argued, ran the risk of marginalizing the more essential surveillance and consensus-building roles of the state itself. The celebrated investigative journalist John Pilger accused Leveson of being essentially concerned with "the preservation of the system" and noted that "Leveson has asked nothing about how the respectable media complemented the Murdoch press in systematically promoting corrupt, mendacious, often violent political power whose crimes make phone-hacking barely a misdemeanor." The monitoring site Media Lens argued that the Leveson Inquiry constituted "yet another instance of established power investigating itself" while the academic Richard Keeble insisted that that the Inquiry should be understood as "spectacular theatre" that provided "the illusion of moral intent by the state and its propaganda institutions—the leading media corporations—when in reality the system is run on ruthless profit-oriented principles."[40]

These are valuable and legitimate criticisms. The emphasis in the Leveson Inquiry on individual "bad apples" and its reluctance to confront any structural issues meant that, despite overwhelming evidence to the contrary, corrupt organizations, complicit relationships, and corrosive institutions were individualized, decontextualized, and stripped of their systemic characters in order to pursue politically pragmatic resolutions.[41] Without challenging the underlying conditions that gave rise to phone hacking—a press system wedded either to private profit or public influence—Leveson was, to a certain extent, captured by precisely the power relations it sought to investigate and to hold to account.

But there is one problem with these critiques: they ignore the possibility that the exposure of media power during the course of the Inquiry might help to radicalize victims' groups, other activists, and indeed ordinary members of the public to ask more fundamental questions about how best to seek not just a more ethical press but a truly accountable media system, not just to introduce a new code but to press for a completely different form of political culture. It is true that the structuring of the Inquiry fits the propaganda model notion of containing debate within acceptable limits but it also raised fundamental questions about the location and exercise of power in the UK that, if acted upon by activist organizations, could have laid the basis for a more sustained challenge to the hegemony of corporate media.

Media activists have a responsibility in this context to amplify these arguments about the flaws of an entrenched media power as part of a broader argument about the operation of the capitalist state. They do not need to make polite requests to tone down the worst excesses of the tabloid press or engage in subdued parliamentary lobbying to secure minimal changes to press self-regulation. Instead, activists should attempt to broaden the debate and to deepen the crisis by campaigning for specific remedies to, for example, media concentration, press scapegoating, and the decline of local news. We should encourage a diversity of approaches that includes everything from academic research that demonstrates the scale of the problems to street protests (as we have seen in Mexico, Istanbul, and Athens in recent years) that seek to mobilize publics in support of efforts to democratize media systems. At the same time we need to insist that the failures of mainstream media and existing policy-making processes are indeed systemic and not incidental or peripheral to the core operations of media and political elites. We need, in other words, to introduce more radical questions and techniques to those traditionally posed by reform-minded policy actors.

Is reform enough?

This is a debate, after all, about the politics of reform in general. Reform has been hijacked in recent years: education reforms, health reforms, welfare reform—all these have been about the further implantation of market values into public services rather than the democratizing of these institutions. But of course these are not examples of genuine reform so much as attempts to concentrate power and wealth in fewer hands. Just because political reform has been re-branded does not mean that activists should abandon the struggle for democratic reforms. The whole point of the anti-slavery movement, attempts to organize labor in the nineteenth century, struggles for the vote for women in the early twentieth century, the struggle for civil rights later on in the twentieth century was that these were reforms that were really fought for by different groups of people using hugely varied tactics from the polite and the parliamentary to the far more risky and revolutionary. That is the nature of reform movements: they combine people who are happy to stick to the immediate demands with those who want to go much further; they consist of fragile coalitions between people who think that the system as it exists can deliver reforms that will satisfy enough people and those who think that there are structural inequalities that cannot be ironed out given the priorities of capitalism.

In these circumstances, the best tactic for those who want to see radical and durable change is not to withdraw from reform-minded movements but to demonstrate that reforms can only be won and protected through systemic critique and radical action such as the boycotts, marches, occupations, and direct action that have won the greatest victories in struggles for justice.

But what is odd is that while many of us are happy to engage in anti-racist, environmental, disability, living-wage, and any number of other campaigns to deal with the injustices meted out every day, we are far more reluctant to place such demands on prospects for media justice. We're simultaneously fascinated and horrified by the mainstream media: we love complaining about it but we also love for our protests to be covered; we want to produce our own media but have to deal with the fact that millions of people continue to turn to corporate outlets for their information and entertainment and not to movement resources. Della Porta actually raises this as an issue when she talks about the difficulties for alternative media "to reach beyond those already sympathetic to the cause"[42] and embraces the need to engage with the mass media in order to disseminate progressive messages more widely.

Media policy activism, as with many other campaigns for social reform and justice, is therefore a way of reaching out to those people who have a healthy and often instinctive critique of the status quo but who maintain some illusions of the status quo. It is a way of working with those who want to see meaningful change but are not yet prepared to junk existing institutions and traditional forms of political campaigning in parliament and civil society.

We can learn a lot from Bob Hackett and Bill Carroll's great book on democratic media activism which argues that it is both defensive and pro-active—in other words that it can be both reform-oriented in practice but also revolutionary and autonomist in spirit.[43] Media activism for them involves a redefinition of the very idea of democracy to include new rights such as the right to share meaning as well as an increased emphasis on participation and equality through acts of media-making. The objective for democratic media activists is "to build coalitions and campaigns to engage with and transform the dominant machinery of representation, in both the media and political fields."[44] Indeed, it is harder and harder to separate media activism from other social struggles and to insulate media reform from political reform in particular because of the lack of autonomy of the media "field"—precisely as we saw in the Leveson Inquiry where complicit relationships between media and political elites were laid bare.

We need therefore to use an inside/outside perspective that takes me back to the dimensions of media activism that I started this chapter with: efforts to secure positive coverage of activist concerns, radical critique of mainstream media, production of independent and alternative media, and attempts to democratize the mainstream media. This is best characterized in a slogan developed by Canadian media activists behind the annual Media Democracy Day: "know the media," "be the media," AND "change the media." We have to employ all three strategies if we are going to achieve more democratic media systems.

In conclusion, to the extent that activists want to precipitate a fundamental shift in political power and social justice, they need to engage in media reform but not from a reformist perspective. In doing this, we can draw on a pamphlet by the German revolutionary Rosa Luxemburg, *Reform or Revolution*, written back in 1899 in which she distinguished between "revisionist" strategies for reform which attempt to administer palliative care to the capitalist system and more radical strategies that seek to win reforms as a fundamental part of a revolutionary strategy to transform the status quo. While the former wants "to lessen, to attenuate, the capitalist contradictions"[45] in order to stabilize society and produce consensus, the latter seeks to struggle for reforms as part of a more widespread challenge to capitalist hegemony. The crucial point for Luxemburg however was that movements for reforms were central to a more profound social struggle: "Between social reforms and revolution there exists for the revolutionary an indissoluble tie. The struggle for reforms is its means; the social revolution, its aim."[46]

Now my point is *not* that Luxemburg would have been active in Free Press or FLOSS movements, or the Media Reform Coalition, or that she would have spent her time lobbying for better rules for internet governance or more effective codes of conduct for journalists. I simply want to stress that media reform, like all other forms of social reform, is a contradictory and uneven process in which different groups are involved and different strategies are mobilized. There is a world of difference between an activist campaign which calls on a handful of the "great and the good" to plead its case and one which seeks to mobilize greater numbers of people using all the tactics that are available—a difference perhaps between "reform from above" and "reform from below."

Of course, if social movements are to secure durable and significant change, then there is little point in aiming only at amelioration: at applying a Band-Aid to deep cuts. It is also the case, however, that there is little point in refusing at least to treat the wound if activist movements are to grow and gain influence. We need to delegitimize and pose alternatives to the highly unequal power structures that dominate the media, but we also need to take seriously all those who want to find solutions to current problems if we are to secure a full mandate for change. A media activism that is based on pressing for policy change in the here and now while simultaneously developing its own structures that go far beyond the constraints of existing media systems may yet bear out Downing's prediction that "only dual activity by radical media makers and radical policy activists has the prospect of letting the public construct for themselves any kind of zone worth inhabiting."[47]

Notes

1 William Hoynes, "Media Research and Media Activism," in *Rhyming Hope and History: Activists, Academics and Social Movement Scholarship*, Eds. David Croteau, William Hoynes, and Charlotte Ryan (Minneapolis: University of Minnesota Press, 2005), 100.

2 See Aidan Ricketts, *The Activist's Handbook: A Step-by-Step Guide to Participatory Democracy* (London: Zed, 2012) and Randy Shaw, *The Activist's Handbook: Winning Change in the 21st Century*, 2nd ed. (Oakland: University of California Press, 2013).
3 See David Edwards and David Cromwell, *Guardians of Power: The Myth of the Liberal Media* (London: Pluto, 2006) and Edward Herman and Noam Chomsky, *Manufacturing Consent: The Political Economy of the Mass Media* (New York: Pantheon, 1988).
4 Chris Atton, *Alternative Media* (London: Sage, 2002); John Downing, *Radical Media: Rebellious Communication and Social Movements* (London: Sage, 2001); Dan Gillmor, *We the Media: Grassroots Journalism by the People, for the People* (Sebastopol: O'Reilly, 2004); Stefania Milan, *Social Movements and their Technologies: Wiring Social Change* (Basingstoke: Palgrave Macmillan, 2013).
5 Adam Vaughan, "Lego Ends Shell Partnership Following Greenpeace Campaign," *Guardian*, 9 October 2014, www.theguardian.com/environment/2014/oct/09/lego-ends-shell-partnership-following-greenpeace-campaign
6 For work on mediatization, see Andreas Esser and Jesper Strömbäch, Eds., *Mediatization of Politics: Understanding the Transformation of Western Democracies* (Basingstoke, England: Palgrave Macmillan, 2014); Stig Hjarvard, *The Mediatization of Culture and Society* (New York: Routledge, 2013); Andreas Hepp, *Cultures of Mediatization* (Cambridge: Polity, 2013). For an account of the informatization of power, see Manuel Castells, *Communication Power* (Oxford: Oxford University Press, 2009).
7 Todd Gitlin, *The Whole World Is Watching: Mass Media in the Making & Unmaking of the New Left* (Berkeley, CA: University of California Press, 1980), 3.
8 Wilma de Jong, Martin Shaw, and Neil Stammers, "Introduction," in *Global Activism, Global Media*, Eds. William de Jong, Martin Shaw, and Neil Stammers (London: Pluto, 2005), 3.
9 Lorenzo Mosca, "Bringing Communication Back in: Social Movements and Media," in *Communication Rights and Social Justice*, Eds. C. Padovani and A. Calabrese (Houndsditch, England: Palgrave Macmillan, 2014), 231–232.
10 Downing, *Radical Media*, 26.
11 Donatella della Porta and Mario Diani, *Social Movements: An Introduction*, 2nd ed. (Oxford: Blackwell, 2006), 220.
12 Alberto Melucci, *Challenging Codes: Collective Action in the Information Age* (Cambridge: Cambridge University Press, 1996), 36.
13 Melucci, *Challenging Codes*, 228.
14 Hoynes, "Media Research and Media Activism," 98.
15 Harvey Molotch, "Media and Movements," in *The Dynamics of Social Movements*, Eds. Mayer N. Zald and John D. McCarthy (Lanham, MD: University Press of America, 1988), 71.
16 William Gamson, *The Strategy of Social Protest* (Homewood, IL: Dorsey, 1975), 166–167.
17 Hoynes, "Media Research and Media Activism," 99.
18 Charlotte Ryan, *Prime Time Activism* (Boston, MA: South End Press, 1991), 10.
19 Ryan, *Prime Time Activism*, 29.
20 Bertolt Brecht, *Brecht on Film and Radio*, Trans. and Ed. Marc Silberman (London: Methuen, 2000); Hans Magnus Enzensberger, "Constituents of a Theory of the Media," *New Left Review* 64 (1970): 13–36.
21 Paul Mason, *Why It's Kicking Off Everywhere: The New Global Revolutions* (London: Verso, 2012).

22 Stefania Milan, *Social Movements and their Technologies*, 9.
23 Bart Cammaerts, "Activism and Media," in *Reclaiming the Media: Communication Rights and Democratic Media Roles*, Eds. Bart Cammaerts and Nico Carpentier (Bristol, England: Intellect, 2007), 270.
24 See Paolo Gerbaudo, *Tweets and the Streets: Social Media and Contemporary Activism* (Basingstoke, England: Palgrave Macmillan, 2013) and Evgeny Morozov, *The Net Delusion: How Not to Liberate the World* (London: Allen Lane, 2011).
25 Milan, *Social Movements and their technologies*; and Marc Raboy, Norman Landry, and Jeremy Shtern, *Digital Solidarities, Communication Policy and Multi-stakeholder Global Governance* (New York: Peter Lang, 2010).
26 della Porta and Diani, *Social Movements*, 220.
27 Downing, *Radical Media*, 394.
28 Bart Cammaerts, Alice Mattoni, and Patrick McCurdy, Eds., *Mediation and Protest Movements* (Bristol: Intellect, 2013).
29 Dieter Rucht, "Protest Movements and their Media Usages," in *Mediation and Protest Movements*, Eds. Bart Cammaerts, Alice Mattoni, and Patrick McCurdy (Bristol: Intellect, 2013), 249–268.
30 Andrew Calabrese, "Media Reform and Communication Rights in the USA," in *Communication Rights and Social Justice*, Eds. Claudia Padovani and Andrew Calabrese (Houndsditch, England: Palgrave Macmillan, 2014), 187.
31 Roger Silverstone, *Media and Morality: On the Rise of the Mediapolis* (Cambridge: Polity, 2007), 174.
32 De Jong, Shaw, and Stammers, *Global Activism*, 12.
33 Mickey Huff, "Project Censored 2012: Moving Beyond Media Reform," *Truthout*, 7 September 2011, www.truth-out.org/opinion/item/3160:project-censored-2012-moving-beyond-media-reform
34 Ronnie Lipschutz, "Networks of Knowledge and Practice: Global Civil Society and Global Communications," in de Jong, Shaw, and Stammers, *Global Activism*, 28.
35 Cammaerts, "Activism and Media," 217.
36 Media Justice Network, "Whose Media? Our Media!" http://web.archive.org/web/20040602043148/http://www.mediajustice.org
37 Joe Karaganis, "Cultures of Collaboration in Media Research," 2009, http://papers.ssrn.com/sol3/papers.cfm?abstract_id=1485181
38 Ibid., 1.
39 Christian Garland and Stephen Harper, "Did Somebody Say Neoliberalism?: On the Uses and Limitations of a Critical Concept in Media and Communications," *tripleC* 10, no. 2 (2012): 419.
40 See John Pilger, "The Leveson Inquiry into the British Press—Oh, What a Lovely Game," *johnpilger.com*, 31 May 2012, http://johnpilger.com/articles/the-leveson-inquiry-into-the-british-press-oh-what-a-lovely-game; also see *Morning Star*, "Leveson: A Tiger With No Teeth?" 9 July 2012.
41 Des Freedman, *The Contradictions of Media Power* (London: Bloomsbury, 2014).
42 Donatella della Porta, "Bridging Research on Democracy, Social Movements and Communication," in *Mediation and Protest Movements*, Eds. Bart Cammaerts, Alice Mattoni, and Patrick McCurdy (Bristol: Intellect, 2013), 29.
43 Robert Hackett and William Carroll, *Remaking Media: The Struggle to Democratize Public Communication* (London: Routledge, 2006), 13.
44 Hackett and Carroll, *Remaking Media*, 16.
45 Rosa Luxemburg, *Reform or Revolution* (London: Bookmarks, 1989 [1899]), 18.
46 Luxemburg, *Reform or Revolution*, 21.
47 Downing, *Radical Media*, 394.

Section III

New political genres

Introduction: New media dialectics

Jonathan Pace

The history of modern media is a dialectical history. Newspapers engendered national publics through acts of solitary reading.[1] In the dark space of the theater, cinema isolated the viewing subject while implicating her in a social and spectatorial ritual.[2] Radio and telephone flourished in domestic milieus yet undermined the integral privacy of the twentieth-century household. Television immobilized viewers and mobilized protesters in one fell swoop, fashioning the couch potato and the activist celebrity as iconic reverse-images.[3] Like M. C. Escher's puzzling prints, which forestall any conclusive establishment of spatial coordinates, the social consequences of media technologies are fundamentally paradoxical.

New media comparably require dialectical thinking: they are vehicles of novelty and tradition, emancipation and power, reverie and solidarity.[4] Neither McLuhan's global optimism nor Adorno's ideological pessimism are finally adequate to the task of digital media studies.[5] This is not to suggest a radical historical break between old and new media, as if the emergence of digital technology outdated past theory and inaugurated a de Manian "true present."[6] Rather, this is to claim that one-dimensional approaches to new media fail to deliver the proverbial goods. Only by tracing the interplay of counterpoised tendencies can digital media studies do justice to the complexity of the current technosocial situation. The essays in this section, "New Political Genres," fulfill these dialectical obligations and offer nuanced perspectives on emergent media technologies.

In "*Cahiers de doleance* 2.0," Paolo Gerbaudo charts the development of a new digital rhetoric on crowd-sourced activist blogs. These platforms aggregate personal testimonies related to prevalent social issues, recasting individual stories as instances of collective political categories. Group solidarity thus emerges through the repetition of personal accounts, and new digital platforms galvanize the traditional form of the grievance list. Gerbaudo's dialectical thesis accordingly counters the popular argument that digital activism is a hyper-individualized product of decentralized networks. Such technological determinism, for Gerbaudo, conceals the sociosymbolic dimension of new-media contestation and elevates the network to a meta-explanatory framework.

Similarly, Leslie Regan Shade, Harrison Smith, and Evan Hamilton consider the interplay of freedom and power in geoweb technologies. Through the collection and curation of spatial data, activist groups map social injustices, political abuses, and environmental disaster sites, thereby generating crowdsourced evidence for policy makers. Still, corporate ownership of these technologies circumscribes their democratic promise, as private companies establish industry standards and maintain property rights over interfaces and datasets. Egalitarian social change thus emerges in conditions of politico-economic hegemony, and constellations of locational data become greater than the sum of their technosocial parts.

Stefania Milan broadens these concerns in her discussion of data activism. For Milan, data has become both the means and the ends of computational politics. She understands the systematic compilation of digital information by an assemblage of social agencies as an emergent form of social control. Through new styles of hacking and traditional modes of campaigning, activists resist and undermine these pervasive surveillance practices. Power relations thereby saturate the field of data, as contestation in civil society extends into the computational sphere.

These essays exemplify the dialectical affinities of contemporary digital media studies. As the techno-utopianism of the late twentieth century gives way to the conceptual reservations of the early twenty-first, new-media theorists are foregrounding paradox in order to balance the possibilities and the limitations of emergent communication technologies. Digital media will not usher in egalitarian social change without the concerted effort of an active citizenry, nor will it institute a global surveillance state with a technological blank check. The dreams of 1968 and the nightmares of 1984 are, in the end, twilight misconceptions. Freedom still emerges within a matrix of power, and whether or not new media tips the scale in favor of the former remains, as always, an open question.

Notes

1 See Benedict Anderson, *Imagined Communities* (London: Verso, 1983).
2 See Jacqueline Rose, "The Cinematic Apparatus," in *Sexuality in the Field of Vision* (London: Verso, 1986).
3 On the immobilizing character of television, see Fredric Jameson, "Surrealism Without the Unconscious," in *Postmodernism* (Durham, NC: Duke University Press, 1991). On the relation between television and mid-century American activism, see Todd Gitlin, *The Whole World is Watching* (Berkeley, CA: University of California Press, 1980).
4 See Alexander Galloway, *Protocol* (Cambridge, MA: MIT Press, 2004) for a discussion of digital control mechanisms. On the legacy of old media, especially cinema, in digital technology, see Lev Manovich, *The Language of New Media* (Cambridge, MA: MIT Press, 2002). W. L. Bennett's controversial thesis in *The Logic of Connective Action* (Cambridge, UK: Cambridge University Press, 2013) centers on the interplay of the personal and the public in contemporary activism.

5 See Marshall McLuhan, *The Gutenberg Galaxy* (Toronto, ON: University of Toronto Press, 1962) and *Understanding Media* (Corte Madera, CA: Gingko Press, 1964). See Theodor Adorno and Max Horkheimer, "The Culture Industry: Enlightenment as Mass Deception," in *Dialectic of Enlightenment* (Stanford, CA: Stanford University Press, 1944).
6 See Paul de Man, "Literary History and Literary Modernity," *Daedalus* 99, no. 2 (1970): 384–404.

Chapter 8

Cahiers de doleance 2.0: Crowd-sourced social justice blogs and the emergence of a rhetoric of collection in social media activism

Paolo Gerbaudo

Introduction

> "We don't claim to speak for anyone, we merely present stories."
> *We Are the 99 Percent* Tumblr blog

Social Justice blogs are one the most interesting forms of political expression to have emerged in the context of social media activism. From Occupy Wall Street in the United States to the indignados movement in Spain,[1] digital activists in post-2008 protest movements have used Tumblr and similar online platforms to create multi-author blogs (MABs).[2] MABs ask internet users to submit their own contributions on a number of different issues: economic deprivation, housing insecurity, unemployment, sexism, health issues, and so forth.

Despite differences in content, all these blogs share a common format. First, they adhere to a crowd-sourcing logic by virtue of the fact that they depend exclusively on user submissions. Second, they customarily display a series of simplified instructions explaining to users how to make their submissions. Third, the submissions are usually only very lightly edited by the operator of the blog, with the assumption that all submissions will be displayed. Fourth, their ostensible aim is to raise awareness about various social issues by showing the extent and gravity of the issue at stake, signalled both by the sheer number of submissions that they receive and in the dramatic content of these submissions. These blogs are thus an interesting manifestation of the web's new culture of collaboration and the way in which it is utilized for activist purposes.

Examples of crowd-sourced social justice blogs now abound. Possibly the most famous such blog to date is Occupy Wall Street's Tumblr blog, *We Are the 99 Percent*, which at the height of the occupations collected the stories of social and economic hardship experienced by different sectors of American society.[3] Another example of an activist blog concerned with social inequality is *No Nos Vamos, Nos Echan* (*We Don't Go, They Kick Us Out*) by the Spanish activist group *Juventud Sin Futuro* (Youth Without a Future), which was able to channel the frustration of thousands of Spaniards forced to leave their country because of the economic crisis. Other examples include the manifold feminist crowd-sourced blogs that have been created in recent years such as Everyday Sexism, a project that documents instances of sexism suffered by people in their everyday life.[4] These projects have attracted several hundred submissions, thousands of views on social media, and garnered coverage in the news media. They have thus played an important role in supporting social movements and representing their cause to the wider public. Looking at crowd-sourced social justice blogs in this chapter I focus on a number of questions: What is the novelty of crowd-sourced activist blogs *vis-à-vis* previous forms of digital activism? What kind of communicative logic underlies them? What are the best concepts that we can use to capture their inner workings? And what do they tell us about digital activism and, more generally, about contemporary protest movements?

My argument in this chapter is that crowd-sourced blogs break with the network logic of communication that lies at the heart of the anti-globalization movement.[5] They testify instead to the rise of a more collective and unifying communicative logic. This is a logic that Jeffrey Juris theorizes as a "logic of aggregation"[6] and what I refer to in my previous work as a "choreography of assembly."[7] In this paper, I approach this issue by developing the idea of a "rhetoric of collection."[8]

This term serves to express the way in which crowd-sourced social justice blogs aggregate different examples of a particular social grievance. This can be understood as a sort of contemporary equivalent of the *cahier de doleances*, the list of grievances drawn up by the Three Estates during the last gathering in March and April 1789 before the French Revolution. Furthermore, it highlights how this rhetoric stands in opposition to the "logic of connection," which has been dominant in current interpretations of digital activism as epitomized in W. Lance Bennett and Alexandra Segerberg's discussion of "connective action" as the overcoming of traditional collective action dynamics through the use of digital tools.[9] Thus, against the view according to which digital activism is dominated by networked individualism, crowd-sourced social justice blogs demonstrate the continued importance of collective identity and solidarity in contemporary movements.

Crowd-sourced blogs thus involve the symbolic construction of a certain grievance in a way which transcends their singularity, presenting them not as stories that are reducible to a particular person, but rather as individual examples of the same collective phenomenon. By assembling together the stories of many people, these blogs help raise social awareness about the grievances affecting different parts of society, be they people from disadvantaged economic backgrounds, citizens affected by the financial crisis, women, people of color, or LGBT communities.

From activist diaries to crowd-sourced blogs

Crowd-sourced social justice blogs can be interpreted as an evolution of activist blogging at the turn of the millennium. Blogging, the practice of keeping a running diary or commentary that is posted on a dedicated website, is an activity that predates the history of the early World Wide Web.[10] Blogs are one of the most obvious manifestations of the online "participatory culture" that has developed in the so-called web 2.0 era.[11] Blogging has introduced new voices into political debates, allowing for a greater diversity of opinions and in-depth discussions.[12] Blogging has also been widely adopted by activists in order to cover social movements from a more sympathetic angle than the mainstream news media.[13]

Initially activist blogs, as with blogs more generally, tended to be individual affairs,[14] with single authors using them as a platform to express their views on a political situation or to ask their audience to participate in a protest action. But since the late 2000s multi-author blogs (MABs) started to emerge,[15] which allow multiple individuals to contribute to the same collective commentary, making use of the affordances of web 2.0 to aggregate user-generated content. "Crowd-sourced blogs" are a subcategory of MABs. They are frequently *ad hoc* blogs lasting for a small period of time that are used to call for contributions from web users who are interested in a specific issue. Tumblr has become a particularly popular platform for this type of project, as seen in Tumblr blogs such as *Everyday Sexism* and *Project Unbreakable*, which collects the stories of female victims of domestic abuse.

Crowd-sourced blogs can be seen as constituting a specific genre, in the sense that they are a category of expression marked by the presence of a number of shared features that revolve around common symbols.[16] Conceptualizing crowd-sourced blogs as a cultural "genre" rather than a technological structure is quite important for the theoretical positioning of this paper. My approach runs against the technodeterministic tendency to view technology as an independent variable that determines all other phenomena. Rather, I allow for the relative autonomy of symbolic processes, and intend to account for the ways in which technological development is accompanied by the development of new rhetorics of communication that are chiefly cultural rather than technological in character.

Crowd-sourced blogs are a genre characterized by a number of features including:

1. A *single-issue orientation* with a focus on a specific social problem (the economy, racism, sexism, etc.).
2. Crowd-sourced blogs are *time-bound*, with projects concentrating on a short period of time during which submissions are received.
3. Contributions are *simplified*, usually taking the form of pictures, short textual messages, or selfies of users holding a sign (which has become a sort of sub-genre in its own right).

4. A *catalogue format* in which individual contributions are presented as an item in a larger set.

Despite their differences, all crowd-sourced social justice blogs reflect these features. Having described the main features of this genre, in the remainder of this chapter I am interested in exploring how they are concretely manifested in specific projects. Furthermore, I am interested in the underlying social and cultural meanings this emerging genre brings forth.

Capturing the cultural logic of crowd-sourced blogs involves questioning the dominant approach to digital activism. This scholarship revolves around an understanding of digital activism as involving centreless networks of individuals connected with one another by loose ties that are also capable of flexibly taking part in protest action. This vision has been strongly informed by Spanish sociologist Manuel Castells' work on the network society. Castells sees contemporary society as moving away from the morphology of the pyramid and towards the morphology of the network.[17] When it comes to understanding digital activism, this analysis implies a view of the protest organization as a "networked," "rhizomatic," and "leaderless" structure.[18] The concept of the network has been used by sociologists to study various associational and kinship structures, the relationships amongst various individuals, and to describe the morphology of the technical infrastructure of information and communication technologies. The implications of this line of theory are highly problematic, since it assumes that the properties of technology do not mediate social action while neglecting social and cultural factors that are involved in activism. My contention is that networks have therefore been elevated to a sort of blanket term used to explain the transformation of organizational processes.

Similar to the work of Manuel Castells, W. Lance Bennett and Alexandra Segerberg have proposed an influential theory of protest that they call "connective action" that is juxtaposed with traditional collective action dynamics.[19] Compared to collective action, "connective action networks are typically far more individualized and technologically organized sets of processes that result in action without the requirement of collective identity framing or the levels of organizational resources required to respond effectively to opportunities."[20] In this context, "taking public action or contributing to a common good becomes an act of personal expression and recognition or self-validation achieved by sharing ideas and actions in trusted relationships."[21] The "collective" gives way to a world of individualized interactions that are fleetingly bound together by flexible network ties.

Bennett and Segerberg's analysis is useful for understanding how current forms of digital protest depart from the paradigm of formal mass membership organization that was dominant in the twentieth century. Yet it is not able to capture the concrete cultural practices that lie at the heart of social media activism, particularly crowd-sourced activist blogs. They do not operate by means of one-to-one connection and therefore they have little to do with the metaphor of the network. To understand this phenomenon, we refer not to networks but to the notion of "category."

A useful reference for developing our understanding of crowd-sourced blogs as categories rather than networks is the work of social movement historian Charles Tilly and his famous notion of "cat-net." A cat-net is "a network within a category" or "a set of individuals comprising both a category and a network."[22] One-to-one ties operate only when they are accompanied by a sense of collective self—as women, youth, gays, citizens, and so on—ranging from the most particularistic to the most general. What is important in this notion is that mobilization not only requires networks, but also forms of categorical identification, whereby a number of individuals come to subscribe to the same collective identity. What is important here is that a category is not an objective datum, but the result of a social and symbolic construction.[23] Workers or women exist as a social and political category not just because of their objective existence, but also because of the meanings and narratives that are associated with these terms.

Crowd-sourced blogs permit the symbolic construction of specific social groupings as "aggrieved categories" of citizens who are framed as subjects entitled to protest against the grievances affecting them, thereby defining them as a group. They allow individuals to subscribe to a collective identity by both participating in the construction of that identity through their own individual contribution and validating it by their participation in the project. They are performances that assert identity and belonging in ways that are instrumental to facilitating protest mobilization. Thus, crowd-sourced blogs evince a very different communicational logic than the individualism often associated with contemporary digital movements. They entail a more collective and solidarity-oriented logic of action than the one that is assumed in the present literature. In the subsequent empirical analysis, I will demonstrate how this hypothesis provides an explanation for the symbolic processes at play in different crowd-sourced blogs and how they reflect the new cultural orientation of post-crash protest movements.

Methodology

This chapter is based on a case-study analysis of two crowd-sourced blogs, Occupy Wall Street's *We Are the 99 Percent* blog and the blog *No Nos Vamos, Nos Echan* associated with the indignados movement. I have selected these case studies because of their importance and the different geographic and social contexts of the two movements. My analysis is based on archival data collected from these blogs, including all of the contributions, the "about" pages, and the submission pages. I have then proceeded to analyse this material from a discursive standpoint, with an interest in the structure of meaning and the underlying narrative of these artifacts as well as the ways each of them reflects the ideology and orientation of social movements.

Submit your experience here ...

My analysis concentrates on two famous cases of crowd-sourced social justice blogs, the *We Are the 99 Percent* Tumblr blog that was developed by activists connected with the Occupy Wall Street movement and the *No Nos Vamos, Nos Echan* blog developed by activists for *Juventud Sin Futuro* (Youth Without a Future), part of the Spanish indignados movement. I will proceed to analyze these two projects separately before identifying some commonalities between them.

The *We Are the 99 Percent* Tumblr blog, created by Occupy Wall Street activists during the Autumn 2011 protests, is arguably the most famous example of a crowd-sourced social justice blog to date. The blog was launched by a 28-year-old New York activist known only as "Chris" and his friend Priscilla Grim, a 36-year-old activist, and social media expert. They opened the website in early August, but only began publishing posts on September 15, two days before the occupation of Zuccotti Park. In fact, it was only in late September, once activists had already pitched their tents in Zuccotti Park, that the website became widely known, eventually attracting tens of contributions per day.

In the text published on the homepage of the blog, the organizers of the blog proposed a simple but compelling description of what they meant by the collective category the "99 percent":

> We Are the 99 Percent. We are getting kicked out of our homes. We are forced to choose between groceries and rent. We are denied quality medical care. We are suffering from environmental pollution. We are working long hours for little pay and no rights, if we're working at all. We are getting nothing while the other 1 percent is getting everything. We Are the 99 Percent.

By taking a picture of themselves holding a sign and submitting it to the website, users could symbolically subscribe to the identity of 99 percent, adding their own individual story to a collective assembling of anger and indignation. Internet users who identified with this description were instructed to photograph themselves holding a small sign with a message no longer than one sentence. However, almost all of the messages entered by participants ended up being several lines long, as they were unable to contain their personal sentiments to a concise statement.

> Make a sign. Write your circumstance at the top, no longer than a single sentence ... Then, take a picture of yourself holding the sign and

submit it to us. The 99 percent have been set against each other, fighting over the crumbs the 1 percent leaves behind. But we're all struggling. We're all fighting. It's time we recognize our common struggles, our common cause. Be part of the 99 percent and let the 1 percent know you're out there.

Among the hundreds of posts published on the Tumblr page, there were stories of people coming from very different walks of life: working mothers incapable of providing for their children, older workers nearing the end of their career without the prospect of a pension, people needing surgery or dental care and unable to pay for it, and Americans of different ethnic backgrounds, classes, and ages confessing that they were regularly going hungry or were "one paycheck away from homelessness" as one message stated.

The blog soon acquired enormous popularity. Hundreds of people ended up contributing their stories to the project, and many more participated by commenting on the blog. This allowed for a collective conversation regarding the reasons for the suffering documented on the website, as well as possible political solutions. The blog in fact acted not just as a space for the documentation of social injustice—a catalog of the suffering experienced by millions of Americans in the post-crash era, marred by unemployment, low pay, and lack of public services—but also as a sort of wailing wall, a space for a highly emotional discussion about the economic hardships that people faced in the aftermath of the 2008 financial crisis.

Similar is the case of the crowd-sourced social justice blog *No Nos Vamos, Nos Echan* (*We Don't Go, They Kick Us Out*) launched by the Spanish activist group *Juventud Sin Futuro* (*Youth Without Future*) in preparation for a demonstration on April 7, 2014. The blog examined the problem of youth migration, which has been a huge issue in Spain since the beginning of the 2008 economic crisis. Over half a million people left the country since the beginning of the economic crisis, the majority of them young and well educated.[24] The header of the blog featured a picture of an airplane tag with the line "*300K de jovenes exiliados*" (300,000 youths exiled). Like the *We Are the 99 Percent* Tumblr, this blog invited young Spaniards forced to move abroad, or considering moving abroad because of the economic crisis, to contribute their story in the form of a picture of themselves holding a message detailing their conditions. Another way people could contribute to this project was by posting short written messages plotted on a Google Map, creating a visualization of the position of Spanish emigrants all over the world.

On its "About" page, the blog is described as "an initiative that denounces the forced exile of the precarious youth. In this map we show cases of youth both outside and within the country." Similar to the *We Are the 99 Percent* Tumblr, the *No Nos Vamos, Nos Echan* project contained a series of instructions for user submissions. The form that was used to submit new stories was accompanied by a number of framing questions: "*¿Te ves / te has visto forzado a emigrar?*" ("Do you feel you've been forced to emigrate?") "*¿Te gustaría volver? / ¿Te gustaría no tener que emigrar?*" ("Would you like to return?" / "Would you like not to migrate?"), and "*¿Ves posible volver? / Si aún no has emigrado, ¿ves una alternativa digna quedándote?*" ("Do you see returning as a possibility?" / "If you have not migrated, do you see a decent alternative by staying?").

These questions reflect the implicit framing by the blog's curators. This framing revolved around the view that migration was not so much a choice for many Spaniards as it was something they had found themselves forced to do out of sheer necessity, a prospect they would have avoided had they been able to find similar working opportunities in their own country. This narrative was also reflected in a YouTube video posted on the blog's main page, which pictured different young people suddenly disappearing from their workplaces, their homes, and from their groups of friends.

Internet users validated this framing by submitting stories that followed the same narrative. They expressed a deep sense of frustration and indignation at having being forced to leave the country in which they were born and raised. Furthermore, the contributions provided important socio-demographic insights about the social composition of migrants, or at least highly educated and highly-skilled migrants. Most contributors to the blog were university graduates who worked in the liberal professions: creative workers, designers, programmers, journalists, and so forth. All in all, the website played an important role inside the indignados movement by raising the question of forced migration, which was the *raison d'être* of a number of activist groups such as the *Marea Granate* (Murray Wave) which developed in the aftermath of the 2011 protests.

The *We Are the 99 Percent* Tumblr blog and the *No Nos Vamos, Nos Echan* blog have common features not just in terms of their content, but also in terms of their publishing logic. First, both websites are characterized by an apparently low level of editorial coordination and control. This is made visible in the simple and practical submission instructions. Yet, even these simple and apparently neutral instructions entail a certain framing and a pre-definition of the subject's grievances. Second, the success of both blogs revolved to a great extent not just around the quality but the quantity of submissions they attracted, which was in the hundreds. This is an important part of the communicative logic of crowd-sourced blogs. Crowd-sourced blogs require a large number of submissions in order to validate the "aggrieved category" they construct. Third, the mission of both blogs is to raise awareness around particular issues. This is seen in the self-descriptions of these blogs on their "About" page, which argue that while the problems they raise are there for everyone to see, they are sometimes ignored by the very people who are affected by them. The presence of these common features reveals that these blogs are animated by a common cultural logic, a "rhetoric of collection" rather than the logic of connection proposed by Bennett and Segerberg.[25]

Collecting indignation

Crowd-sourced blogs such as Occupy Wall Street's *We Are the 99 Percent* Tumblr or the indignados blog *No Nos Vamos, Nos Echan* demonstrate how activists in the post-2008 protest wave have utilized the affordances of social network sites to construct new forms of collective identity. These movements make use of blogs not only to promote the creation of so-called user-generated content, but also because of the ability of blogs to *aggregate* user-generated content that speaks to the specific topics and grievances that people feel affected by. At the heart of these projects thus lies a rhetoric of *collection* rather than a logic of connection, which is hegemonic in contemporary interpretations of digital activism. The rhetoric of collection revolves around the construction of a *catalog of grievances*, which aims at gathering in the same digital space manifold individual experiences of people who are affected by a variety of social problems such as economic injustice, racism, sexism, or forced emigration.

These projects highlight the complex articulation between the individual and the collective in contemporary social movements. On the one hand, it is apparent that individual social experience has a central role, affirming Bennett and Segerberg's emphasis on the personalized character of current forms of protest action.[26] These crowd-sourced blogs rely on personal accounts of suffering, frustration, and hardship. Yet at the same time, individual experiences are not understood as simply personal and individual. Submissions are catalogued together because of the way they *exemplify* collective grievances, as examples of the general issues at stake. Furthermore the underlying spirit of the rhetoric of collection is that these grievances are not just problems, but also a source of collective identification. *The collective is constructed through collection.* Thus, these blogs highlight the continued importance of collective identity in digital protest. They revolve around the creation of a sense of unity across a mass of users, divided by their specific biography, yet united in 1) their common grievances, and 2) their common engagement with a particular communicative platform.

Crowd-sourced social justice blogs thus appear as a contemporary equivalent of the *cahier de doleances* of the French Revolution, the lists of grievances presented to the King by the Three Estates. Similar to the *cahier de doleances*, the logic of crowd-sourced blogs revolves around creating a catalog of discontent and bringing together testimonies of aggrievement by different individuals. To a great extent, the impact of these blogs is not due to the uniqueness of the stories that are posted, but about the repetition of very similar grievances across diverse personal stories and backgrounds. The quantity of posts that are added to the blogs is vital to their success. This is why crowd-sourced blogs resemble social experiments. They are launched as a hypothesis, which is then validated if the blogs are met with a sufficient quantity of responses, either confirming or disproving the assumptions of the project's initiators. The hope is that the accumulation of personal stories will lead to the construction of a critical mass and ultimately to a collective mobilization that addresses the grievances expressed on the blog.

By collecting the grievances affecting different sectors of society, crowd-sourced blogs demonstrate the continued existence of social inequality and forms of injustice. The aggregation of individual submissions on crowd-sourced blogs is proof that people continue to share more with the people in their social category than they do with society as a whole. Obviously some of these categories are broader than others. In particular the *We Are the 99 Percent* blog puts forward one of the largest categories that one could possibly think of: the entirety population of a given country, in this case the United States. However, even in this extreme case which aims at being all encompassing, people feel the need to locate themselves in a category that relies on the exclusion of an Other—in this case, of the numerically inferior, yet economically dominant, 1 percent.

Crowd-sourced blogs also illuminate the changing nature of authorship and editorial control in contemporary digital activism. Crowd-sourced blogs are different from individual blogs because they express a collective intentionality. Furthermore, in launching these projects activists do not aim at putting forward a well-thought-out and self-enclosed narrative. Rather they adopt the role of "social media curators," organizers who frame the general space in which a conversation is to unfold by carefully wording a call for submissions and then filtering and editing the contributions they receive in a most light-handed manner. This does not mean that elements of leadership or authorship are absent from this process: even "light" forms of framing can be quite prescriptive in indicating the narrative that the project will convey. What matters is that such leadership and authorship is only successful to the extent that people actually submit their stories to the blog and that the content of these submissions adheres to the general framing put forth by the blog's organizers.

The rhetoric of collection evident in crowd-sourced blogs thus invites us to rethink the paradigms that are used to understand the role of digital communication in contemporary social movements. As discussed at the beginning of the chapter, in recent years the imaginary of the network has acquired a dominant position in current debates about online activism. However, the network imaginary overlooks the continued importance of collective identity and leadership in providing unity and coherence in highly complex and fragmented processes of online interaction. Crowd-sourced blogs operate according to a digital mass logic rather than a network logic,[27] and manifest new possibilities for mobilizing. Crowd-sourced blogs point to the emergence of new forms of "digital solidarity"[28] within contemporary movements, inviting us to develop new concepts and methods for understanding online activism.

The findings emerging in this chapter offer an opportunity for developing a more systematic analysis of crowd-sourced blogs and their relation to other forms of digital activism that have emerged in the aftermath of the 2008 crash. We urgently need a way to come to grips with these new forms of political expression by making sense of how they differ from earlier forms of digital activism. What appears clearly from the present research, as in my previous work, is the fact that the imaginary of the network is not capable of capturing the mass communicative logics that arise on the internet, which is increasingly dominated by digital monopolies including Facebook, Twitter, and Google. In order to analyze the genres of political expression emerging in this context we need new theories beyond the tired metaphor of the network.

Notes

1 Manuel Castells, *Networks of Outrage and Hope: Social Movements in the Internet Age* (Malden, MA: John Wiley & Sons, 2012); Paolo Gerbaudo, *Tweets and the Streets: Social Media and Contemporary Activism* (London: Pluto, 2012); Jeffrey S. Juris, "Reflections on #Occupy Everywhere: Social Media, Public Space, and Emerging Logics of Aggregation," *American Ethnologist* 39, no. 2 (2012): 259–279; Sarah van Gelder, *This Changes Everything: Occupy Wall Street and the 99% Movement* (San Francisco: Berrett-Koehler Publishers, 2011).
2 Marti A. Hearst and Susan T. Dumais, "Blogging Together: An Examination of Group Blogs," in *Proceedings of the International Conference on Weblogs and Social Media (ICWSM)*, 2009.
3 See http://wearethe99percent.tumblr.com/
4 See http://everydaysexism.com/
5 Jeffrey S. Juris, *Networking Futures: The Movements Against Corporate Globalization* (Durham, NC: Duke University Press, 2008).
6 Juris, "Reflections on# Occupy Everywhere."
7 Gerbaudo, *Tweets and the Streets.*
8 Kenneth Burke, *A Rhetoric of Motives* (Berkeley: University of California Press, 1969).
9 W. Lance Bennett and Alexandra Segerberg, "The Logic of Connective Action: Digital Media and the Personalization of Contentious Politics," *Information, Communication & Society* 15, no. 5 (2012): 739–768; W. Lance Bennett and Alexandra Segerberg, *The Logic of Connective Action: Digital Media and the Personalization of Contentious Politics* (Cambridge: Cambridge University Press, 2013). See also Castells, *Networks of Outrage and Hope.*
10 Jill Walker Rettberg, *Blogging* (Cambridge: Polity, 2008).
11 Henry Jenkins, *Fans, Bloggers, and Gamers: Exploring Participatory Culture* (New York: New York University Press, 2006); Brian D. Loader and Dan Mercea, *Social Media and Democracy: Innovations in Participatory Politics* (London: Routledge, 2012).
12 Antoinette Pole, *Blogging the Political: Politics and Participation in a Networked Society* (New York: Routledge, 2010).
13 Richard Kahn and Douglas Kellner, "New Media and Internet Activism: From the 'Battle of Seattle' to Blogging," *New Media & Society* 6, no. 1 (2004): 87–95;

Tom Isherwood, "A New Direction or More of the Same? Political Blogging in Egypt," *Arab Media & Society* 6 (2008): 1–17; Geert Lovink, *Zero Comments: Blogging and Critical Internet Culture* (London: Routledge, 2013).
14 Rettberg, *Blogging*.
15 Hearst and Dumais, "Blogging Together."
16 Carolyn R. Miller, "Genre as Social Action," *Quarterly Journal of Speech* 70, no. 2 (1984): 151–167.
17 Manuel Castells, "Informationalism, Networks, and the Network Society: A Theoretical Blueprint," in *The Network Society: A Cross-cultural Perspective*, Ed. Manuel Castells (Northampton, MA: Edward Elgar, 2004): 3–45.
18 Castells, *Networks of Outrage and Hope*.
19 Bennett and Segerberg, "The Logic of Connective Action."
20 Ibid., 750.
21 Ibid., 752.
22 Charles Tilly, *From Mobilization to Revolution* (New York: McGraw-Hill, 1978), 62.
23 Anthony P. Cohen, *Symbolic Construction of Community* (London and New York: Routledge, 2013).
24 See www.bde.es/f/webbde/SES/Secciones/Publicaciones/InformesBoletinesRevistas/BoletinEconomico/14/Sep/Fich/be1409-art5.pdf
25 Bennett and Segerberg, "The Logic of Connective Action"; Bennett and Segerberg, *The Logic of Connective Action*.
26 Ibid.
27 Paolo Gerbaudo, "Populism 2.0: Social Media Activism, the Generic Internet User and Interactive Direct Democracy," in *Social Media, Politics and the State: Protests, Revolutions, Riots, Crime and Policing in the Age of Facebook, Twitter and YouTube*, Eds. Daniel Trottier and Christian Fuchs (New York: Routledge, 2014), 67–87.
28 Felix Stalder, *Digital Solidarity* (Lüneburg, Germany: Mute Publishing and PML Books, 2013).

Chapter 9

Data activism as the new frontier of media activism

Stefania Milan

Haiti, January 2010: a catastrophic earthquake hits the capital Port-au-Prince, affecting an estimated three million people. A global network of technologists, student volunteers, and diaspora Haitians join forces to operate a live crisis map of the country, repurposing a piece of open source software called Ushahidi. Over 40,000 eyewitness accounts submitted via email, mobile text and Twitter are plotted on the map, providing crucial information for disaster relief operations.[1]

The ability of generating and making sense of ever-larger quantities of data has prompted observers to speak of a new breakthrough phase in human history, which Hellerstein termed the "industrial revolution of data."[2] Big data include the various databases generated by governmental agencies in their functions; the text, video, and audio files, links, and tags that result from online distribution and archiving; the communication metadata ensuing from mass-interception and government snooping; the information generated by human interactions in social networking platforms and by the indexing processes of web activities. But they can result also from the process of "datafication," that is to say the "ability to render into data many aspects of the world that have never been quantified before,"[3] such as friendships in the form of "likes." Immense datasets are continuously generated by technologies as diverse as aerial sensors, radio-frequency identification readers, surveillance cameras, and personal mobile devices. Each day in 2013 Google alone handled 24 petabytes of data (24 million gigabytes); over 10 million pictures were uploaded to Facebook.[4] People leave behind digital footprints of their doings and whereabouts in a myriad of software logs and communications metadata incessantly collected by service providers. "Open data" (i.e. data that citizens can use, reuse, and redistribute) have become a crucial governance tool in the era of the government-as-platform:[5] as the editor of the *Guardian Data Blog* Simon Rogers recently explained, "we are surrounded by data. Governments around the world are opening up their data vaults, allowing anybody access to it."[6] Citizens can contribute to improve public services like education, transport, and health care by actively participating in monitoring and overseeing.

But dark shadows hang over the data revolution. As we know from whistleblower Edward J. Snowden, a former US intelligence contractor, national security agencies consistently engage in blanket data collection to the detriment of their citizens' privacy, and often in cooperation with the industry.[7] In the "informational" state, characterized by "shifts in the nature of power and its exercise via information policy," "governments deliberately, explicitly, and consistently control information creation, processing, flows, and use to exercise power."[8] For example, social media monitoring is increasingly employed for predictive policing and prevention of protest.[9] Data profiling has been used to reinforce social exclusion and inequalities for poor people, communities of color, and migrants.[10] The rise of "computational politics" goes hand in hand with a "shift away from demographics to individualized targeting, the opacity and power of computational modeling ... and the growth of new power brokers who own the data."[11] Data end up "standing in" for the individual, who is made to disappear in favor of a representation that can be effortlessly classified and manipulated.[12]

We are at a critical juncture, where governments and firms are taking advantage of the "new oil"[13] of big data, thanks to blurred legislation and the users' inclination to trade privacy for better services. Citizens face a moral paradox, typical of phases of rapid change, when legislation and corporate and/or state practices are not yet aligned with social norms. On the one hand, they see big data as a set of novel opportunities for social change, while, on the other, they equal them with social control. Slowly, however, people become increasingly aware of the critical role of information in modern societies. This growing awareness nurtures new social practices rooted on data and technology, which I have termed "data activism."

Data activism embraces the broad range of social mobilizations taking a critical stance toward massive data collection and big data more generally. From the sociological point of view, we can consider data activism as an "emergent movement praxis."[14] It represents the new frontier of media activism, as it appropriates information and technological innovation for political purposes. Like some previous forms of citizens' media, it identifies spaces for people to enact their democratic agency beyond traditional means of civic participation.[15] Similar to the media activism of the 1990s, which seized the nascent digital technology to spread the voices of the streets,[16] data activism aims at uncovering stories of injustice or change. Data activism, too, emerges from the fringes of society, and taps into the broker and sense-making role of a relatively small group of tech-savvy activists. However, contrary to earlier instances of media activism, data activism does not remain confined to small circles of experts who are the repositories of the know-how, but aims at reaching out to laymen, thanks to software that makes complex tasks such as data analysis and visualization or encryption much easier to perform.

This theoretical chapter explores data activism as the newest form of media activism. It puts forward the notion of data activism as a heuristic tool able to bring democratic agency back into the analysis of how big data affect contemporary society.[17] It straddles three streams of literature, namely media studies (and the subfield that scrutinizes alternative media in particular), social movement studies, and science and technology studies (STS), in view of offering an all-round theoretical and empirical approach to investigate people's critical engagement with massive data collection.

In the context of this chapter, I take big data to indicate "things that one can do at a large scale, that cannot be done at a smaller scale, to extract new insights or create new forms of value, in ways that change markets, organizations, the relationship between citizens and governments, and more."[18] This definition emphasizes the transformative and empowering potential of data, focusing on the complexity of the tasks that can be performed, rather than data magnitude. In addition, it stresses the human agency aspect—that is to say, what people can do with data.

In what follows, I provide an analytical definition of data activism, and I place it in relation to the current social movement ecology. Second, I distinguish between two forms of data activism, namely proactive and reactive. Third, I provide historical grounding to the concept, placing data activism within the contemporary movement ecology and analyzing its role in relation to technological innovation and to media activism in its historical and current interpretations. Finally I offer some epistemological and methodological notes that in my view could successfully guide the empirical study of data activism, and explore three possible approaches to data activism, seen respectively as an incipient data epistemology, a set of new forms of civic participation, and a range of emerging forms of social organizing.

Defining data activism

Data activism is a rapidly growing empirical phenomenon at the intersection of the social and technological dimensions of human action—hence it is sociotechnical in nature because while it is technologically animated, it unfolds in the context of socio-political processes and seeks to alter power distribution.[19] It interrogates the politics of big data, assuming that both data collection and the manifold ways data are put to use are not neutral but carry socio-political agendas and programs. It calls into question the overall epistemology of big data, and interrogates our way of making sense of the "political" in relation to information—but also our ways of understanding development, change, and the relation between individuals and society.

The action repertoire of data activists includes examining, manipulating, leveraging, and exploiting data, along with resisting and meddling their creation and use: in other words, the "antiprograms"[20] citizens enact as "line[s] of escape from the determinism" of algorithmic-mediated big data.[21] They are mostly counterhegemonic tactics, that is to say, defensive tactics that seek to alter the relationship between citizens and big data/massive data collection by empowering users to be more critical.[22] Similar to what Hackett and Carroll termed "democratic media activism,"[23] data activism is unique in the panorama of contemporary social movements to the extent that it treats big data simultaneously as the tool and the end of struggle.

Data activism is both enabled and constrained by software, which can be seen as the *sine qua non* condition of this genre of organized collective action to emerge and develop. Code, that is to say the technical environment that supports software and the internet,[24] takes central stage not only in the activists' analysis of the socio-economic forces that animate the informational state, but also in the actual activist practices. On the one hand, activists acknowledge that code does "format our action,"[25] and as such is a locus of power in societies that are highly reliant on algorithms: by underpinning the technological environment in which people move, code both enables and sets boundaries to human action. On the other, activists develop and use code to facilitate a series of actions of resistance and subversion, as well as of data manipulation, making the engagement of the non-tech-savvy sectors of the population possible.

The geographical span of data activism extends over different territorial levels, from local to transnational. At the local or national level we see activists leveraging the availability of open data to support campaigning efforts, or advocating for governments to adopt Freedom of Information Acts giving their citizens access to data. At the global level, more and more thematic networks emerge in both the proactive and reactive subfields: for example, the global network Hacks/Hackers, with its several national or city-bound chapters, is an innovative alliance of journalists ("hacks") and technologists ("hackers") for skill exchange in the area of data journalism—that is to say, the craft of getting stories out of complex datasets by means of social science and computational methods; the platform OpenSpending allows non-experts to explore over 28 million government financial transactions from 75 countries around the world. It is worth noting that local, national, and transnational networks often show similar features for what concerns tactics, identities, and organizational forms, in line with what I have noted elsewhere for other forms of tech-oriented mobilizations.[26]

Not unlike other contemporary mobilizations, data activism is characterized by a complex articulation of individual and collective practices which are inscribed in the very same object of activism: data and the material cultures associated with it. As Renzi and Langlois observed, "data bridges individuals, modulating the relation between the *I* and the *We*—our sense of ourselves both alone and as members of a community"; because data has the ability to establish new relations, it is also "a vector for the circulation of affective and emotional bonds."[27] While promoting individual action, as, for instance, individuals can also effectively engage in data tinkering, data activism is essentially collective because knowledge and skills become relevant in the context of the group of peers. However, individual action and critical practices of technology use such as the adoption of encryption also constitute activism when they are not explicitly shared within the group on the ground that, as social movement scholars have observed, "there is protest even when it is not part of an organized movement."[28] These individual forms of protest, in the vein of collective ones, provide people with a "moral voice," and "an opportunity to articulate, elaborate, alter, or affirm one's moral sensibilities, principles, and allegiances."[29] They activate imagined communities of resistance that can be mobilized at need, for example in case of threats to established norms and practices, or when a political opportunity for change arises.[30]

Culturally and ideologically, data activists look back at the hacker and open source tradition,[31] at the radical tech activism of the 1990s,[32] at statactivism, or activism that targets statistics,[33] and at the do-it-yourself culture of hacklabs and hackerspaces.[34] From their forerunners, data activists have borrowed the hands-on attitude and the enthusiasm for code tinkering, collaboration, access to information, and world improvement through technical fixes.[35] But, not unlike those portions of the media reform movement preaching direct engagement with technology as a way of confronting elite expertise,[36] data activists actively seek to overcome the elitist character of tech activism to involve ordinary users. For instance, activists organize "cryptoparties," which have been likened to "a Tupperware party for learning crypto,"[37] in view of introducing the basics of cryptography to the general public.

At the heart of the antiprogram

Analytically, we can distinguish two forms of data activism, namely reactive and proactive collective action. Reactive and proactive are two facets of the same phenomenon: both take information as a constitutive force in society able to shape social reality.[38] Further, both have as an ultimate objective the "development of new or alternative forms of material culture."[39] By increasingly involving average users, they signal a change in perspective toward massive data collection emerging within the citizenry at large.

We have reactive data activism when citizens resist the threats to civil liberties, and privacy in particular, that derive from corporate intrusion and government surveillance. They do so primarily by means of technical fixes or by creatively subverting and hijacking the monitoring and snooping with tactics like counterveilance and obfuscation,[40] but adopt also more traditional movement strategies such as campaigning. For example, in 2014 the American Civil Liberties Union and other US-based nonprofits launched a charter of civil rights principles for the era of big data.[41] But while advocacy efforts are still in their infancy, much has been taking place in the realm of data and technology, and their software and hardware architecture in particular, on the ground that "[r]esistance to power programmed in the networks also takes place through and by networks."[42] In order to protect users' privacy, activist developers run proxy servers, maintain software enabling anonymous browsing, or create new privacy-minded platforms from scratch. Examples include privacy-minded alternatives to commercial social networking platforms such as Crabgrass (US), and Lorea (Spain), which put users in control of their data, and the Tor network, which allows users to conceal the destination of the information they send from network surveillance and traffic analysis. These tactics are reactive, in that they provide technical fixes to external hazards that are normally outside of their remit and reach, namely corporate intrusion and government profiling. Contrary to earlier initiatives of this kind, activists seek to move beyond the expert niche to also engage ordinary users. For example, in Facebook Resistance workshops, activists develop adds-on that non-tech-savvy users can also easily use.[43]

Proactive data activism, on the contrary, actively takes advantage of the possibilities for advocacy and campaigning that big data offer, and uses and appropriates data to foster social change. It articulates the link between the right to use data and a functioning public sphere on the ground that access to data equals empowerment.[44] However complex, data show patterns and tell stories, and civil society is progressively acknowledging the value of such stories for civic engagement. Access alone, however, is not enough: users willing to put data to new uses need advanced data-analysis skills. Proactive data activists position themselves as interpreters of data, acting as facilitators thanks to the growing availability of user-friendly data-analysis tools facilitating the engagement of laymen. They take advantage of the decentralized peer production and distributed human capital of the global networks of developers and users of data-crunching tools and platforms, as the live crisis mapping in post-earthquake Haiti illustrates. For example, Occupy Data, a spin-off of the Occupy Wall Street mobilizations, which emerged in the fall of 2012 in New York but rapidly spread across the world, seeks to support the "initiatives of the Occupy Wall Street Movement through data gathering, analysis, and visualization"; journalists and hackers collaborate more and more often;[45] the nonprofit Tactical Tech Collective has published a manual on visualizing information for advocacy, encouraging activists to empower their advocacy efforts by representing facts in ways that are at the same time "emotionally powerful, morally compelling and rationally undeniable."[46] A variety of online platforms ease the task: for instance, the non-profit Open Knowledge Foundation has developed the open source data portal CKAN, used by civil society as well as institutional actors like the US government to explore data.

Within the contemporary movement ecology

Data and data-based advocacy are gaining terrain in the realm of contentious politics: for example, the very same slogan of the Occupy mobilizations was a data query, calling attention to the disempowered 99 percent being disenfranchised by the 1 percent.[47] While "metadata corrals activism into processes of capital accumulation (e.g. through data mining)," it might likewise "create the conditions for the development of new activist practices (e.g. campaigns around hashtags); data, in addition, is "actively implicated in circulating affects and fostering social relations."[48] At the same time, movements are growing more concerned about government and corporate snooping, and are increasingly eager to learn how to defend themselves from surveillance and repression. It should then not surprise that contemporary data activism does not exist in isolation, but is embedded in the complex ecology of contemporary social movements. But what are the role and space of the data activist in relation to contemporary movements, and media activism in particular?

Like media activism, data activism is "more about constructing a 'politics of connections' than it is about constructing its own composite action system."[49] It occupies the spaces in between, more often than not serving other causes and movements, spread as it is across the field of movement politics. In that respect, it has a "boundary-spanning" capacity and works as a "point of articulation *between* movements" rather than a movement *per se*.[50] For example, reactive data activists provide training in the use of encryption to other activists and like-minded people, while proactive data activists, too, offer training but also engage in interpreting and visualizing data at need. Further, it is worth noting that data activists might themselves be directly involved in other forms of political action. Finally, data activism is supported by a variety of social sources outside the movement sphere and only occasionally intersecting with the path of data activists: they include professionals like data analysts, data journalists, and software developers, and advocates and social groups that might need access to data to advance their demands.

In earlier writings, I distinguished three decades in the emergence of communications and information as a site of struggle, from the 1970s onwards. The 1995–2005 decade, in particular, saw a renaissance of media activism, thanks to the unprecedented availability of cheap and easy-to-use digital technology like camcorders, as well as the expansion of the World Wide Web. It was back then when the "media activist," who embodied a particular skillset, and was the repository of expert cultures of critical usage of technology, became a distinct identity within the social movement ecology: a specific figure at the service of movements, and instrumental to other struggles.[51]

The figure of the media activist changed substantially with the diffusion of commercial web 2.0 platforms, such as microblogging and social media. On the one hand expertise in media usage became seemingly irrelevant, as everyone could master the tools. On the other, however, with social media introducing "new patterns of protest that shape movement dynamics beyond the realm of technological practice,"[52] media activists took up the role of "'soft leaders' or choreographers, involved in setting the scene, and constructing an emotional space within which collective action can unfold."[53] So, while everyone, including non-tech-savvy individuals, can become a media activist, media activists are not solely concerned with the management and production of information, but have moved to the core of action itself.

The advent of data activism, however, gives back to media activists the role of the bearers and interpreters of technological innovation. Tactics of resistance to massive data collection and appropriation of data for social change (still) require the filter of experts, in particular for software development, training and the crucial interactive "meaning work"[54] associated with making sense of technology and its potential for political action. But, similar to what happened to the media activist in times of social media, data activists have the ability to act not only in the sphere of communicative action, but also in connection with direct action itself.[55]

In what follows I offer some epistemological and methodological notes for the empirical study of data activism.

An agenda for the study of data activism

The notion of data activism represents a conceptual innovation at the crossroads of a sociological process (organizing collectively in order to take action), a cognitive activity (making sense of complex information), and a sociotechnical practice (software is central to data activism). How do we study a social phenomenon that is rooted in communications technology (and information) and is positioned between the social and communicative dimensions of human action? Adopting an interdisciplinary approach able to take into account the multidimensional nature of the phenomenon is key. Potential disciplines include political sociology, and social movement studies in particular, for their ability to understand collective action dynamics and activists' sense-making activities and strategies; media studies to appreciate the communicative action inherent in data activism, as well as its intersections with journalism, alternative media, social media, and so on; international relations to track the shifts of power within the transnational civil society brought about by big data; software and platform studies to unpack the specifics of the technological supports; science and technology studies for its ability to simultaneously think about the "technological" and the "social."

In consideration of its sociotechnical nature, data activism is best studied through a mixed-method approach able to allow the researcher to capture several layers of human action: what people think and say (i.e. how they perceive big data and massive data collection), what people do (i.e. how people mobilize in reaction to massive data collection, or engage proactively with data), and how algorithms mediate what people think and do (i.e. the role of software in empowering and shaping activism). In addition, it allows us to explore both the "social" and the "technological" dimensions of data activism. In the STS fashion of considering technology as an interpretively flexible object,[56] I argue that in order to capture the multilayered nature of data activism we have to allow for some flexibility in the combination of methods that do not necessarily share the same ontological and epistemological assumptions. First, qualitative data, in their nature of "data enhancers" that boost data to make it possible to see aspects of the object of research that might otherwise be neglected,[57] are particularly apt to the study of relatively unexplored realms of human action such as data activism. In-depth interviews and focus groups aid to capture what activists believe they do, their stated motives and interpretations of their social world; ethnography of infrastructure[58] can help to uncover how software shapes activism practices. Second, computational methods can prove useful to address data collection to the ways "in which social practices are defined and experienced."[59] In other words, I argue in favor of adopting algorithm-based methods to explore a social phenomenon that is rooted in algorithms. Computational methods might, for example, help to explore code repositories like GitHub, which hosts much of the software used by data activists: one might, for instance, mine "fork & pull" projects—in other words, branches of existing software developed starting from existing software available on the platform—looking for the evolution of software functionalities or the developers' social graphs.[60]

Finally, what can we look for in addressing data activism as a field of study? Here I briefly outline three possible approaches to the study of data activism: albeit proving only partial views, each helps to illuminate a specific aspect of the phenomenon, while having the added value of leveraging different literatures and disciplinary traditions. The first way to look at data activism is its nature of emerging data epistemology.[61] Data is a way of making sense of our realities:[62] what do we gain or lose from the shift toward massive, quantitative data? How do people's perceptions of themselves, their social reality, and their relational being-in-the-world evolve under the pressure of these developments? How does this impact activism and democratic participation? A second lens through which we can interpret data activism is its ability to bring about "new" forms of civic participation, which range from data journalism to data visualization, from video streaming to app-mediated engagement. How do these new forms contribute to changing the tactical repertoire of social movements? How do they influence the tension between the individual and the collective typical of much of contemporary activism? What do they mean for the sustainability of political activism over time? Last, we can investigate data activism by analyzing the emerging forms of social organizing it promotes. The notion of "social movement rhizomes"— in other words, the horizontal and network-like form of contemporary social movements[63]—might be useful to approach the question. What new, unexpected rhizomes emerge, which bring together groups and identities that have rarely interacted before? How do these rhizomes work in terms of decision-making and internal structures? Are they sustainable over time?

In conclusion

This chapter has introduced the notion of data activism as a heuristic tool that allows us to investigate how big data affect contemporary society without dismissing the democratic agency of citizens. It argued that we need to develop a new vocabulary of interdisciplinary concepts and mechanisms, as well as innovative methodological approaches if we want to capture the complex sociotechnical nature of this emerging empirical phenomenon.

Data activism indicates the complex and dynamic ecosystem of organized collective action and individual engagement that takes a critical stance at big data and massive data collection. It examines, manipulates, leverages, and takes advantage of existing data, but also resists and meddles data creation and use—and these tactics can be seen as antiprograms to pre-set hegemonic uses of data and software. Data activism can take two forms: when activists seek to resist corporate and government snooping, we are in the presence of reactive data activism; conversely, we are in the presence of proactive data activism when people appropriate and use big data for advocacy and social change. Present-day data activism has its roots in earlier movement traditions, such as the hacker culture, statactivism, and the open source software movement. It is rooted in and enabled by software, comprises both individual and collective practices, and has a geographical span from local to global. *Vis-à-vis* contemporary movement scenes, data activism occupies a space in between, putting skills at the service of other causes and groups.

We have seen how data activism returns to the long tradition of media activism, undertaking its historical role of bearer and interpreter of technological innovation, as critically engaging with massive data collection still requires a certain amount of skills and expertise. It remains to be seen whether data activism will be able to fascinate a broader sector of society, and whether, and how, its various tactics and approaches will be able to bring about change in the ways big data are collected, used, and redistributed.

Acknowledgments

This research was made possible by a Starting Grant from the European Research Council (ERC-2014-STG—639379—DATACTIVE), with the author as Principal Investigator (see https://data-activism.net).

Notes

1 Patrick Meier, "How Crisis Mapping Saved Lives in Haiti," *National Geographic*, 2 July 2 2012, http://voices.nationalgeographic.com/2012/07/02/crisis-mapping-haiti/

2 "The Commoditization of Massive Data Analysis—Data," 2008, http://strata.oreilly.com/2008/11/the-commoditization-of-massive.html
3 Kenneth Cukier and Viktor Mayer-Schoenberger, "The Rise of Big Data: How It's Changing the Way We Think about the World," *Foreign Affairs* 92, no. 3 (2013): 28–40, www.foreignaffairs.com/articles/139104/kenneth-neil-cukier-and-viktor-mayer-schoenberger/the-rise-of-big-data
4 Viktor Mayer-Schönberger and Kenneth Cukier, *Big Data: A Revolution That Will Transform How We Live, Work, and Think* (Boston: Houghton Mifflin Harcourt, 2013).
5 Anne-Marie Slaughter, "Government as Platform," *The Wired World in 2013*, 2012, http://scholar.princeton.edu/sites/default/files/slaughter/files/13_wired_world_in_2013.pdf
6 Michele Bonechi, *Interview with Simon Rogers, Editor Guardian Data Blog*, London, 2012, www.youtube.com/watch?v=bU8DiD2J-tw
7 David Lyon, "Surveillance, Snowden, and Big Data: Capacities, Consequences, Critique," *Big Data & Society* 1, no. 2 (2014): doi:10.1177/2053951714541861
8 Sandra Braman, *Change of State: Information, Policy, and Power* (Cambridge MA: MIT Press, 2009), 1.
9 Lina Dencik and Oliver Leistert, Eds., *Critical Approaches to Social Media Protest* (London: Rowman & Littlefield, 2015).
10 Seeta Gangadharan, "Digital Inclusion and Data Profiling," *First Monday* 17, no. 5 (2012), http://journals.uic.edu/ojs/index.php/fm/article/view/3821/3199
11 Zeynep Tufekci, "Big Data: Pitfalls, Methods and Concepts for an Emergent Field," 2013, http://papers.ssrn.com/sol3/papers.cfm?abstract_id=2229952
12 John Cheney-Lippold, "A New Algorithmic Identity Soft Biopolitics and the Modulation of Control," *Theory, Culture & Society* 28, no. 6 (2011): 164–181.
13 Perry Rotella, "Is Data the New Oil?," *Forbes*, 4 February 2012, www.forbes.com/sites/perryrotella/2012/04/02/is-data-the-new-oil
14 Robert A. Hackett and William K. Carroll, *Remaking Media: The Struggle to Democratize Public Communication* (New York and London: Routledge, 2006), 84.
15 Clemencia Rodríguez, *Fissures in the Mediascape: An International Study of Citizens' Media* (Cresskill, NJ: Hampton Press, 2001).
16 M. Pasquinelli, Ed., *Media Activism: Strategie E Pratiche Della Comunicazione Indipendente* (Roma: Derive Approdi, 2002); Stefania Milan, *Social Movements and their Technologies: Wiring Social Change* (Hampshire and New York: Palgrave Macmillan, 2013).
17 It is worth noting that as an analytical category data activism is a theoretical construct: although data activism does exist as a composite and dynamic empirical reality, the unity of the conceptualization presented here is the result of the author's active framing. In other words, many of these activists might not refer to themselves as "data activists" but as "open data activists," "hackers," "data journalists," and so on (see also Miren Gutierrez, *Bits and Atoms: Proactive data activism and social change from a critical theory perspective*. PhD dissertation (2017), University of Duesto, San Sebastian).
18 Mayer-Schönberger and Cukier, *Big Data*, 6.
19 For a definition and contextualization of sociotechical objects in STS, see Madeleine Akrich and Bruno Latour, "A Summary of a Convenient Vocabulary for the Semiotics of Human and Nonhuman Assemblies," in *Shaping Technology/Building Society. Studies in Sociotechnical Change*, Eds. Wiebe E. Bijker and John Law (Cambridge, MA and London, England: MIT Press, 1992), 259–264.
20 Wiebe E. Bijker and John Law, Eds., *Shaping Technology/Building Society* (Cambridge, MA: MIT Press, 1992).

21 Berardi in Geoff Cox, *Speaking Code. Coding as Aesthetic and Political Expression*, Software Studies (Cambridge, MA and London, England: MIT Press, 2013), x.
22 For a distinction between counterhegemonic and reformist tactics, see R. A. Hackett, "Taking Back the Media: Notes on the Potential for a Communicative Democracy Movement," *Studies in Political Economy*, 63 (Autumn 2000): 61–86.
23 Hackett and Carroll, *Remaking Media*.
24 Lawrence Lessig, *Code 2.0* (New York: Basic Books, 2006), http://codev2.cc/download±remix/Lessig-Codev2.pdf
25 Berardi in Cox, *Speaking Code*, ix.
26 Milan, *Social Movements and Their Technologies*.
27 Alessandra Renzi and Ganaele Langlois, "Data Activism," in *Compromised Data: From Social Media to Big Data*, Eds. Greg Elmer, Ganaele Langlois, and Joanna Redden (London: Bloomsbury, 2015), 202–225. Italics in the original.
28 James Jasper, *The Art of Moral Protest: Culture, Biography, and Creativity in Social Movements* (Chicago: Chicago University Press, 1997), 5.
29 Ibid., 15.
30 For a definition of political opportunities in social movement studies, see S. Tarrow, *Power in Movement. Social Movements and Contentious Politics* (Cambridge: Cambridge University, 1998).
31 Steven Levy, *Hackers: Heroes of the Computer Revolution* (New York: Dell/Doubleday, 1984); Gabriella Coleman, *Coding Freedom: The Ethics and Aesthetics of Hacking* (Princeton and Oxford: Princeton University Press, 2013), http://codingfreedom.com
32 Milan, *Social Movements and Their Technologies*.
33 Isabelle Bruno, Emmanuel Didier, and Tommaso Vitale, "Statactivism: Forms of Action between Disclosure and Affirmation," SSRN Scholarly Paper (Rochester, NY: Social Science Research Network, 2014), http://papers.ssrn.com/abstract=2466882
34 Maxigas, "Hacklabs and Hackerspaces—Tracing Two Genealogies," *Journal of Peer Production*, no. 2 (2012), http://peerproduction.net/issues/issue-2/peer-reviewed-papers/hacklabs-and-hackerspaces/
35 D.M. Berry, *Copy, Rip, Burn: The Politics of Copyleft and Open Source* (London: Pluto Press, 2008).
36 Christina Dunbar-Hester, "Producing 'Participation'? The Pleasures and Perils of Technical Engagement in Radio Activism," *Public Culture* 26, no. 1, 72 (2014): 25–50, http://publicculture.dukejournals.org/content/26/1_72/25.short
37 Cory Doctorow, "CryptoParty: Like a Tupperware Party for Learning Crypto," *BoingBoing*, 12 October 2012, http://boingboing.net/2012/10/12/cryptoparty-like-a-tupperware.html
38 Braman, *Change of State*.
39 David J. Hess, "Technology-and Product-oriented Movements: Approximating Social Movement Studies and Science and Technology Studies," *Science, Technology & Human Values* 30, no. 4 (2005): 515–535.
40 Rita Raley, "Dataveillance and Countervailance," in *"Raw Data" Is an Oxymoron*, Ed. Lisa Gitelman, Infrastructure Series (Cambridge, MA and London, England: MIT Press, 2013); Finn Brunton and Helen Nissenbaum, "Vernacular Resistance to Data Collection and Analysis: A Political Theory of Obfuscation," *First Monday* 16, no. 5 (2011), http://firstmonday.org/ojs/index.php/fm/article/viewArticle/3493; respectively.
41 Leadership Conference on Civil and Human Rights, "Civil Rights Principles for the Era of Big Data," 27 February 2014, www.civilrights.org/press/2014/civil-rights-principles-big-data.html

42 Manuel Castells, *Communication Power* (Oxford: Oxford University Press, 2009), 49.
43 Marc Stumpel, "Facebook Resistance: Augmented Freedom," in *Unlike Us Reader. Social Media Monopolies and their Alternatives*, Eds. Geert Lovink and Miriam Rasch (Amsterdam: Institute of Network Cultures, 2013), 274–288.
44 Stefania Milan and Miren Gutierrez, "Medios Ciudadanos Y Big Data: La Emergencia Del Activismo de Datos," *Mediaciones*, no. 14 (2015): 10–26.
45 Seth C. Lewis and Nikki Usher, "Open Source and Journalism: Toward New Frameworks for Imagining News Innovation," *Media, Culture & Society* 35, no. 5 (2013): 602–619; Victor Sampedro, *El Cuarto Poder En Red. Por Un Periodismo (de Código) Libre* (Barcelona: Icaria, 2014).
46 Tactical Tech Collective, *Visualising Information for Advocacy* (Bangalore: Tactical Tech Collective, 2013), 3.
47 Bonechi, *Interview with Simon Rogers*.
48 Renzi and Langlois, "Data Activism."
49 William K. Carroll and Robert A. Hackett, "Democratic Media Activism through the Lens of Social Movement Theory," *Media, Culture & Society* 28, no. 1 (2006): 93.
50 Ibid.; Hackett and Carroll, *Remaking Media*, 199.
51 Pasquinelli, *Media Activism*.
52 Jeffrey S. Juris, "Reflections on #Occupy Everywhere: Social Media, Public Space, and Emerging Logics of Aggregation," *American Ethnologist* 39, no. 2 (2012): 277.
53 Paolo Gerbaudo, *Tweets and the Streets: Social Media and Contemporary Activism* (London: Pluto Press, 2012), 151–161.
54 For an elaboration of meaning work, see William A. Gamson, *Talking Politics* (Cambridge, MA: Cambridge University Press, 1992).
55 Renzi and Langlois, "Data Activism."
56 Wiebe E. Bijker, *Of Bicycles, Bakelites, and Bulbs. Toward a Theory of Sociotechnical Change* (Cambridge, MA and London, England: MIT Press, 1995).
57 Kathleen M. Blee and Verta Taylor, "Semi-Structured Interviewing in Social Movement Research," in *Methods of Social Movement Research*, Eds. Bert Klandermans and Suzanne Staggenborg (Minneapolis and London: University of Minnesota Press, 2002), 109.
58 Susan Leigh Star, "The Ethnography of Infrastructure," *American Behavioural Scientist* 43, no. 3 (1999): 377–391.
59 Christine Hine, *Virtual Methods* (Oxford and New York: Berg, 2005), 1.
60 See, for example, https://github.com/datactive/bigbang.
61 Milan Stefania and Lonneke van der Velden, "The Alternative Epistemologies of Data Activism", *Digital Culture & Society*, 2(2) (2016): 57–74.
62 José van Dijck, "Datafication, Dataism and Dataveillance: Big Data Between Scientific Paradigm and Ideology," *Surveillance and Society* 12, no. 3 (2014): 197–208.
63 S. Uzelman, "Hard at Work in the Bamboo Garden: Media Activists and Social Movements," in *Autonomous Media: Activating Resistance and Dissent*, Eds. A. Langlois and F. Dubois (Montréal: Cumulus Press, 2005), 16–29.

Chapter 10

The use of the geoweb for social justice activism

Leslie Regan Shade, Harrison Smith, and Evan Hamilton

What is the geoweb?

The geoweb refers to a set of geospatial social networking tools and services that are used to curate and interact with web-based locational content and new forms of spatial data generated through participatory mapping or crowdsourcing of information. Popular examples include Google Earth, Google Maps, OpenStreetMaps, Yahoo Maps, and the Ushahidi platform. Alongside access on the web, social media tools and smartphones have popularized everyday uses of the geoweb and provided "accessible," and often "free" interrelated platforms. Location-based services—the provision of the geoweb on mobile platforms utilizing GPS, and other forms of location awareness to deliver customized information services—are also creating new forms of spatial awareness.[1]

The geoweb can transform how we make, use, and share mapped information. It can offer innovative modes for many stakeholders—citizens, civil society groups, private firms, and governments—to build applications that "mash up," aggregate, or crowdsource geographic data from diverse sources: social media, open data provided from federal governments and municipalities, and information from citizen journalists and civil society groups.

The informational opportunities afforded by the geoweb herald a belief in the increasing accessibility of geospatial data to a wide variety of audiences, including academics, civil society, government, policy makers the private sector, and the general public. One of the core tenets of the geoweb is that maps and geospatial media can be produced, distributed, and used by non-experts; people with little or no training in cartography or geographic information systems (GIS) are increasingly using geospatial media for a variety of political, economic, and social applications. The creation of content by the public (or the amateur cartographer) is often referred to as VGI, volunteered geographic information, and in many ways represents a shift from top-down to bottom-up forms of participatory or user-generated mapping content.[2]

With the popularity of Google Maps, which emerged in 2005, crowdsourcing has been seen as a new approach to mapping. Crowdsourcing involves peer production and collaboration in knowledge creation. As Dodge and Kitchin describe:

> [In] geocrowd mapping projects such as OpenStreetMap (OSM), people voluntarily collect, clean, and upload GPS tracks and add attribute data in order to produce surveyed geospatial information. Novel works can also be constructed in the form of mash-ups that use application programming interfaces (APIs) to combine multiple sources of data in ways not prescribed or necessarily anticipated by the providers.[3]

Geoweb discourses include those promoting civic engagement, democracy, equality, and public participation. These claims pose important questions about whether and how citizens are indeed empowered through the geoweb. Assessing the extent to which such claims stand up to empirical scrutiny requires that we examine issues of geoweb accessibility, ownership, and diversity.

The geoweb has been used for social justice activism in diverse ways. It has been used as a new tool in digital humanitarianism, for instance in crisis mapping of environmental catastrophes or political uprisings. Mapping has been used to monitor political abuses in repressive regimes, to give testament, especially for human rights abuses and political corruption, for visibility ("to make the invisible visible" as Take Back The Tech proclaims), to tell stories that can lend credence to evidence-based policy making to document, archive, and preserve protest movements, to conduct investigative work, to coordinate activities and actions with on-the-ground activists and citizens and other organizations, to manage environmental disasters, and to map social phenomenon through participatory crowdsourcing and storytelling.

A recent example is the Umbrella Movement Visual Archives and Research Collective that is documenting, preserving, and archiving the prolific public art created by and in support of the pro-democracy protesters in Hong Kong.[4] Created by local artists, arts administrators, and academics, the Collective is using Google Maps and open data platforms to map the location of the street art. Their mission statement: "to systematically document and research into the creative spatial practices realised by protesters; to protect the artifacts and items that are deemed relevant and important to the movement from being damaged and confiscated during police clearing operations."[5]

In what follows we provide an overview of specific instances of how the geoweb has been used for social activism, focusing on digital humanitarianism and crisis mapping, violence against women, and some recent uses of mapping in Canadian activism.

Digital humanitarianism and crisis mapping

In their report, "Humanitarianism in the Network Age," the UN Office for the Coordination of Humanitarian Affairs affirmed the principles that "information is a basic need, anyone can generate valuable information, and information creates most value when it can be shared widely and freely."[6] OCHA recognized the value and utility of new forms of social mapping technologies for existing humanitarian organizations and as a way to coordinate with local communities and virtual volunteers. Burns states that digital humanitarianism as "a technological corollary to the geoweb, should be conceptualized as the enacting of social and institutional networks, technologies, and practices that enable large, unrestricted numbers of remote and on-the-ground individuals to collaborate on humanitarian management through digital technologies."[7] Techniques and strategies in digital humanitarianism include crisis mapping, crowdsourcing, social media monitoring, and the integration of "more traditional, techniques applied in the areas of emergency management, political crisis response, and general social causes."[8]

Interdisciplinary in nature, crisis mapping—the sourcing, aggregation, visualization, documentation, and analysis of data (economic, political, ecological, financial, humanitarian)—has been heralded as a tangible way for volunteers to support global humanitarian crises. States Patrick Meier, one of the pioneers in this field: "live crisis maps are almost as good as having your own helicopter. They provide a bird's-eye view of an unfolding event and thereby create more situational awareness."[9]

Crisis mapping has emerged from humanitarian responses to environmental or political situations with maps becoming a mode to report and circulate instances of physical devastation, political repression, intimidation, violence, or crimes committed by the state. Crisis mapping consists of data acquisition, visualization, analysis and response and its process "is an emergent one, driven by individuals, networks, and loose affiliations"[10] that can take advantage of "real-time information to shed light on a situation as it happens."[11]

The value of crisis mapping was abundantly clear during the aftermath of the 2010 Haiti earthquake. Critical infrastructure was wiped out, and responders faced a steep task in trying to reach those impacted; street maps consisted of major roads but little detail about street names, the location of major buildings, etc. Facilitated by over 600 remote volunteers, OpenStreetMap became the default basemap for numerous responding organizations such as search and rescue teams. Satellite firms Digital Globe and GeoEye released, free of charge, high definition images of the islands, and details were then added to the map, including aerial photographs from the US military, the Central Intelligence Agency (CIA), various GPS coordinates, and reliance on the memories of inhabitants regarding the location of landmarks. Coordination of essential services such as water, food, health supplies, and medical attention was thus facilitated. After the Haiti crisis the OpenStreetMap Humanitarian OpenStreetMap Team (HOT) continued their work with the community, imbuing the map with local knowledge and values.[12]

Mobilizing students at Tufts University, Meier and his colleagues created the Ushahidi Haiti Crisis Map consisting of over 2,000 live reports from social media and news reports. Ushahidi (the Swahili name for "testimony") was initially developed by Ory Okolloh during the 2008 post-Kenyan election to allow citizens to submit, via mobile phone and the web, reports of violence and peace efforts that were then mapped onto a website. Its key feature was the ability to integrate text messages from mobile phones into the crisis map. As Okolloh blogged during the crisis:

> Last week, in between nightmares about where my country was going, I was dreaming of a Google Mashup to document incidents of violence, looting etc. that have occurred during the post-election crisis.
>
> We believe that the number of deaths being reported by the government, police, and media is grossly underreported. We also don't think we have a true picture of what is really going on—reports that all have us have heard from family and friends in affected areas suggests that things are much worse than what we have heard in the media.[13]

Ushahidi's mission statement is "to change the way information flows in the world and empower people to make an impact with open source technologies, cross-sector partnerships, and groundbreaking ventures."[14] Growing to 45,000 users, the original web mash up was then developed into the Ushahidi platform. The free and open source platform collects data from crowdsourcing (SMS, email, Twitter, and web-forms) and visualizes the information on a map. Information can be mapped, tracked over time, filtered, and refined.

Ushahidi now has several distinct products. Crowdmap is a map-making tool built on open API (application programming interface) allowing for real-time collaborative mapping.[15] Swiftriver is an emergency support system allowing for real-time crowdsourced analysis of data, email, Twitter, text, and news.[16] It has been used as an emergency response system for the municipality of Puget Sound, Washington.[17] CrisisNET is the "firehose of global crisis data" allowing for the location, formatting, and exposure of crisis data in an "intuitive" structure.[18] To map violence in Syria, CrisisNET is being used to aggregate and cross-monitor social media posts (reportedly 10K per day), to monitor YouTube channels and Facebook pages.[19] Ping is a multi-lingual SMS and email alert system allowing for group check-in during emergencies, designed to allow families, colleagues, and organizations to check-in with each other ("Are you OK?"), and is not dependent on a platform or device.[20]

Several organizations serve as global networks for crisis mapping. Humanitarian Tracker is a forum for citizen journalists to "share reports of what they witness on the ground, worldwide, about human rights violations, disease spread, rape, conflicts, or disasters. We also tap into a wide network of professionals, media, and policy makers to help share information and tackle the issue from all sides."[21] Working with a range of organizations (Ushahidi, Health Map, and the Women's Media Center), projects focus on health (Ebola Screening, Epidemic Tracker, Syrian Polio Vaccination), and on the conflict in Syria. The International Network of Crisis Mappers,[22] founded by Patrick Meier and Jen Ziemke, consists of over 5,000 members from academia, government, the private sector, and nonprofit organizations. The Standby Volunteer Task Force for Live Mapping (SBTF) is a global volunteer network of over 1000 volunteers based in 79 countries who are trained in live crisis mapping and situational analysis. They have developed geo-location and verification techniques, media monitoring, and other strategies to assist on-the-ground humanitarian organizations. A recent intervention is in assistance to the organization NetHope in the collection and management of information related to the Ebola outbreak in West Africa.[23]

Mapping violence against women

Mapping is increasingly being used by women's groups and feminists to record and map violence against women, whether by and through information and communication technologies (ICTs) themselves or through documenting instances of war crimes, human rights abuses, or street harassment. This section looks at the following global initiatives: APC's Take Back the Tech, HarrassMap, Women Under Siege, and Hollaback.

Take Back the Tech: Mapping Technology-based Violence Against Women (their motto: "Map It. End It") is a campaign from the Association for Progressive Communication (APC) that provides a platform to map digital acts of violence against women (VAW), including "cyberstalking, sexual harassment, surveillance, privacy violations, and the unauthorised use and manipulation of personal information including images and videos."[24] Using the Ushahidi platform to facilitate interactive mapping and visualization, reports can be submitted categorizing type of violation and harm, technology platform, abuser/violator, strategies to respond to the incident, and providing links to news/video sources, allowing for the uploading of photographs and mapping the location of the incident via OpenStreetMap. Anonymity is suggested to protect the identity (or identities) of the persons affected. Reports can be submitted online, through email, via the Ushahidi Android or iPhone app, or tweeting #takebackthetech. A Take Back the Tech project in Cambodia is designed to produce evidence-based material on gender-based violence to inform policy makers and local councilors in their prevention efforts of VAW and the implementation of the Cambodian National Action Plan to End Violence Against Women.[25] Localized for the Khmer language, the website also provides links and references to legislation, regulations, and law about gender-based violence, and prevention services.[26]

Women Under Siege is a project of the Women's Media Center (a NY-based nonprofit founded in 2005 by Jane Fonda, Robin Morgan, and Gloria Steinem with a focus on media monitoring, training women to work in media institutions, and promoting women experts in the media).[27] Women Under Siege aims to document sexualized violence in Syria, crowdsourcing information from activists and citizens in Syria, the news media, social media, and human rights organizations. Ultimately director Lauren Wolfe hopes the data can be used as evidence in war crimes trials and to highlight where women need help for psychosocial services. Also using the Ushahidi platform, detailed reports can be submitted documenting the date, time, and mapping of the exact location of the incident, the category of sexualized assault using a comprehensive menu of descriptors, and providing links to news/video sources and uploading of photographs.

HarassMap was initiated before the revolution in 2010 to allow women in Egypt to report the pervasive instances of sexual harassment in the country. They write that they are "working to end the social acceptability of sexual harassment and assault in Egypt. All our activities are geared towards encouraging bystanders—normal people like you and me everywhere around Egypt—to speak up against harassers and have a zero-tolerance attitude towards sexual harassment."[28]

The prevalence and normalization of sexual harassment in Egypt is "a display of gendered power and the result of underlying sexist, patriarchal social and cultural discourses and performances."[29] Co-founder Rebecca Chiao explained that the genesis of HarassMap was:

> [to] do something positive about this issue ... it's an issue that we face everyday, and we were tired of complaining ... we wanted to do something other than advocacy that happens behind closed doors, and we wanted to engage the public to get active on this issue, and making a change in our neighborhoods from the ground up.[30]

Initially run by volunteers, the organization then received a two-year grant from the Canadian International Development Research Centre (IDRC) allowing the founders to work on the project full-time and hire others to assist with technical and community coordination. HarassMap's information is collected and reported by hundreds of female and male volunteers using Twitter, Facebook, SMS, email, mobile phone apps, and the HarassMap website. The widespread adoption of mobile phones in Egypt has facilitated the reporting of incidences.[31]

HarassMap is not only involved in documenting harassment against women using online mapping, but in community mobilization to discuss sexual harassment and gender stereotypes. Spread out over 21 communities and 18 governorates in Egypt, the teams are comprised of men and women:

We talk mainly to people who spend a lot of time on the street—shopkeepers, police officers, doormen, restaurant and café owners: basically people who have the power to influence the "culture" and atmosphere of the street. These people can decide to ignore or even participate in harassment, or they can decide to intervene and stop it. Most of the people we talk to (about 8 out of 10) become convinced and decide to do just that: make their part of the street a zero-tolerance zone for harassment.[32]

Along with community mobilization, women that submit reports of harassment via SMS are sent back a text message with information about victim services (psychological help, legal aid, self-defense classes). HarassMap has been reaching out to other institutions; their Schools and Universities project drafts anti-sexual harassment policies, which so far has been adapted by Cairo University.[33]

Initiatives similar to HarassMap have spread to other countries in the Middle East including Lebanon, Palestine, Syria, and Yemen along with countries such as Bangladesh, India, Algeria, and Japan, Cambodia, and Saudi Arabia.[34]

Hollaback is a nonprofit international movement whose objectives are to end street harassment around the world. Galvanized by local leaders and community volunteers, its mission is to "better understand street harassment, to ignite public conversations, and to develop innovative strategies to ensure equal access to public spaces."[35] Hollaback defines street harassment as forms of sexual harassment that take place in public spaces. At its core is a power dynamic that constantly reminds historically subordinated groups (women and LGBTQ folks, for example) of their vulnerability to assault in public spaces. Further, it reinforces the ubiquitous sexual objectification of these groups in everyday life. Street harassment can be sexist, racist, transphobic, homophobic, ableist, sizeist, and/or classist. It is an expression of the interlocking and overlapping oppressions we face and it functions as a means to silence our voices and "keep us in our place."[36]

Hollaback's strategy is to put the focus not on the women who are harassed, but on the harassers themselves. Says Executive Director Emily May, women "wanted us to be the Craigslist of street harassment."[37] But as they recognized, alongside providing a website and blog where people can report stories about their harassment, or harassment they witnessed, in order to create more fulsome awareness they needed to mobilize local activism. Hollaback has thus grown from a handful of US cities to encompass a presence in over 79 cities, 26 countries, 14 different languages, and since 2011 they have trained over 300 leaders as community leaders. Site leaders are diverse: 75% are under the age of 30; 50% under the age of 25; 41% LGBTQ; and 33% people of color.

Submissions to Hollaback can be made online through the website (where contributors can post their stories and map the location of the incident) or through an Android or iPhone app. Does Hollaback provide a "safe space" for women to report their stories? The reported stories are open for reading, and other participants may comment back, or press a green "I've got your back" button beside the story. In research on how storytelling serves as a conduit to activism, several Hollaback participants pointed to their sense of empowerment and as a way of "doing activism" and as "an act of resistance in response to harassment" and a conduit to engage in offline training and conversations with their peers and family about harassment.[38] However, given the unknown identity of Hollaback readers,

> participants were afraid of those invisible audiences, that they would be criticized by the way they reacted the situation. One participant was worried that it would impede their ability to contact the police or they were worried about their safety by posting the story. This fact is also variable depending on laws in different countries.[39]

New Canadian initiatives

Crowdsourcing is being used for several Canadian activist initiatives related to Indigenous rights, censorship and freedom of speech, and telecommunications sovereignty.

Indigenous rights

Idle No More is one of the largest Indigenous mass movements in Canadian history. It started out as a series of teach-ins in Saskatchewan, spearheaded by Jessica Gordon, Sylvia McAdam, Nina Wilson, and Sheelah McLean, who were concerned with the government's omnibus Bill C-45 legislation that called for drastic changes to land management on reservations, and the weakening of environmental laws to protect waterways. Its mission grew to encompass a range of Indigenous sovereignty issues: "Idle No More calls on all people to join in a peaceful revolution, to honour Indigenous sovereignty, and to protect the land and water."[40] Mapping was used in 2012 and 2013 to list (and document) the myriad activities—teach-ins, rallies, blockades, hunger strikes, and flash-mob round dances—that were happening in Canada, and globally. The 2012 map was organized by Tim Groves of the Media Co-Op. Initially Groves set up a simple Google map where he placed markers on the map about events, but realizing the enormity of the job he crowdsourced the information, setting up an online form for event submissions. The limitations of Google Maps became obvious:

> It turns out I could only store about 200 markers on one page. This is due [to] the server requirement to serve up more dots on a map. If I were more experienced with other mapping platforms I could

have transferred it over, but I decided to cap the map as a list of events in 2012.[41]

He also added,

> I am incredibly happy with the response and impact that my first Idle No More map has had. That said I am also excited to learn more mapping skills so I can make something more powerful next time I undertake a project like this one.[42]

Censorship/freedom of speech

In Canada, the *Canadian Charter of Rights and Freedoms* guarantees the right to freedom of expression, but as Tasleem Thawar, Executive Director of PEN Canada stated,

> Recent incidents where expression has been controlled, prevented, or silenced have made national headlines ... the silencing of scientists, the auditing of charities for political activity, and the rise in SLAPP suits are just a few examples of what has brought our organizations together to create this tool.[43]

Censorship Tracker is a recent initiative co-sponsored by the Canadian Civil Liberties Association (CCLA), Canadian Journalists for Free Expression (CJFE), PEN Canada, and the British Columbia Civil Liberties Association (BCCLA). Its goal is to allow citizens, civil society groups, activists, journalists, and government workers to report and crowdmap cases across Canada where freedom of expression has been stifled, threatened, or limited. Reports may be made anonymously and project coordinators will attempt to verify all submitted reports.

IXmaps.ca maps internet exchanges and the pattern of internet traffic as it passes through sites where the National Security Agency (NSA) has splitter operations, or surveillance points. They do this through collecting traceroute data that is generated by volunteers through a crowdsource approach, and then geolocating that information to map the global routes of internet traffic on a Google Maps mashup. The IXmaps team has built a software application called TrGen to facilitate the mapping. As of 2014 IXMaps had collected over 26,000 traceroutes contributed from over 200 submitters from over 180 originating addresses in North America in excess of 2600 destination URLs. Looking at only US-based routes (numbering 2927), 2839 passed through one of 18 cities they identified as likely sites for NSA splitter operations: "In other words, installing splitters in the major internet exchange points in just these cities would be sufficient for the NSA to intercept 97% of our US only traceroutes!"[44] Project leader Andrew Clement suggests that this finding "justif[ies] our claim that these cities are strongly suspected of hosting NSA warrantless surveillance facilities."[45]

Clement is particularly concerned with ensuring Canadian network sovereignty. As his study shows, very often Canadian data passes through US exchange points in the United States and this data—even the most sensitive—is subject to Patriot Act legislation.[46]

Tensions in the geoweb for social justice activism

The use of the geoweb for social justice activism raises many pertinent challenges, especially related to the ownership of the platforms; the security and privacy of the information, and the potential for surveillance, access, and data literacy; and the verifiability of crowdsourcing.

Platform ownership and the political economy of the geoweb

While mapping was always a function performed by the state, Leszczynski argues that the rise of neoliberalism, resulting in an evisceration of state funding, has allowed states to give up their traditional mapping functions.[47] As a result, spatial mapping, also enabled by the digitization of new mapping tools, has become outsourced to the public and to private concerns. "These reconfigurations are manifesting as pronounced shifts within regimes of spatial data governance—the production, dissemination, and institutionalization of geographic information."[48]

Political economy, with its focus on understanding the power relationships that structure the ownership, production, distribution, and consumption of media content and infrastructure, is a useful framework for understanding the geoweb.[49] Two main platforms for mapping include Google Maps/Google Earth and OpenStreetMaps.

Google's quick ascent to dominance over many aspects of the World Wide Web, particularly search, email, and maps markets, is in part explained by its fast acquisition of firms. This includes Google Maps and Google Earth, which follow a strategic history of Google's purchase of Keyhole and other firms engaged in geospatial and remote-sensing activities.[50] Exploring the strategic acquisitions made by Google in the mapping market highlights how they have become the dominant player in geoweb-mapping platforms. The first and perhaps most important acquisition was in 2004, when Google purchased Keyhole Inc., for an undisclosed sum.[51] Keyhole Inc., founded in 2001, was a key corporation in the production of satellite and aerial imagery funded in part by In-Q-Tel, a venture capital arm of the Central Intelligence Agency; Sony's Broadband Entertainment unit and graphics-chip manufacturer NVidia.[52] The strategic acquisition of Keyhole eventually culminated in the Google Maps and Google Earth products, as well as their Keyhole Markup

Language XML notation, otherwise known as KML, which became a standard geospatial data notation of the Open Geospatial Consortium in 2008 for visualizing geographic information. Securing KML as an international data standard solidified Google Maps' market dominance.

Google has made seven known acquisitions in the construction of Google Maps. One of these was Google's acquisition of Waze, an Israeli-based firm specializing in GPS-based real-time traffic and navigation services for $966 million USD, according to Securities and Exchange Commission 2013 quarterly filings. The strategic acquisition of Waze has been speculated by some as a means of further enriching Google Maps and deterring users from alternate mapping services from rival companies such as Facebook and Apple.[53] In addition, the Waze service platform utilizes real-time GPS information about its users to construct maps, which can, for instance, respond to changes in traffic such as accidents. This can effectively strengthen Google Maps' reliance on user-generated content. At the time of the announcement, the US Federal Trade Commission (FTC) considered investigating the acquisition on grounds of potential antitrust violations, but has since abandoned their pursuit.[54]

Google's market dominance should be examined by those interested in using the geoweb as a tool for activism. First, ownership influences what kind of skills or training will be in demand. Because Google's acquisition strategy led to KML as an open standard for geospatial media, it follows that cartographic and geospatial knowledge producers must be expected to have a certain degree of familiarity and competency with KML. Second, KML secures Google as a key player at the infrastructural level of the geoweb, meaning that it becomes a key force in determining the overall direction of the geoweb by setting industry standards. In effect, KML as an open standard "locks in" Google Maps and Google Earth as platforms for any geoweb application. Finally, because Google is a for-profit corporation, there is a monetary interest to maintain ownership and control over the geoweb. Although the geoweb is "free" to access, it is only free insofar as determined by Google's terms of service,[55] meaning that Google Maps and Google Earth retain key rights over their interface and datasets in such a way that maintains their particular position of power and authority over geospatial media and infrastructure.[56]

Corporate ownership of the platform can trouble knowledge politics. For instance, in her analysis of the Crisis in Darfur project, Summerhayes points to the authority of Google in data visualization and geoweb mapping.[57] Created by the United States Holocaust Memorial Museum (USHMM), the project involves "a complex, multi-layered document of the massacres, massive displacement of people, and the destruction of villages occurring in Darfur as a result of the 1983 civil war in the Sudan."[58] The site consists of photographs, videos, stories, and statistics that are embedded within the map itself, showing "a vast topography of human destruction, with some icons introducing us to higher resolution shots of the earth, zooming across landscapes of 19 burnt villages and tent cities."[59] Lisa Parks critiques the project's lack of historical contextualization and notes that Google Earth is a prime exemplar of the synergies of digital capitalism and disaster capitalism, profiting from the "erosion of public, state, NGO funding for all kinds of programs, but especially conflict, disaster and security-related services."[60] As a dominant corporate player, Google has provided public access to images collected by the CIA and National Reconnaissance Office, in turn muddying the nature of what constitutes public and private information, rendering the ownership status unclear.

The Terms of Service for many popular geoweb-mapping platforms reveal a much more complex legal entanglement of content licensing and restrictions of use and ownership. Google Maps and Google Earth, for example, grant users a license to use their services, but this is subject to numerous restrictions of use, as well as proprietary restrictions. Google's general terms of service also include provisions that grant Google "a worldwide license to use, host, store, reproduce, modify, create derivative works (such as those resulting from translations, adaptations or other changes we make so that your content works better with our Services), communicate, publish, publicly perform, publicly display and distribute such content."[61] This license continues, "even if you stop using our Services."[62] If the geographic information produced through geoweb applications remains the intellectual property of the service provider then larger issues of power and participation, particularly on one's own terms, are questionable.

The interoperability and harmonization of intellectual property across platforms is also a concern. Often there needs to be complex copyright negotiations to use particular data emanating from open data and proprietary data; Chamales and Baker cite the example of Ushahidi deployments collecting Twitter data which is placed on top of OpenStreetMap base maps.[63]

Security, privacy, and surveillance

The pervasive use of social media exposes our personal information to third-party marketers zealous to monetize this data, or even to governments, law officials, and potential employers, eager to compile a dossier of our activities without our knowledge and consent. The architecture and terms of service on social media have a significant impact on the security and privacy of our personal information related to data collection, retention, distribution, and control.

Geo-referenced information, collaborative mapping, use of social media, and mobile phones create metadata that leaves a digital trail of personally identifiable information. This data can be subjected to unlawful intrusion from governments, or from social media companies themselves, who are often asked to provide information to the state.[64]

Protecting the safety and security of individuals and organizations is particularly important in crisis mapping. Shanley, Burns, Bastian, and Robson identified vulnerabilities for working on volatile issues, including protecting the identity of journalists, organizations, and individuals, verifying volunteers, handling unverified reports, controlling the security of communication networks, and accounting for intentional misinformation.[65]

In the Women Under Siege project, ensuring the security of the information and anonymity of contributors is crucial. Reports can be submitted via a webform, through the Twitter hashtag #RapeinSyria, or via email. Digital security precautions are outlined, with suggestions to use the PGP encrypted email service HushMail, to protect against internet surveillance by using the security software Tor, and use of https proxies for common use of websites such as Google and Yahoo.[66]

Hollaback's Privacy Policy responds directly to concerns about unlawful access and the sharing of information:

> Your contact information will never be sold or shared. Ever. Not with the police, government, academics, or journalists. If anyone wants to get in touch with you, they may either post in the comments section or we may directly email you. But we will never share your contact information without your written permission.[67]

Access, diversity, and data literacy

The geoweb also raises important issues related to diversity: who is producing and using geoweb content? For instance, recent research highlights how women's contributions to geoweb content, including their participation via volunteered geographic information (VGI), such as through OpenStreetMap and Google Maps, and their paid labor in the geoweb industry itself, has been unequal, compared to their male counterparts.[68]

Concerns emanate from earlier entreaties to consider critical, participatory and feminist GIS as a key grounding for VGI to foster more integrated sociotechnical approaches[69] as well as the use of GIS for gender and development initiatives.[70] With new geospatial media, gender still matters, contend Leszczynski and Elwood, especially as "the things we do with them have material consequences that are deeply gendered."[71] Three primary dimensions they identify in which gender matters include data creation and curation practices, the affordances of technologies, and digital–spatial mediations of everyday life.[72] Increasing dependencies on geospatial media for employment and work, and the incentivization structures of social media can not only erode personal privacy, but also exacerbate social exclusion should we choose to opt out from participating.

Cultural relevance is also important. Burns, in assessing digital humanitarian projects, cautions that "an exclusion may happen when individuals do not find mapping to be culturally relevant for conveying and visually representing their knowledges."[73]

Digital literacy is key to ensuring that all citizens can function and participate in a networked society. While there has been much research and concern about the changing nature of digital literacy, and digital policy literacy,[74] we need to think more about data literacy. With the move toward open data and the release of various datasets by municipal and federal governments, we need to pay attention to the nuances and key attributes of data literacy.[75] Increasing broadband access does not generate an engaged public. Developing fluency in spatial thinking and visualization, mapping structures, remote sensing, and GIS are necessary literacy strengths.

Crowdsourcing: Authenticity and verifiability of information

Crowdsourcing is essentially the outsourcing of discrete tasks, such as data production and processing, gathering diverse social media data, and problem solving, to a large group of distributed individuals (who may not be known to each other except in a community of interest). Crowdsourcing is an inherently social activity: "The apparent willingness of many people to participate for 'free' in crowdsourcing projects is undoubtedly based on the fact that they provide genuinely effective platforms to connect socially, communicate meaningfully, and contribute collectively."[76]

Questions about crowdsourcing necessarily arise because of concerns regarding data quality, data consistency, data reliability, data ownership, and data retention.[77] Because much of crowdsourcing emanates from voluntary contributions, the ethics and politics of labor also need to be considered and situated amidst recent interrogations of virtual and precarious digital labor.[78]

There is potential for crowdsourcing to be used for evidence-based policy-making and social change. For instance, HarassMap has studied how crowdsourcing can be used as a data collection method and its efficacy for understanding patterns, bringing to light unexpected findings, and stimulating social change. One unexpected finding from the HarassMap is that many harassers are not, as Egyptian authorities have cited, under-employed and economically deprived men, but rather that 8.5% are pre-pubescent boys who bully. Online mapping was shown to be a valuable tool: "We argue that online open source platforms have the potential to elicit more detailed stories of sexual harassment than person to person settings, and may provide additional perspectives on sexual harassment that would otherwise be missed in traditional research."[79]

Conclusion

As this chapter has illustrated, the use of the geoweb for social justice has taken many different dimensions—from building up maps to assist in humanitarian work in environmental catastrophes, to documenting injustices from repressive and corrupt regimes, to data visualization illustrating trends in social issues, to organizing protests and mobilizing awareness of social justice issues. Much of this work is done by volunteers and through crowdsourcing. When asked what motivated her to work as a crisis mapper volunteer, a woman interviewed for BBC Radio 4 stated,

> It's addictive ... there is no job in the world that could pay for the way this makes you feel ... when you actually know you have saved someone's life, from sitting in your sitting room in your pajamas at 2 o'clock in the morning. It's priceless.[80]

But alongside the potentialities of the geoweb for social justice are a host of attendant policy issues, including ownership, security, privacy and surveillance, and copyright. We need to remain vigilant about how best to use these (often proprietary, such as Google) platforms to protect the lives and livelihoods of activists. Further research needs to also consider how to leverage crowdsourcing as a mode of evidence-based policy making and social change, and produce an understanding of the diverse knowledge politics where stakeholders define, negotiate, and leverage the geoweb for social and political awareness and change.[81]

Acknowledgments

This research is part of Geothink.ca, a 5-year partnership research grant funded by the Social Sciences and Humanities Research Council of Canada (SSHRC). Geothink's goals are to examine new forms of map making (Geospatial Web 2.0), and the "implications of increasing two-way exchanges of locational information between citizens and governments and the way in which technology shapes, and is shaped by, this exchange." See http://geothink.ca/project-description/

Notes

1 Adrianna de Souza e Silva, "From Cyber to Hybrid: Mobile Technologies as Interfaces of Hybrid Spaces," *Space and Culture* 9, no. 3 (2006): 261–278.
2 Sarah Elwood, Michael F. Goodchild, and Daniel Sui, "Prospects for VGI Research and the Emerging Fourth Paradigm," in *Crowdsourcing Geographic Knowledge: Volunteered Geographic Information (VGI) in Theory and Practice*, Eds. Daniel Sui, Sarah Elwood, and Michael F. Goodchild (New York: Springer, 2013), 361–375; Michael F. Goodchild, "Citizens as Sensors: The World of Volunteered Geography," *GeoJournal* 69, no. 4 (2007): 211–221; Stephane Roche, Eliane Propeck-Zimmermann, and Boris Mericskay, "GeoWeb and Crisis Management: Issues and Perspectives of Volunteered Geographic Information," *GeoJournal* 78, no. 1 (2013): 21–40.
3 Martin Dodge and Rob Kitchin, "Crowdsourced Cartography," *Mapping* (2013): 20.

4 "Occupy Central Hong Kong Turns Streets Into Art Galleries," *Art Radar*, 20 October 2014, http://artradarjournal.com/2014/10/10/occupy-central-hong-kong-streets-art-galleries/; Joyce Lau, "Art Spawned by Hong Kong Protest; Now to Make It Live On," *New York Times*, 14 November 2014, www.nytimes.com/2014/11/15/world/asia/rescuing-protest-artwork-from-hong-kongs-streets.html#

5 "The Umbrella Archives: Hong Kong Artist Collective Fights to Preserve Protest Art," *Art Radar*, 24 October 2014, http://artradarjournal.com/2014/10/24/the-umbrella-archives-hong-kong-artist-collective-fights-to-preserve-protest-art/

6 UN Office for the Coordination of Humanitarian Affairs, *Humanitarianism in the Network Age* (New York: United Nations Policy Development and Studies Branch (PDSB), 2013), 55, https://docs.unocha.org/sites/dms/Documents/WEB%20Humanitarianism%20in%20the%20Network%20Age%20vF%20single.pdf

7 Ryan Burns, "Moments of Closure in the Knowledge Politics of Digital Humanitarianism," *Geoforum* 53 (2014): 52.

8 Ibid.

9 Patrick Meier, "Crisis Mapping in Action: How Open Source Software and Global Volunteer Networks Are Changing the World, One Map at a Time," *Journal of Map & Geography Libraries: Advances in Geospatial Information, Collections & Archives* 8, no. 2 (2012): 100.

10 Jen Ziemke, "Crisis Mapping: The Construction of a New Interdisciplinary Field?" *Journal of Map & Geography Libraries: Advances in Geospatial Information, Collections & Archives* 8, no. 2 (2012): 104.

11 Ibid., 105.

12 Robert Soden and Leysia Palen, "From Crowdsourced Mapping to Community Mapping: The Post-Earthquake Work of OpenStreetMap Haiti," in *COOP 2014—Proceedings of the 11th International 311 Conference on the Design of Cooperative Systems*, Eds. C. Rossitto *et al.*, 27–30 May 2014, Nice (France); see also http://hot.openstreetmap.org/projects/haiti-2

13 See www.kenyanpundit.com/2008/01/09/ushahidicom/

14 See www.ushahidi.com/mission

15 See www.ushahidi.com/product/crowdmap/

16 See https://wiki.ushahidi.com/display/WIKI/SwiftRiver

17 See http://firsttosee.org/

18 See www.ushahidi.com/product/crisisnet

19 Jonathon Morgan, "Syrian Social Media, Journalists' Secret Weapon in the Crisis Data Revolution," *Crisis Net*, 3 June 2014, http://blog.crisis.net/syrian-social-media-journalists-secret-weapon-in-the-crisis-data-revolution/

20 See www.ushahidi.com/product/ping/

21 See www.humanitariantracker.org/#!aboutus/csgz

22 See http://crisismappers.net

23 See www.standbytaskforce.org/about-us/

24 See www.takebackthetech.net/mapit/page/index/2

25 Open Institute, "Gender Based Violence Project in Cambodia," 2013, www.open.org.kh/en/gender-based-violence-gbv-project#.VHtNhOcnjP8

26 See http://spider.apc.org/main

27 See https://womenundersiegesyria.crowdmap.com/main

28 See http://harassmap.org/en/what-we-do/

29 Amel Fahmy, "Towards a Safer City—Sexual Harassment in Greater Cairo: The Effectiveness of Crowdsourced Data," *HarassMap Youth and Development Consultancy Institute (Etijah)*, 2014, 73, http://harassmap.org/en/wp-content/uploads/2013/03/Towards-A-Safer-City_full-report.pdf

30 CBC Radio, "HarassMap: Mapping Sexual Assaults as they Happen in Egypt," *The Current*, 29 January 2013, www.cbc.ca/thecurrent/episode/2013/01/29/harassmap-mapping-sexual- assaults-as-they-happen-in-egypt/
31 Matthew L. Smith and Katherine M. A. Reilly, *Open Development: Networked Innovations in International Development* (Cambridge, MA: MIT Press, 2014), 1.
32 See http://harassmap.org/en/what-we-do/community-mobilization/
33 See http://harassmap.org/en/press-release-harassmap-cairo-university-adopts-anti-sexual-harassment-policy/
34 See http://harassmap.org/en/what-we-do/around-the-world/
35 See www.ihollaback.org/about/
36 Ibid.
37 Ibid.
38 Jill P. Dimond, Michaelanne Dye, Daphne LaRose, and Amy S. Bruckman, "Hollaback!: The Role of Collective Storytelling Online in a Social Movement Organization," *CSCW '13* (23–27 February 2013): 486.
39 Ibid.
40 See www.idlenomore.ca/vision
41 Tim Groves, "Making a Map of Idle No More," 3 January 2013, http://timgrovesreports.wordpress.com/2013/01/03/making-a-map-of-idle-no-more/
42 Ibid.
43 "PEN Canada, BCCLA, CCLA AND CJFE Launch Censorship Tracker," 20 November 2014, www.prnewswire.com/news-releases/pen-canada-bccla-ccla-and-cjfe-launch-censorship-tracker-283340171.html
44 Andrew Clement, "NSA Surveillance: Exploring the Geographies of Internet Interception," paper presented at iConference, 2014, Berlin (4–7 March 2014), www.ideals.illinois.edu/bitstream/handle/2142/47305/119_ready.pdf
45 Ibid.
46 Geothink Newsletter Number 2. Partner Spotlight: Prof. Andrew Clement at KMDI. Geothink.ca, January 2014.
47 Agnieszka Leszczynski, "Situating the Geoweb in Political Economy," *Progress in Human Geography* 36, no. 1 (2011): 72–89.
48 Ibid., 73.
49 Harrison Smith, "Open and Free? The Political Economy of the Geospatial Web 2.0, Working Paper for Geothink," 2014, http://geothink.ca/wp-content/uploads/2014/06/Geothink-Working-Paper-001-Shade-Smith1.pdf
50 Jeremy W. Crampton, "Keyhole, Google Earth, and 3D Worlds: An Interview with Avi Bar-Zeev," *Cartographica* 43, no. 2 (2008): 85–93.
51 Google, "Google Acquires Keyhole Corp," 2004, http://googlepress.blogspot.ca/2004/10/google-acquires-keyhole-corp.html
52 "Meet the CIA's Venture Capitalist," *Bloomberg Businessweek*, 9 May 2005, www.businessweek.com/stories/2005-05-09/meet-the-cias-venture-capitalist; "Google Acquires Keyhole: Digital-mapping Software Used by CNN in Iraq War," *Wall Street Journal*, 2004, www.wsj.com/articles/SB109888284313557107
53 Peter Cohan, "Four Reasons Google Bought Waze," *Forbes*, 2013, www.forbes.com/sites/petercohan/2013/06/11/four-reasons-for-google-to-buy-waze/
54 Sara Forden and David McLaughlin, "Google Said to Avoid US Antitrust Challenge over Waze," *Bloomberg*, 2013, www.bloomberg.com/news/2013-10-01/google-said-to-avoid-u-s-antitrust-challenge-over-waze.html
55 Google, "Google Terms of Service," 2013, www.google.com/policies/terms; "Google Maps/Earth Additional Terms of Service," 1 March 2012, www.google.com/intl/en-US_US/help/terms_maps.html
56 See www.google.com/intl/en-US_US/help/terms_maps.html

57 Catherine Summerhayes, "Embodied Space in Google Earth: Crisis in Darfur," *MediaTropes eJournal* 3, no 1 (2011): 113–134.
58 Ibid., 120.
59 Ibid., 120; see also www.ushmm.org/learn/mapping-initiatives/crisis-in-darfur
60 Lisa Parks, "Digging into Google Earth: An Analysis of 'Crisis in Darfur,'" *Geoforum* 40, no. 4 (2009): 542. Reprinted in *Human Geography: Five Volume Set*, Eds. Derek Gregory and Noel Castree (London: Sage, 2012).
61 Google, "Google Terms of Service."
62 Ibid.
63 George Chamales and Rob Baker, "Securing Crisis Maps in Conflict Zones," Conference paper for the Global Humanitarian Technology Conference (GHTC) IEEE, Seattle, WA (2011), http://roguegenius.com/wp-content/uploads/2011/11/Securing-Crisis-Maps-in-Conflict-Zones-Chamales_BakerIEEE-Formatted.pdf
64 Ann Cavoukian, "A Primer on Metadata: Separating Fact From Fiction," July 2013, Toronto: Information and Privacy Commissioner Ontario, www.ipc.on.ca/wp-content/uploads/Resources/metadata.pdf; Ronald J. Deibert, *Black Code: Inside the Battle for Cyberspace* (Toronto: McClelland & Stewart, 2013).
65 Lea H. Shanley, Ryan Burns, Zachary Bastian, and Edward S. Robson, "Tweeting Up A Storm: The Promise and Perils of Crisis Mapping," *Photogrammetric Engineering & Remote Sensing* (2013): 871, www.wilsoncenter.org/sites/default/files/October_Highlight_865-879.pdf
66 See https://womenundersiegesyria.crowdmap.com/page/index/2
67 See www.ihollaback.org/share/
68 Monica Stephens, "Gender and the GeoWeb: Divisions in the Productions of User-generated Cartographic Information," *GeoJournal* 78, no. 6 (2013): 981–996.
69 Sarah Elwood, "Volunteered Geographic Information: Key Questions, Concepts and Methods to Guide Emerging Research and Practice," *GeoJournal* 72, nos. 3–4 (2008): 133–135.
70 Keith Bosak and Kathleen Schroeder, "Using Geographic Information Systems (GIS) for Gender and Development," *Development in Practice* 15, no. 2 (2005): 231–237.
71 Agnieszka Leszczynski and Sarah Elwood, "Feminist Geographies of New Spatial Media," *The Canadian Geographer/Le Géographe canadien* (2014): 2.
72 Ibid., 3.
73 Burns, "Moments of Closure in the Knowledge Politics of Digital Humanitarianism," 59.
74 Leslie Regan Shade and Tamara Shepherd, "Viewing Youth and Mobile Privacy Through a Digital Policy Literacy Framework," *First Monday* 18, no. 12 (2013).
75 Javier Calzada Prado and Miguel Ángel Marzal, "Incorporating Data Literacy into Information Literacy Programs: Core Competencies and Contents," *Libri* 63, no. 2 (2013): 123–134; Michael Twidale, Catherine Blake, and Jon Gant, "Towards a Data Literate Citizenry," in *iConference 2013 Proceedings* (iSchools, 2013), 247–257, http://hdl.handle.net/2142/38385
76 Dodge and Kitchin, "Crowdsourced Cartography," 20.
77 Dodge and Kitchin, "Crowdsourced Cartography"; Michael F. Goodchild and Linna Li, "Assuring the Quality of Volunteered Geographic Information," *Spatial Statistics* 1 (May 2012): 110–120.
78 Jessica Lingel and Bradley Wade Bishop, "The GeoWeb and Everyday Life: An Analysis of Spatial Tactics and Volunteered Geographic Information," *First Monday* 19, no. 7 (2014), http://firstmonday.org/ojs/index.php/fm/article/view/5316; see also http://dynamicsofvirtualwork.com/

79 Fahmy, "Towards a Safer City," 19.
80 Kate Arney "Mapping the World," *BBC Radio 4*, 23 February 2014, www.bbc.co.uk/programmes/b03s6mf0
81 Sarah Elwood and Agnieszka Leszczynski, "New Spatial Media, New Knowledge Politics," *Transactions of the Institute of British Geographers* 38, no. 4 (2013).

Section IV

Feminism's digital wave

Introduction

Rosemary Clark

On October 25, 1997, hundreds of thousands of women from across the United States converged on Philadelphia to participate in the Million Woman March, a protest staged to highlight the effects of institutional racism in black neighborhoods and bolster the voices of black women, who had been doubly silenced in both the white-centered feminist movement and the male-dominated Civil Rights movement. The March's grassroots organizers—Asia Coney and Phile Chionesu—bypassed the leaders and organizations that had historically structured these movements, instead spreading the word through online discussion boards, chat rooms, emails, and an official March webpage, which community members printed and distributed to neighbors without internet access. Scholars would eventually refer to the March as one of the earliest instances of online feminism. A decade later, in the same city, a pirate radio collective endeavors to empower the underprivileged, particularly women and people of color, through hands-on technical experience-building community radio stations. Elsewhere in the US and beyond, free and open source software communities, hackerspaces, and tech corporations grapple with issues related to diversity. Meanwhile, activists working at the intersection of race and gender use social media to mobilize collective action online.

These are the stories Aisha Durham and Christina Dunbar-Hester unravel in the following chapters. Their ethnographically informed work follows activists channeling political energies through a variety of media, driven by do-it-yourself values that connect empowerment with grassroots participation. While their case studies span the gender justice spectrum from hip hop feminism to geek feminism, both Durham and Dunbar-Hester tease out tensions underlying egalitarian access to movements and their technologies.

In her chapter on black feminists' digital activism, Durham traces the history of hip hop feminism, a post-civil rights movement that centers women of color and recognizes culture, particularly media, as a powerful site for resistance. She sketches out the movement's development through three key events: the 1997 Million Woman March, the 2008 "We are the 44 Percent" campaign against sexual violence within communities of color, and the 2013 Twitter hashtag protest #SolidarityIsForWhiteWomen, which critiqued mainstream liberal feminism's privileging of whiteness. Online feminism in the US, known variously as cyborg feminism, cyberfeminism, virtual feminism, digital feminism, networked feminism, or hashtag feminism, has been the subject of much scholarly[1] and popular[2] discourse. Little research, however, historicizes this contemporary repertoire of feminist media practices within the broader history of the movement. Durham fills in this gap, framing the Million Woman March as a precursor to the organizational strategies characteristic of today's online feminism while simultaneously disrupting white-centric narratives regarding feminism's history that erase women of color. The March, with its grassroots origins and intersectional values, drew on analog black feminist strategies that circumvented white and male political leadership to connect the specific concerns of local communities with national movements and prioritize the situated knowledge of women of color. Following suit, the digitally networked activism of "We Are the 44 Percent" and #SolidarityIsForWhiteWomen enabled participants to mobilize collective action, emphasize personal experiences, and reach a broad audience without the restrictions of exclusive movement organizations. Durham establishes the March as the foremother of online participatory cultures, productively reimagining how black feminists have shaped contemporary media activism, especially as reflected in the #BlackLivesMatter movement.

Dunbar-Hester's chapter focuses on feminist activism in two different arenas—FM radio activism and open-technology cultures—to evaluate the political potential and limitations of projects seeking to increase women's involvement in technological development. Drawing on data from four years of ethnographic research on a Philadelphia-based community radio collective, Dunbar-Hester identifies the ways in which the collective's democratic values of accessibility and emphasis on empowerment through technical participation conflicted with the legacy of computing as an elite, white, masculine domain. She cautions that, by clinging to democratic ideals without purposefully intervening on structural inequalities that restrict access to technological capital, activist groups like the radio collective run the risk of reinforcing existent patterns of exclusion. In contrast, the hackerspaces, conferences, corporate events, and software training meetups along with the free and open source software listservs and websites Dunbar-Hester studied work from an explicit critique of the Habermasian citizen,[3] openly acknowledging the social, cultural, political, and economic inequalities affecting users' experiences (or lack thereof) with technology, with a primary focus on the inclusion of women. These groups and spaces range in political agenda from conservative—the neoliberal, postfeminist urge to boost women's technical abilities to participate in capitalism as effective laborers or consumers—to more radical—the formation of intersectional communities that explicitly and implicitly critique structural inequalities. However, while all of these initiatives make important strides toward confronting the white male dominance of technology, Dunbar-Hester contends that they run the risk of privileging white educated women, excluding queer, trans*, and gender-nonconforming individuals, and restricting empowerment to workplace performance. Through her careful delineation of the paradoxes surrounding activists' emancipatory ideals for technology, Dunbar-Hester underscores the importance of foregrounding issues related to gender and access against the broader context of sociohistorical inequalities.

Read together, Durham's and Dunbar-Hester's chapters uncover gendered and racialized histories of contemporary media activism that are often lost in the unending struggle to keep pace with technological advancements. Both offer accounts built on sustained, thorough, and participatory observations of activists working on the ground, adding much-needed historical analysis and fruitful complexity to ongoing discussions concerning digital media, social movements, and identity. Durham and Dunbar-Hester challenge academics and activists alike to be mindful of the enduring legacies of historical inequalities across multiple axes when considering empowerment through technology. At stake is the political project of an intersectional approach to feminist media activism in theory and praxis.

Notes

1 See for example the three special sections of commentary on hashtag feminism published in *Feminist Media Studies* 14, no. 6; 15, no. 1; and 15, no. 2.
2 See for example Michelle Goldberg, "Feminism's Toxic Twitter Wars," *The Nation*, 29 January 2014, www.thenation.com/article/feminisms-toxic-twitter-wars/
3 Jürgen Habermas, *The Structural Transformation of the Public Sphere: An Inquiry into a Category of Bourgeois Society* (Cambridge, MA: MIT Press, 1991).

Chapter 11

Feminists, geeks, and geek feminists: Understanding gender and power in technological activism[1]

Christina Dunbar-Hester

Framework

Both radio activism and gender advocacy within F/OSS[2] illustrate how technologies acquire political meanings within technical communities. In examining these sites, we can observe how activists who are concerned with expressing political beliefs do so through engagement with technologies. Geek communities are important because they are situated between "downstream" end-users of technology and "upstream" social groups like policy makers and designers. "Geek" as a social identity is constructed around the formation of strong affective relationships with highly specialized pursuits (including fan cultures, though in recent decades "geek" has a dominant meaning related to technology, especially electronics, and computers). While geek pursuits may sometimes appear idiosyncratic to those outside their communities, the significance of technologically oriented geeks is the interpretive work they conduct. They mediate between those who build and regulate technology and everyday users of technology. Geeks' interventions into the politics of artifacts have a profound impact on how technology may be built, enabled or constrained by policy, or taken up by those of us who are not geeks.

Contemporary social studies of technology treat technology as neither wholly socially determined nor as conforming to or flowing from an internal rational logic. Technologies and technical practices are understood as durable (but not immutable) assemblages of social relations and technical artifacts. In keeping with this tradition, but specifically in relation to gender, feminist social studies of technology conceive "of technology as both a source and a consequence of gender relations."[3] Gender structure and identity[4] are materialized in technological artifacts and practices, and technology is implicated in the production and maintenance of a relational system of gender.[5] Technical domains such as electronics tinkering, including computers and ham radio, have historically served as sites of masculine identity construction.[6] Looking at these issues in their present-day context, Sara Diamond has noted that:

> In spite of the possibility of emancipation from corporeal realities imagined by early theorists and boosters of new media and cyberspace, bodies and social positions are anything but left behind in relationships with computers ... it is still the case within the so-called high tech and new media industries that what kind of work you perform depends on how you are configured biologically and positioned socially.[7]

In other words, social context and position, including gender, matter greatly as we consider who participates in technical practices, and who possesses agency with regard to technology, both historically and in the present.

Having established that geeks act as mediators of technology, and that technology is a site of gender production and maintenance, I turn to two empirical cases.

Technical DIY and tinkering for change: FM radio activism

The first case I present is a group of media activists whose work foregrounded engagement with communication technologies. Working in a self-consciously collaborative mode, the activists approached technical work as a site to enact DIY (do-it-yourself) politics. This practice was understood to be in service of a broader goal of facilitating technical and political engagement through "demystification" of technology.

These activists came together in the mid-1990s as a pirate radio collective in Philadelphia, PA, in the United States. After they were raided and shut down by the Federal Communications Commission in 1998, they stopped broadcasting, and turned toward policy advocacy and building radio stations. Expanding access to low-power FM radio (LPFM) was their main issue, but they also considered how to expand their mission to "free the airwaves" to include not only radio but also Internet-based technologies, especially community wi-fi. They espoused radical left politics and considered their work to occur against the backdrop of a social movement for media democracy and a wide social change agenda; they conceived of their work as supporting an "international movement for people to own their own voices."[8] The data in this chapter are drawn from a much larger ethnographic project, including participant-observation and around thirty semi-structured interviews, conducted from 2003–2007.[9]

The activists presented technical engagement as a strategy for leveling expertise and increasing political participation. In this, they recognized that tinkering is as much a form of cultural production as a technical one;[10] the activists sought to produce not just technical artifacts but egalitarian social relations, by eroding boundaries between experts and laypeople. Activists suggested that demystification of technology through widespread hands-on making could provide an alternative to prevalent technical cultures in which authority is not distributed, but resides exclusively with experts. By emphasizing technical *participation*, these activists distinguished themselves from and mounted a challenge to volunteer projects where technical *virtuosity* is paramount (notably, many free and open source software projects, for example). This enabled them to focus on the deliberate cultivation of a radically participatory technical identity, enacting DIY as a mode of technical and political decision-making that rests on technical empowerment, where the notion of active political and technological agency is key.

Technical engagement held a special symbolic value within a diverse repertoire of activist practice. The activists convened weekly tinkering groups to build or repair electronics hardware, other tinkering workshops, and radio station "barnraisings," events where participants put a new radio station on the air over the course of a weekend. Barnraisings were highly symbolic events where the radio activists reinforced their twin missions of community radio and community organizing. The barnraising concept was a self-conscious reference to the Amish practice of people joining together to accomplish a project that an individual or small group alone would struggle to achieve, thereby emphasizing interdependence and cooperation.

The activists' stated ideal was that "no one is allowed to do what they already know how to do" at a barnraising; expert engineers and activists were supposed to guide novice volunteers through the assembly of the new radio station, handing tools off to other people to learn new skills. This was seen as an exercise in community empowerment, and the technical practices were explicitly linked to political engagement. A staff activist reflected on this, invoking DIY: "[A] big part of the barnraisings [is that] it is a demystification, and making people feel like ... oh, if I just did this enough, I could do this just as well ... as this engineer."[11] Whether the activists' ideals were matched by the social reality (and in practice, they were not), the symbolic importance of the barnraising for the activists was that by "getting their hands dirty," volunteers and activists forged a sense of engagement in a common technological and political project, and people who did not regularly participate in technical pursuits would feel a sense of agency and empowerment. These practices were intended as a radical opportunity for groups who have traditionally been excluded from technical expertise, including women.

But in practice, difficulties arose. One afternoon during a weekend workshop where volunteers were building a new low-power FM radio station, a middle-aged electrician approached me and apologized for making me cry. This was puzzling to me, because I had not interacted with him at any point. I looked at him quizzically, and he quickly realized his error: he had mistaken me for another young white woman with short dark hair. Naturally I wondered what was going on. We figured out he had thought I was a volunteer named Louisa,[12] and he asked me to tell her he was looking for her if I saw her. A few hours later, I bumped into Louisa, and alerted her that she was being sought. She declined to explain the situation in the moment, but later, in an interview, she briefly described what had happened:

> I tried to get involved in some carpentry [to build the radio studio]. And I didn't understand what [the electrician] was saying, and I just ... walked away ... But I [had] really wanted to be a part of the carpentry and I wanted to learn and I wanted to get involved.
>
> [Specifically,] he was talking about some kind of nail, and measuring from this point to that point, and I was kind of like, "which point again?" and he got snappish and was just like "just let me do it!" And once you start with the "just let me do its," you don't feel welcome and you don't want to be involved.[13]

The promotion of technical participation as a route to wider empowerment reveals two paradoxes of participation, both foreshadowed above. Louisa's informal and *ad hoc* attempt to "plug in" to the carpentry work in the radio studio was a result of the radio activists' deliberate choice to leave much of the work to build the radio station relatively unstructured. Their vision for "participation" included the experience of self-guided discovery and learning, and the formation of affective connection to activism through making one's own way. Ironically, though, the putatively self-directed exploration of new skills could backfire. This ideal left Louisa, a novice, dependent on the electrician building the console to learn about carpentry and electronics; it also made the electrician responsible for helping Louisa move from absolute beginner status toward a burgeoning sense of technical engagement. In this case, the electrician was not only trying to engage Louisa technically and pedagogically according to the activists' vision, he was trying to build a working console in a compressed amount of time. This raised the stakes of his and Louisa's encounter, putting his and her goals at odds with each other, which in turn undermined Louisa's ability to explore and learn. Thus, a "participatory" mode that made peers responsible for producing the console together was itself responsible for frustrating and alienating a novice, to the point of tears.

In addition, there were patterned gaps in the radio-activist organization and volunteer base that undercut the activists' commitment to egalitarian participation. Louisa and the electrician came together at the workshop bearing the full weight of their social identities, which preceded and included relationships with technology. Men were more likely than women to know how to use the tools the activists touted, to build electronics, to be excited by tinkering, and to have the know-how to teach neophytes. This troubled the activists, who fervently hoped to provide a participatory experience that was universally attainable; the last thing they wished to do was to reproduce a hierarchy of technical participation based on gender roles.

In an interview, one staff activist described the challenge he faced in trying to make sure that barnraisings were attended by "techies" who shared Prometheus' radical vision, which he felt was at odds with a more traditional engineering "culture of exclusion."[14] He said:

> A lot of the old-school dude engineers, they don't always get it ... [They can be stand-offish, exclusive, have problems with approachability] ... like [J—, who] is a prime example of a not-approachable engineer, he's a fucking grump, and if he weren't such a genius I don't think we would want him there.
>
> [But i]t's tough because we have to balance people who can get shit done [possess the greatest expertise] with people who can teach, and ultimately there are a couple of things that are beyond me [technically] and there are a couple of other [more expert] people I need to rely on. ... It's a struggle to find people who can do everything. ... I try really hard to get people of color and women engineers there, but I don't know that many, there just aren't that many.
>
> [Like] look at me, I'm a white guy, I'm one of millions of white dudes who went to engineering school, I just happen to have more of a lefty attitude than most of them.[15]

A technically skilled volunteer, who is a woman, also shared her impressions:

> I've been sensitive to [the radio activists'] sensitivity. [They] make no bones about saying "It's a dudefest. We need more women." [But] ... I feel an odd responsibility. I definitely feel like I'm extra visible and like I should be extra visible. I understand what I have to contribute ... Chicks with Ethernet cables, there's a certain inherent value in that, even in just seeing that, especially for people who aren't used to seeing it.[16]

For this volunteer, her technical skills made her feel extra visible in the barnraising setting, like she was a part of the radio activists' display of their egalitarian vision, as someone who clearly displayed a feminine identity coupled with technical expertise. She also felt that, at least amongst the radio activists themselves, the unequal distribution of technical skills was not primarily due to sexism or exclusionary behavior on the part of the men, but to a shortage of women willing to learn and display technical skills. Like the staff activist, she felt that part of the problem here was a shortage of women who have the range of competence and comfort with technology; she feels that the feminist men's attempts to be inclusive toward women were genuine and mostly adequate.[17] As a woman who was not intimidated by technology and who already possessed a high degree of technical expertise, she may have felt differently than neophytes (both women and men), who are potentially derailed by competitive, "stand-offish," or masculine displays as they try to engage with technology, which is exactly what happened to Louisa in her attempt to plug into carpentry.

Thus technical participation was vexed by the gendered legacy of the activities the activists prized. Try as the activists might to ferret out technically skilled women and put them in leadership roles at barnraisings, this volunteer was a relative anomaly. Many women were instead likely to exhibit comfort with cooking, cleaning, and managing logistical work. For them to move toward technical participation meant not only taking up new skills and tools but leaving behind familiar activities, a daunting proposition when *all* of these tasks—from soldering to cooking—needed to be accomplished in the activists' work site. The activists' greater attention to the technical side of work left them unprepared to address gender parity across the multiple domains of work that their practice encompassed.

The radical inclusion this group strove for mounts a significant challenge to participatory cultures that take for granted democratic potential in self-organized projects, without committing to the hard work often required to truly open up participation (either because their practitioner base is monolithically elite already, or because commitment to nonhierarchy is more nominal). But even with strong egalitarian ideals firmly in place, there may be real risks in fetishizing technology as a platform for political action; activists may inadvertently reinforce patterns of exclusion that have already formed around technical practice, limiting participation to those already inclined toward affective pleasure in technology. In attempting to break conventions of "expert expertise" in order to promote an egalitarian ideal, the activists ran afoul of real differences in knowledge and familiarity with electronics. The divide between novice participants and others deeply familiar with electronics (including some with formal engineering training) was not easily overcome by a simple prescription to include novices or to disallow anyone from doing anything he or she already knew how to do; the technical and affective training this proposition required could not be imparted over a weekend. In other words, the activists' ideals represented fantasy, driven by well-intentioned political aspiration and affection for technology.

Gender activism in open-technology cultures

In the second site, which is "diversity" advocacy in F/OSS and hackerspaces, we see some very related issues, but they are not quite the same. Self-consciously feminist activists and allies, among others, have identified low rates of participation by women in particular in these spaces. Here they confront technical cultures around the issue of "diversity" itself. In contrast to the first case, these initiatives begin with a critique of the liberal Habermasian citizen in how the activists frame and address the problem: they openly admit that there is inequality in their communities, and acknowledge the effects of positionality in producing different rates of participation between men and women. (Not everyone in these technical communities agrees with this assessment, but amongst the advocates addressing "diversity," it is not controversial.)[18]

Diversity advocacy is multi-sited and multi-vocal. My research methods here are informed by an ethnographic sensibility, but lack the "deep hanging out"[19] component that is a hallmark of traditional single-site ethnographic studies (including my radio activism study). Instead, I have sought to mirror the distributed nature of this advocacy, conducting participant observation at a number of sites (North-American hackerspaces, fablabs, software conferences, "unconferences" for women in open technology, corporate events, and software training events/meetups).[20] Fieldwork and data gathering spans 2011 to 2014, with continuous attention to listservs and online traffic, and punctuated conference attendance and interviewing. This period is meaningful because it has seen several feminist hackerspaces appear as well as growing attention to gender in mainstream open source; at the same time, it is a snapshot of an unfolding story with both a prehistory and a future that are outside the scope of the present research. It is significant that several initiatives that became research sites were born during this period; while this indicates that I "have my finger on the pulse" of a meaningful social phenomenon, it also means that the objects of study were a moving target and hard to identify before the fact, which creates a methodological challenge.

One illustrative vignette is as follows: In July 2006, a few attendees of the Hackers on Planet Earth (H.O.P.E.) Conference in New York City offered for sale homemade silk-screened t-shirts that riffed on a recent gaffe by Senator Ted Stevens (R-AK). Stevens, a senator charged with regulating the Internet, had recently remarked, "The Internet is not something you just dump something on. It's not a truck. It's a series of tubes."[21] This comment was widely circulated online and roundly mocked by many who insisted that Stevens understood neither the technical aspects nor the principles of the regulation he oversaw, which concerned "net neutrality" and whether Internet service providers should be barred from giving delivery priority to favored content.[22]

However, the activists hawking t-shirts at the H.O.P.E. Conference not only swiped at Stevens' lack of support for net neutrality, but lobbed a separate critique at their own community: the shirt featured the Stevens quote "The Internet is a series of tubes" as the caption for an anatomy-book representation of the female reproductive system. One woman claimed that she would not sell shirts to men unless they first said out loud to her, "uterus" or "fallopian tubes."[23] In other words, these activists creatively and humorously challenged the notion that a technical domain such as the Internet is a masculine one.[24] Significantly, they did so at a conference for computer hackers, an event dominated by male speakers and audience members (participants estimated the ratio of men to women as 40:1, though there is no way of verifying this officially).

And this episode is only one minor, fleeting example: our contemporary moment is saturated with exhortations for women (and members of other under-represented groups, but particularly women) to take up participation in science and technology (the common abbreviation is STEM, for Science, Technology, Engineering, and Math). The rationales for this push vary, but common ones are national competitiveness, and women's empowerment. Both can be found on the White House's website in 2015: 1) "Supporting women STEM students and researchers is ... an essential part of America's strategy to out-innovate, out-educate, and out-build the rest of the world"; and 2) "Women in STEM jobs earn 33 percent more than those in non-STEM occupations and experience a smaller wage gap relative to men."[25]

Industry, too, often regards increased women's participation as desirable. Google neatly summarizes the corporate agenda surrounding women in the technology on a webpage: "Technology is changing the world. Women and girls are changing technology ... We always believed that hiring women better served our users."[26] In other words, the corporation's full market potential is not being realized without a developer base that can cater to diverse users. On another page, entitled "Empowering Entrepreneurs," Google explicates the global reach of its vision and reiterates that "technology" is a route to empowerment: "Archana, an entrepreneur from Bangalore, shows how women are using technology to better their businesses, improve their lives and make their voices heard around the world."[27] (Note that while my research sites are predominantly North American, Archana is in India; technical work is used to bring people into globalized capitalism, literally and figuratively.)[28]

These agendas reflect the complex social reality within computing and technical fields, in which "what kind of work you perform depends on how you are configured biologically and positioned socially," as noted above. They also provide a backdrop for the object of focus in this project, "diversity" initiatives in technology emanating from F/OSS and hackerspace projects. Consciousness about diversity (including but not limited to gender) is evident across a wide swath of groups and sectors, including F/OSS development projects, informal hacker groups, and technology-based political collectives (loosely lumped together as free-culture or open-technology projects). Activists, advocates, and developers are increasingly addressing disparities including gendered divisions of technical labor and the gendered "baggage" of some media and information technologies, including computer hardware and software. Indeed, among some free and open source software (F/OSS) practitioners and media activism groups, there is has been a veritable explosion of interest in holding conversations and debate about the gender implications of their work with communication technology.[29]

Beginning in the mid-2000s, the F/OSS community reacted not only to a longer trajectory of men's dominance in computing but to a policy report released by the European Union in 2006. This report showed that while women's presence in proprietary software was around 28 percent, in F/OSS it was an astonishing 1.5 percent.[30] And it served as a rallying cry: this statistic was mobilized to justify increased attention to women's participation in F/OSS. As one person stated in 2009 on a newly launched listserv for women in F/OSS, "There is nothing particularly male about either computers or freedom—and yet women account for fewer than 2 percent of our [F/OSS] community."[31] Notably, the agendas of F/OSS and amateur technical projects that seek to promote diversity may exhibit contiguity with, but are not necessarily identical to corporate and policy diversity initiatives.[32] But similarities are rampant: on a post, one advocate for diversity in open source writes, "our [diversity imbalance] is reducing our ability to bring the talent we need into our profession, and reducing the influence our profession needs to have on society."[33]

My project here is distinctly *not* to ask (or answer) questions pertaining to the issue of "why aren't there more women in STEM?" or "how can we bring more women into STEM?," for example. Rather, I uncover a range of motivations behind amateur interventions into diversity questions, in order to evaluate the political potentials and limitations of such projects, including the placement of technology at the center of a project of social empowerment. In other words, the multiple framings of who participates in technology development, and to what end, are taken to be objects of inquiry in their own right.

Many scholars of hacking and tinkering have focused on the fact that these activities often take on meaning as communal and shared actions.[34] Anthropologist Gabriella Coleman has demonstrated that hackers deploy a range of stances including agnosticism and denial of formal politics (exceeding software freedom),[35] though implications for intellectual property in particular are at least implicit and often explicit in the technical and social practices of hacking.[36] Scholars have noted that the denial of formal politics makes F/OSS an unlikely site for gender activism, at least historically.[37] But F/OSS projects are not monolithic, and have matured over time.[38] They are also in dialogue with the wider culture, which is, as noted above, currently awash in "women in tech" discourses (including the publication of and reaction to Facebook COO Sheryl Sandberg's 2013 *Lean In*). It is in this context that we must place the raft of initiatives around "diversity."

A salient reason that F/OSS participants emphasize diversity is because they believe that free software is emancipatory, and they seek to build a broad commitment to its use, development, and principles.[39] The following quote is a neat summation of this sentiment:

> The free software movement needs diverse participation to achieve its goals. If we want to make proprietary software extinct, we need everyone on the planet to engage with free software. To get there, we need people of all genders, races, sexual orientations, and abilities leading the way.

That gives the free software movement a mandate to identify underrepresented groups and remove their barriers to access.[40]

Here the aspirational goal is nothing less than to have "everyone on the planet" engaged with free software, as the underpinning of an inchoate political agenda tying user empowerment and "freedom" to the ethics and practices of free software. Proponents of F/OSS also express this desire to open up free software user communities as a commitment to furthering affective pleasure, the *jouissance* that will bind empowered users and user developers to free software and thus build its reach. In general, even when the "why" of F/OSS was underspecified, the reflexive self-importance of participation in this pursuit was unquestioned; in the words of anthropologist Jelena Karanovic, "many ... internet professionals ravenously read books by communication theorists on the ways in which the [I]nternet was transforming sociability and [are] very interested in how their own practices might contribute to realizing the revolutionary potential of the [I]nternet."[41] For our purposes, it is important to note that like the government and industry agendas discussed above, free software proponents also believe that computing technology is an engine driving society[42] and its use is empowering. Note also that the first quote occurred on the occasion of Ada Lovelace day (Lovelace is a nineteenth-century mathematician famed for working on Charles Babbage's difference engine; she is, along with Grace Hopper and Anita Borg, commonly referenced as a figurehead representing women in computing).

Within "diversity," gender diversity is commonly understood to be a primary goal, most often expressed as the inclusion of women. Groups with titles like LinuxChix (founded ca. 1998), Debian Women (the Debian operating system project) (ca. 2004), Ubuntu Women (2006), the Geek Feminism project, and, more recently, PyLadies (from the Python computer language community) (2011) proliferate, and the list goes on and on.[43] A discussion occurred on a listserv [Womeninfreesoftware], about picking a logo for the list/initiative, in 2009. One list subscriber proposed, "If we took the picture of a GNU used by FSF (Free Software Foundation) added lipstick, eye shadow, and mascara, replace the beard by a string of pearls, and replaced the horns by a feminine hat, with a flower sticking up from the hat, I think that would convey the idea."[44] (The GNU-symbol being she references is the logo of a Unix-like, Linux-related operating system, a line drawing of the antelope-like GNU, replete with beard and horns as described in the email.) In other words, the subscriber proposed adorning the GNU with normative markers of femininity.

Responses to this suggestion indicated discomfort with it. One person commented,

> I ... am not a big fan of this idea. Most women in free software do not adhere to traditionally feminine styles of dress/grooming—I have seen

very few wearing makeup let alone pearls at free software events—and I think this sort of appearance would be alienating to many of us.[45]

The original poster agreed with this ("You're right ... Most of us don't dress over-the-top feminine. I certainly don't")[46] and added that the original suggestion was intended to be a humorous way of depicting women in F/OSS. Posters to the list struggled with how to represent the presence of women without falling back on representations of normative femininity that many of them found "alienating." (They also touched on race, as one commenter wrote "I think the gnu is more appealing than the wasp-y [WASP-y] noses and dainty lips [in ideas for logos].")[47]

But they also identfied another issue. One person commented,

> I think the question of gender identity goes deeper than "do we all wear pearls here at [Womeninfreesoftware]" to, are we really limiting our reach to "women" or is there also room for gender queer techies who don't identify with the gender binary?[48]

In other words, using normatively feminine images to represent women in F/OSS was problematic for two reasons. First, these images invoked and threatened to reinscribe a version of femininity that many geek women did not relate to. Second, they also undermined a commitment to gender diversity common in techie circles, where the prevalence of nonbinary-gendered and trans*-identified people seems relatively high (or is, at least, visible and vocal). Gender diversity did not stop with "women." (As noted above, many projects and hackerspaces with a commitment to gender inclusion explicitly address and include people who identify as queer, nonbinary, etc. One representative example is from a hackerspace, who describes their community as, "We are intersectional feminists, women-centered, and queer and trans-inclusive."[49])

Scholars of postfeminism have persuasively argued that much of the cultural work to single out and hail women and girls *as women and girls* in the contemporary moment has to do with constructing feminine, consumerist, individual subject positions within capitalism, aligned with and enacted through neoliberalism.[50] Those insights are useful here, especially as many strains of diversity advocacy align with values of bootstrapping, workplace preparedness, and configuring consumers (often, diverse developers/producers are assumed to better serve consumers). As noted above, reasons for diversity advocacy span a spectrum of political possibility; many do plainly configure subjects for the workplace with an ultimate goal of constructing and serving diverse consumers (difference is mobilized in order to be commodified). And others leave the "why" of "diversity" underspecified, potentially ripe for appropriation by multiple and possibly incommensurate agendas (e.g. Boston PyLadies, whose website states, "Our goal is to get a larger number of women coding and involved in the open source community"[51]).

Nevertheless, some strands of diversity activism exhibit collectivity formation that is more politicized, and often more attuned to structural issues of social inequality. The Geek Feminism site and wiki (founded 2008) is devoted to providing a community for feminist techies to come together. It conjoins the project of feminism with the culture and aesthetics of geekdom: Wiki pages address, for example, fan fiction, "recreational medievalism," and cosplay (dressing up as a character from a story, particularly anime):[52] "Things that are on-topic … 1. geeky discussion about feminism; 2. feminist discussion about geekdom; 3. geek feminist discussion of other things."[53] Crucially, the website also offers a wiki on feminist topics in order to "avoid Feminism 101 discussions"; it assumes conversance in topics such as "privilege, sexism, and misogyny" and recommends visitors to the site unfamiliar with such concepts start by reading as opposed to contributing to discussion.[54]

The space is moderated and various forms of behavior are not tolerated, contra the more anarchic and libertarian strands of open source culture where "anything goes" and norms of free expression trump other boundaries, at least rhetorically.[55] Geek feminist actors have advanced a series of critiques of tech cultures, among them lobbying for codes of conduct at tech conferences, establishing a series of "unconferences" for women in open technology (which are explicitly separatist, as people who do not identify as women may not attend), and, in general, placing priority on the creation of "safer spaces." Such an emphasis is informed by the Geek feminists' collective understanding that women in the wider culture (and in tech culture in particular) routinely suffer systemic and gender-based harassment and abuse. The lesser status and routine mistreatment of women in these communities is assumed to stem from structural inequalities, including different levels of privilege and protection for men and women (again, both in the society at large and in the tech community).

Having sketched the differing impulses guiding "diversity in open technology" initiatives, we can step back and assess them. On the positive side, some strands of this advocacy offer an acknowledgment that—the "openness" ideal of open source notwithstanding—some people have historically been more equal than others when it comes to work with these technologies. In this, activists have begun to confront the legacy of electronics and computing as white, elite, masculine domains, as discussed by historians of radio and computing, with an eye to change. The geek feminists' emphasis on the formation of feminist collectivity and safer spaces for people in technical fields and hobbies who have experienced isolation and harassment within these communities are also positive developments.

That said, these initiatives seem to come up short in other ways. First and foremost, the emphasis on gender diversity often misses an opportunity to frame "diversity" more broadly, especially attending to issues of class, race, and disability status.[56] Though exceptions exist, and emerging feminist hackerspaces in particular often gesture toward "intersectionality," the dominant discourse is around gender, which critics note has the potential to allow white women to stand in for all women, and to give white, educated women the possibility of forming alliances with and moving into greater positions of power *vis-à-vis* white, educated men, with little change to technical cultures beyond the relative empowerment of white women. This serves to perpetuate the marginalized status of poor white women and women of color in technical cultures.[57]

In addition, as noted above, gender diversity initiatives struggle with how to represent the presence of women without reinscribing normative feminities. Ironically, the struggle to render women's presence visible means coming into contact with gender stereotypes and symbolism that have been critiqued by both feminists and geek women as problematic for them. Programmatically making women visible is hard to do without inadvertently presenting them as a monolithic class of people. And this is additionally complicated by the salience of queer, nonconforming, trans*, etc., identities within technical cultures.

Finally, whether technical engagement is empowering in domains exceeding workplace preparedness is underspecified.[58] It is fair to say that at present, geek communities are struggling with how a formerly marginal and derided social identity[59] is colliding with the exaltation of computers and tech work and the celebration of Silicon Valley as the seat of cultural innovation. In other words, while geeks are enjoying a cultural moment where they are at least as revered as reviled, they have not historically been a monolithically politicized constituency.[60] Having social power conferred upon their class may not lead them to goals greater than building better products, or taking home better pay under more stable working conditions. Job precarity in tech fields is legion.[61] Programmers have struggled to retain their autonomy in the face of managerial control for decades (even as the idea of a looming shortage of workers leading to "software crisis" is also a decades-old discourse).[62] Women in these communities are entirely right to suspect that they have it harder than male peers, given the statistics on the wage gap and the punishing conditions of startup culture, etc. Yet it is unclear that many of the collectivities of "women in tech" are pressing for more than the opportunity to be valued as workers ticking boxes for corporations who are exploring diversity as a means to capture a "diverse" consumer market. While job security or value as a worker is hardly something we can fault people for pursuing, the wider emancipatory politics imagined by some who pursue and promote technical engagement is not consistently audible here.

Conclusion

We cannot dismiss technical practice as a platform for activist politics, as these two cases both show. The radio activists show that "expert expertise" can be challenged, offering instead a more egalitarian notion of expertise and technical participation. Their explicit political goal was to propagate not only radio and electronics hardware, but social relations. They vested DIY with emancipatory goals, believing that if people can "look under the hood," take something apart, break it and repair it, this will have an effect on how people understand themselves as agents in society. They promoted these beliefs through hands-on work with technology, providing workshops and other events that symbolically elevated technical practice (e.g. learning to solder a radio transmitter) in a self-consciously participatory, skill-sharing mode.

This is in contrast to technical expertise that disempowers people. We are very accustomed to seeing technocratic discourse that collapses wider social, political, and moral questions into narrow technical questions, and to seeing expertise constructed in ways that favor elites and does so by appealing to seemingly narrow technical values. Instead, the radio activists strove for a model of technical expertise in which everyday people were encouraged to move from novice status toward greater skill and affinity. This represents a challenge to technical cultures predicated on exclusivity and using expertise to draw social boundaries.[63]

But for the radio activists, the legacy of technical expertise, white, middle-class masculinity remained durable. The activists' deployment of DIY was a universalist move ("everyone should be able to do this") but all participants in radio activism are not equal in terms of social identity, and therefore this universalist DIY politics did not map smoothly for all participants.[64] In practice, the activists wound up either reinscribing patterns of exclusion that had already grown up around electronics, swimming upstream to reach out to women and "techies" of color, or both.

But equally distributed technical expertise may be the wrong focus for activism. Why should everyone want to build a radio transmitter (or program a computer), let alone be able to? Rather than imposing the dictum that everyone should possess these skills, which is arguably its own form of technocratic coercion (however well-intentioned), we might reframe the issue as one of social power. Elite social power and technical participation are imbricated to such an extent that they may at first glance seem interchangeable, but increasing participation in technology (defined as consumption, production, or both) is no guarantee of movement into a more empowered social position.[65]

Thus attention to multiple axes along which people can be empowered is likely to yield better outcomes than addressing narrower technical "divides" as if they were not part of much larger social and political configurations. Hypothetically, we might still find, in a more equal society, that technical expertise is not universally distributed. But we also might not find this to be such a problem if multiple avenues to opportunity and agency exist for all. Furthermore, the exhortation that various groups under-represented in technology fields "learn to code" (or solder) in order to improve their social position shoulders *individuals* with the onus to bootstrap or lean in.[66] This draws attention away from social and economic policies that contribute to their occupying more marginalized social positions in the first place, and places an immense burden on people most afflicted by conditions of precarity and structural inequality.

What is so appealing about activism around technology for some is perhaps the way that technology as a focus can seem to skirt or avoid some of the problems that attend movements for social change. At first glance, technology seems more neutral; thorny issues of identity and positionality are not visibly at the fore.[67] But of course, they are there, baked into the legacy of electronics tinkering, computer programming, and all manner of technical pursuits. As shown in the above cases, technical communities focused on equality and emancipation are quickly faced with the question, *do we change the dominant culture or start our own space?*

The above cases represent partial answers to that charge. In taking their measure, we might conclude that activism around technological participation is useful for changing technologically oriented communities, but it is more limited as a strategy to build a more just social world. Social movements centered on technology are likely to reinscribe the placement of men, college-educated people, and whites at the center of social power.[68] Gender advocacy in technical cultures challenges the primacy of masculinity, but does little to destabilize other ways in which power and privilege have consolidated around communication technologies.

Notes

1 Supported by NSF, awards no. 0432077, 1026818. Any opinions, findings, and conclusions or recommendations expressed in this material are those of the author and do not necessarily reflect the views of the National Science Foundation.
2 Alternately referred to as free-software, Free/Libre-software, and open-source-software production (with each label carrying different emphases), for shorthand this chapter lumps all of these forms of practice into the label "F/OSS." I also include related informal hacker groups and technology-based political collectives, with the acknowledgment that this category of practice is certainly not monolithic.
3 Judy Wajcman, "From Women and Technology To Gendered Technoscience," *Information, Communication & Society* 10 (2007): 287–298.
4 It is widely acknowledged that gender occurs not in isolation but within a matrix of factors that affect social identity, which include class, nationality, ethnicity, and race.
5 In spite of the attention given to gender identity, I mean in no way mean to discount social structure (along with gender symbolism) as an important site of production of gender (Nina Lerman *et al.*, *Gender & Technology: A Reader* (Baltimore: Johns Hopkins University Press, 2003), 4); see also Wendy Faulkner, "'Nuts and Bolts and People': Gender-Troubled Engineering Identities," *Social Studies of Science* 37 (2007): 331–356. It is tricky business, but both individual agency (individuals "doing") and social structure (which may act on individuals and groups) are tenets of gender identity.

6. Susan Douglas, *Inventing American Broadcasting* (Baltimore: Johns Hopkins University Press, 1987); Christina Dunbar-Hester, *Low Power to the People: Pirates, Protest, and Politics in Low Power FM Radio* (Cambridge, MA: MIT Press, 2014); Kristen Haring, *Ham Radio's Technical Culture* (Cambridge, MA: MIT Press, 2006); Paul Edwards, "The Army and the Microworld: Computers and the Politics of Gender Identity," *Signs* 16 (1990): 102–127; Jennifer Light, "When Computers Were Women," *Technology & Culture* 40 (1999): 455–483; Judy Wacjman, *Feminism Confronts Technology* (University Park, PA: Pennsylvania State University Press, 1991).
7. Sara Diamond quoted in Lucy Suchman, "Feminist STS and the Sciences of the Artificial," in *New Handbook of Science, Technology and Society*, Eds. E. Hackett, O. Amsterdamska, M. Lynch, and J. Wajcman (Cambridge, MA: MIT Press, 2008), 149.
8. Notably, groups across the political spectrum have weighed in on media issues, especially to oppose media consolidation; it would be misleading to represent all groups engaged in media activism as holding left politics. It would also be inaccurate to represent electronics tinkering as necessarily linked to politics or to left politics.
9. For more on this case, see Dunbar-Hester, *Low Power to the People*.
10. See Carolyn Marvin, *When Old Technologies Were New* (New York: Oxford University Press, 1988), 7.
11. Interview, July 5, 2006, Philadelphia, PA.
12. This is a pseudonym.
13. Interview, July 25, 2006, Philadelphia, PA.
14. Marvin, *When Old Technologies Were New*.
15. Interview, July 5, 2006, Philadelphia, PA.
16. Interview, June 27, 2006, Philadelphia, PA.
17. See Tom Digby, *Men Doing Feminism (Thinking Gender)* (New York: Routledge, 1998).
18. For more on hostility to issues of gender parity in FOSS communities, see Dawn Nafus, "'Patches Don't Have Gender': What is Not Open in Open Source," *New Media & Society* 14, no. 4 (2012): 669–683; Joseph Reagle, "'Free as in Sexist?': Free Culture and the Gender Gap," *First Monday* 18, no. 1 (2013).
19. Clifford Geertz, "Deep Hanging Out," *New York Review of Books* 45, no. 16 (1998).
20. George Marcus discusses "multi-sited ethnography" as a way to adapt to more complex objects of study in "Ethnography In/Of the World System," *Annual Review of Anthropology* 24 (1995): 95–117.
21. Wired Blogs. "Your Own Personal Internet," *Wired Magazine*, 30 June 2006.
22. The mockery of Stevens appeared as widely as Jon Stewart's *Daily Show* on the Comedy Central (for example, *The Daily Show* "Net Neutrality Act" segment, 19 July 2006).
23. Christina Dunbar-Hester, "If 'Diversity' is the Answer, What is the Question? Understanding Diversity Advocacy in Open Technology Projects," *digitalSTS Handbook*, eds. Janet Vertesi and David Ribes (Princeton, NJ, Princeton University Press, under review, 2016).
24. Cleverly extending the metaphor into reproductive politics and women's right to choice, the back of the t-shirt read "Senator Stevens, don't tie our tubes!"
25. "Women in STEM" page on Whitehouse.gov, Office of Science and Technology Policy (www.whitehouse.gov/administration/eop/ostp/women, accessed 2/17/15). The page also quotes President Barack Obama as having said in February 2013, "One of the things that I really strongly believe in is that we need to have more girls interested in math, science, and engineering. We've got half the population that is way underrepresented in those fields and that means that we've got a whole bunch of talent … not being encouraged the way they need to."

26 "Google Women," www.google.com/diversity/women/, accessed 2/17/15. The page "Google Women, Our Work" additionally states, "Our goal is to build tools that help people change the world, and we're more likely to succeed if Googlers reflect the diversity of our users" (www.google.com/diversity/women/our-work/index.html, accessed 2/17/15).
27 "Google Women, Our Future," www.google.com/diversity/women/our-future/index.html, accessed 2/17/15.
28 See Carla Freeman, *High Tech and High Heels in the Global Economy: Women, Work, and Pink-collar Identities in the Caribbean* (Durham, NC: Duke University Press, 2000).
29 For historical background, see Light, "When Computers Were Women"; Janet Abbate, *Recoding Gender* (Cambridge, MA: MIT Press, 2012).
30 Rishab Ghosh. "Free/Libre/Open Source Software: Policy Support," *FLOSSPOLS Deliverable D* 3, 2005, www.flosspols.org/deliverables/FLOSSPOLS-D04-openstandards-v6.pdf, accessed 9/10/2009.
31 [Womeninfreesoftware] listserv, 24 September 2009. It should be noted that within the United States, women's presence in academic and industry computing fields fell in the 1990s and 2000s. National context matters and there are significant cultural and national variations in whether women do tech work.
32 Nafus *et al.* write, "The goals of rectifying the loss of a talented labour pool and with it the opportunity to build better technologies is something that is already recognised as a problem within F/LOSS communities, and is far more likely to motivate action than social justice concerns" (FLOSSPOLS D16 2006: 6).
33 DiversityMediocrityIllusion, 13 January 2015, http://martinfowler.com/bliki/DiversityMediocrityIllusion.html, accessed 2/25/15.
34 See, for example, Gabriella Coleman, *Coding Freedom* (Princeton, NJ: Princeton University Press, 2012); Dunbar-Hester, *Low Power to the People*.
35 The Free Software Foundation explains, "To use free software is to make a political and ethical choice asserting the right to learn, and share what we learn with others. Free software has become the foundation of a learning society where we share our knowledge in a way that others can build upon and enjoy." Free Software Foundation, "What is Free Software?," www.fsf.org/about/what- is-free-software, accessed 2/17/15.
36 Coleman, *Coding Freedom*.
37 See Nafus "'Patches Don't Have Gender'"; Reagle, "'Free as in sexist?'."
38 The current attention to "diversity" represents a turning point within a collectivity focused on F/OSS as a product. Hess TPM's.
39 See, e.g. Johan Soderberg, *Hacking Capitalism* (London and New York: Routledge 2008); Coleman, *Coding Freedom*.
40 "Happy Ada Lovelace Day!," *Free Software Foundation,* 16 October 2012, https://www.fsf.org/blogs/community/happy-ada-lovelace-day, accessed 2/16/15.
41 Jelena Karanovic, "Activist Intimacies: Gender and Free Software in France," Conference paper for the American Anthropological Association, 2009.
42 Merritt Roe Smith and Leo Marx, *Does Technology Drive History?* (Cambridge, MA: MIT Press, 1994).
43 It is beyond the scope of this paper to comment on the prehistory of gender activism in F/LOSS but it would certainly include WELL and Usenet discussion groups; Systers (a play on "sisters" and "sys," as in "sys admin"), a mailing list for technical women in computing founded in 1987; the Anita Borg Institute's Grace Hopper Celebration (begun in 1994); and various cyberfeminist efforts of the 1990s.
44 [M—] to [Womeninfreesoftware], email, 9/24/09.
45 [K—] to [Womeninfreesoftware], email, 9/24/09.
46 [M—] to [Womeninfreesoftware], email, 9/24/09.

47 [A—] to [Womeninfreesoftware], email, 9/24/09.
48 [Womeninfreesoftware], email, 9/24/09.
49 www.doubleunion.org/, accessed 2/25/15.
50 Sarah Banet-Weiser, *Authentic™: The Politics of Ambivalence in a Brand Culture* (New York: NYU Press, 2012); Angela McRobbie, *The Aftermath of Feminism: Gender, Culture, and Social Change* (London: Sage, 2008).
51 www.meetup.com/PyLadies-Boston, accessed 2/17/15.
52 Geek Feminism Wiki, http://geekfeminism.wikia.com/wiki/Geek_Feminism_Wiki, accessed 2/16/15.
53 Geekfeminism.org, "About," http://geekfeminism.org/about/, accessed 2/15/15.
54 Feminism 101, http://geekfeminism.wikia.com/wiki/Feminism_101, accessed 2/15/15. See Joseph Reagle, "The Obligation to Know: From FAQ to Feminism 101," *New Media & Society* (2014).
55 Reagle, "'Free as in sexist?'." Coleman (2012) argues that free software communities frequently form collective rules, but the norm of individual freedom is extremely salient nonetheless.
56 Certain F/OSS projects have imagined the (dis)abilities of users for a long time and include attention to accessibility issues in their practice and rhetoric fairly consistently (e.g. GNOME), while others are less attuned to these topics (and, for example, the F/OSS graphics editor project GIMP (an acronym of GNU Image Manipulation Program) has been criticized for its name).
57 bell hooks, "Dig Deep: Beyond Lean In," *The Feminist Wire*, 28 October 2013, www.thefeministwire.com/2013/10/17973/, accessed 9/13/2016.
58 Dunbar-Hester, "'Freedom from Jobs' or Learning to Love to Labor? Diversity Advocacy and Working Imaginaries in Open Technology Projects," *Revista Teknokultura* 13, no. 2 (2016): 541–666.
59 Christina Dunbar-Hester, "Geeks, Meta-Geeks, and Gender Trouble: Activism, Identity, and Low-Power FM Radio," *Social Studies of Science* 38 (2008): 201–232.
60 See e.g. Matthew Wisnioski, *Engineers for Change* (Cambridge, MA: MIT Press, 2012).
61 Fred Turner, "Burning Man at Google: A Cultural Infrastructure for New Media Production," *New Media & Society* 11, nos. 1–2 (2009): 77; Gina Neff, *Venture Labor* (Cambridge, MA: MIT Press, 2012).
62 Nathan Ensmenger, *The Computer Boys Take Over* (Cambridge, MA: MIT Press, 2010).
63 Marvin, *When Old Technologies Were New*.
64 Feminist social studies of technoscience are instructive here; they urge us to replace universalist ways of knowing with "views from somewhere." See e.g. Lucy Suchman, "Located Accountabilities in Technology Production," *Centre for Science Studies, Lancaster University*, Lancaster, UK, 2003, www.comp.lancs.ac.uk/sociology/papers/Suchman-Located-Accountabilities.pdf; and Donna Haraway, "Situated Knowledges," in *Simians, Cyborgs, and Women* (New York: Routledge, 1991).
65 Eglash *et al.*, *Appropriating Technology: Vernacular Science and Social Power* (Minneapolis: University of Minnesota Press, 2004), xv; Virginia Eubanks, *Digital Dead End: Fighting for Social Justice in the Information Age* (Cambridge, MA: MIT Press, 2011).
66 For more on bootstrapping and romantic individualism in the context of the Internet, see Thomas Streeter, *The Net Effect* (New York: NYU Press, 2010).
67 Thanks to Lucas Graves for discussion on this point.
68 See Dunbar-Hester, *Low Power to the People*; Todd Wolfson, *Digital Rebellion* (Urbana, IL: University of Illinois Press, 2014).

Chapter 12

Analog girl in a digital world: Hip hop feminism and media activism[1]

Aisha Durham

I got on the bus. Philadelphia-bound, I boarded the college charter with other young black women who made a Saturday sojourn to the city of brotherly love for a sistah-centered march that would mark the beginning of a movement.[2] The 1997 Million Woman March foreshadowed a hip hop-invested, politically engaged, tech-savvy cadre of women who would adapt the communicative and community organizing strategies from the civil rights generation and use a new medium to raise awareness about homegirls, produce criticism crafted from intersectional analyses, and mobilize culturally diverse groups to engage in direct collective action. In this chapter, I situate hip hop feminism[3] within and against dominant narratives about movement feminism. I point to three media events that galvanized the hip hop generation artists, academics, and activists alike. I describe how the events characterize hip hop feminist media activism and I provide a historical lens to frame the feminist-inspired millennial-led movements today.

The march is a remarkable moment for understanding the poetics and politics of hip hop feminism as well as the contemporary white-wave model defined by digital media, DIY (do-it-yourself) or "make-do" feminist praxis, and difference.[4] First, the march was one of the largest African-American political gatherings that did not rely on longstanding male-led national organizations, such as the National Association for the Advancement of Colored People (NAACP) or the Nation of Islam.[5] Second, it was one of the earliest examples of cyberfeminism,[6] virtual feminism,[7] cyberwomanism,[8] or cyborg feminism[9] because black women harnessed the Internet as an "oppositional technology of power."[10] They used it to announce a community-based 12-point platform[11] for the march through listservs and emails, to coordinate travel logistics through chatrooms and discussion boards, and to publish self-authored news reports and real-time messages through its official homepage.[12]

Media skeptics all but dismissed how an unknown entrepreneur and public-housing activist could pull off a national rally with international appeal using only "two telephone lines and no fax" and with no major civil rights connections for attracting news reporters.[13] But, organizers Asia

Coney and Phile Chionesu connected with other community leaders across different regions and instructed these wired black women to share their technical expertise and promotional material with those who lacked digital literacy or computer-printer access.[14] Akin to a virtual word of mouth, or what media coordinator Tabiyah Ngozi called the Underground Railroad, news about the march spread despite the blackout. The organizers adapted old-school approaches to networking using the new medium, which served as a catalyst for hip hop feminist forms of activism.[15]

In addition to the new, unconventional route to mobilize marchers provided by the Internet, the coordinators also employed a tried tradition of grassroots activism endemic of black women's organizing efforts. Again, the "face" of large-scale political protests has privileged the lone charismatic black man over the (work) "force" of black women who labor to engender such gatherings.[16] This was true for the 1963 March on Washington, the 1995 Million Man March, and the 2004 Hip Hop National Political Convention (HHNPC)—the latter of which set an agenda for the post-civil-rights generation. Black feminist political scientist Zenzele Isoke suggested the HHNPC framed the hip hop agenda within a masculinist perspective, from the top-down decision-making model right down to the phallic logo of a microphone.[17] Volunteers recalled the gendered division of labor in which women handled communications and convention logistics while suit-satchel-loafer-wearing men addressed the attendees and the broader media public.[18]

Isoke and others point to the political role of black women as "bridge leaders" or activists who have historically connected local communities to male-led national organizations.[19] At the national level, these organizations often redefine gender issues or drop gender altogether.[20] Redefining reproductive justice as genocide is one example that I recall from my participation at a 2004 HHNPC meeting. Another example of erasure is the recent hashtag #SayHerName. While black, queer founders frame #BlackLivesMatter through an intersectional lens, Kimberlé Crenshaw coauthored #SayHerName to call attention to black girls and women who are also victims of state violence but receive little media coverage or comparable campaigns like our male counterparts.[21] Given this kind of historic erasure, organizers Coney and Chionesu intentionally emphasized grassroots organizing to make sure that community concerns could be heard at the national level during the march and that women, particularly economically and politically vulnerable ones, would remain at the center of black liberation.[22]

Along with gender, the attention to class as a political rallying point cannot be overstated. The 12-point platform identifies structural issues and proposes structural solutions from a community-based, working-class perspective.[23] Prisoner re-entry, gentrification, homelessness, and human rights, for example, highlight the precarious relationship that poor black women have with the state (at one time, Coney had been a teen mother who lived in public housing and received welfare). The march makes a radical departure in movement politics by rejecting the rhetoric of personal responsibility, which Coney and Chionesu heard while volunteering at the Million Man March, as well as the rhetoric of respectability echoed by some established black women's organizations.[24] Some personal reflections penned by black women applauded the spirit of sisterhood while others lambasted the coordinators for poor planning, poor sound equipment, and poor communication with potential sponsors and attendees.[25]

It would appear the lukewarm media reception had been connected to the perception that both the gathering and the organizers lacked class. That said, the march did appeal to young black women now fashioning feminism from working-class sensibilities prominently represented in hip hop culture. In step with the platform posted online and contemporary popular culture, coordinators featured artists from the hip hop generation, such as writer Sister Souljah, singer Faith Evans, and actor Jada Pinkett-Smith. For many of us in attendance, the Million Woman March invited us to think about when and where black women enter (cyber)feminism and how we might imagine this "make-do" use of new media and old grassroots politics as an intersectionally driven, bridge-building prototype for hip hop feminist activism today.

Breaking waves: Hip hop feminism as a counter model

Hip hop feminism is situated within and against the wave model. Contemporary narratives of movement feminism are defined by the third (1998–2010) and fourth (2010–today) waves.[26] The model integrates race without actually decentering whiteness. The third wave privileges the indigenous intellectual work by feminists of color who acknowledge multiple, constantly shifting bases of oppression in relation to interpenetrating axes of identities.[27] The fourth wave plays with difference via digital media on a global scale in which challenges to heteropatriarchy morphed from "zines and songs" to videos and blogs in the new wired world.[28]

Despite the early contributions of Third-Wave Foundation black feminist Rebecca Walker, the hip hop feminist scholarship by Joan Morgan in *Chickenheads* and Gwendolyn Pough and Shani Jamila in *Colonize This!*, and the mass mobilization of the Million Woman March, the wave model still struggles to outline an intersectional approach that can account for complex gender politics entrenched in race relations.[29] This is exemplified in popular and scholarly books about the third wave. After *Manifesta* and *Grassroots* introduced the third wave to a general audience, Jennifer Baumgardner contends the wave model is still useful despite its omissions or generalizations.[30] There is also no mention of the grassroots Philadelphia march in those books dedicated to contemporary feminist activism. The same can be said of her edited two-volume *Encyclopedia of Third-Wave Feminism*.[31] To be clear, overlooking the march is not as problematic as the overall investment in a model that remains exclusionary. It is a model that simultaneously requires the representation of racial difference to generate new waves (or new ways) to understand gender, and yet the model makes the contributions of women of color from the same generation ancillary to both feminist theory and praxis. Hip hop feminism breaks waves by privileging the creative–intellectual–political work of women of color in the ongoing struggle for self-determination.

Examining the Philadelphia march can shift the discussion about racialized gender and feminist media activism, especially as it pertains to black women. In her book *Digital Diaspora*, Anna Everett calls the marchers "midwives to the birth of a digital nation."[32] She does so to change the e-conversations that broach race only to describe the digital divide. Blackness often is imagined through lack rather than the (re)productive ways black communication and "technical capital"[33] have helped to create the ways all of us use digital media and engage in participatory culture. It is not a stretch to suggest that social media is grounded in African-American communication patterns and styles, considering black and nonblack users alike interact with each other by playing the dozens or signifyin', integrating phonetics for shorthand communication endemic of Black Vernacular English, and emphasizing connectedness through call-and-response and lived experience.[34] Whether it is a YouTube twerking tutorial reenacted by singer Taylor Swift, a Vine video describing a high schooler's makeup as "on fleek" later repeated in a Taco Bell commercial, or the appropriation of the celebratory Twitter hashtag #blackgirlsrock for #whitegirlsrock, black girls and women actually set trends in popular culture.[35] Still, black women are constructed as disconnected from modernity and perpetual earth mothers in order to render technology white (and male).[36] Blackness, in this way, becomes static against the technological progress of whiteness, which is a narrative that is not markedly different from the forward-moving, white-centered wave itself.

Just as black women have pushed feminism forward by theorizing power as it pertains to racialized gender and class, black women have also demonstrated how mass communication—specifically, advocacy-oriented and investigative journalism—could be used as a form of media activism. In fact, the black press remains critical in cultivating a vital counter-public, which has been necessary to challenge African enslavement, black political disenfranchisement, and overall differential treatment of marginalized groups under the law historically.[37] Apart from Mary Ann Shadd Cary, Ida B. Wells is perhaps the best known early black woman journalist and independent newspaper owner who championed full citizenship for black women during the suffrage movement (i.e. the first wave). Wells published extensively about domestic terrorism, which worked to impede the political advancement of black women. In pamphlets and columns, she presented rape and lynching as interrelated forms of racial–sexual extralegal violence initiated by southern white men and ignored by white women activists to subjugate black women after slavery.[38] The race–gender critique that Cary and Wells levy a century earlier would be echoed by Coney and Chionesu at the march and by other black women online. Placing the e-work of black women within a broader historical context provides an alternate genealogy of media activism in movement feminism today. In the following section, I point to three moments of cyberfeminism. The three moments represent both intraracial and interracial conversations about sexual and symbolic violence in what has been characterized as the new civil rights movement.[39]

Flashpoints in feminist media activism from the (post-)hip hop generation

Social media event one: We are the 44 percent

In 2012, 45-year-old rapper Todd Shaw "Too Short" provided "fatherly advice" in a video for a popular hip hop online magazine, *XXL*, where he instructed middle-school-aged boys how to sexually assault girls by pushing them against the wall to digitally penetrate them. The famous pimp-style rapper intended the "turn girls out" video to be a joke. Promoting rape culture was no laughing matter for the 2008 Green Party vice-presidential candidate Rosa Clemente, who launched the "We are the 44 percent" campaign that brought together a coalition of black and Latina activists, academics, and artists to demand the publisher fire editor Vanessa Satten, issue an apology, donate to advocacy organizations, and publicize information about sexual violence in the magazine. The Facebook fan page and Twitter campaign using the hashtags #itsbiggerthantooshort and #firevanessasatten were followed by an online petition that generated more than 47,000 signatures within two weeks with little attention from white-dominated legacy media.

Clemente and others adopted the language of the Occupy movement, whose slogan, "We are the 99 percent," is itself a riff off the popular hip hop saying: We are hip hop. The open letter listing the demands laid the foundation for town halls across the country and anchored writing campaigns about sexual violence by black and Latina journalists and bloggers, such as those from Bossip, For Harriet, Crunk Feminist Collective, and established minority media sites such as Colorlines, *The Root, the Grio, Essence*, and *Ebony*. *Ebony* magazine, for example, featured hip hop journalist dream hampton's painfully revelatory interview with Too Short, who shared his own story of coercive sex as a minor with a woman.[40] The intimate conversation served as a kind of public pedagogy about rape culture within communities of color.

Social media event two: #Solidarityisforwhitewomen

Blogger Mikki Kendall launched the Twitter hashtag #Solidarityisforwhitewomen in the wake of the self-proclaimed male feminist Hugo Schwyzer's admission of targeting women of color who challenged white-centered third-wave feminism about its race myopia. Schwyzer had professional ties to popular white feminist bloggers and writers, some of whom refused to engage with feminists of color because they believed themselves to be inclusive. In the same moment, third-wave feminist music icon Ani DiFranco advertised a "righteous" writers retreat at an old Louisiana plantation. DiFranco refused to change the location until online public pressure by feminists of color prompted her to eventually cancel it. In an article for *The Guardian*, Mikki Kendall said the hashtag "was intended to be Twitter shorthand for how often feminists of color are told that the racism they experience isn't a feminist issue."[41] Since its launch in 2013, the hashtag has been used to speak directly to Schwyzer, DiFranco, and later *Jezebel*-supported Lilly Allen, who used twerking black women as props in her pimp-parody music video. The hashtag also has been extended to challenge how the perspectives and experiences of girls and women of color are sometimes silenced within popular brands of feminism.

Social media event three: #Oscarsowhite

In 2016 presenters from the 88th Academy Awards announced another year of all-white nominees, including those in the writing category, which included *Straight Outta Compton*, a black hip hop biopic that earned critical acclaim and box office success. Magazine editor April Reign responded by reviving her old Twitter hashtag #Oscarsowhite to call attention to the continued lack of diversity in Hollywood.[42] It caught fire. The hashtag sparked a global conversation about the nominees and the predominantly white male voters and studio executives who determine what film projects are produced and are prize-worthy. Reign and others suggested industry whiteness did not make sense when recent reports showed that profitable movies included a diverse cast and diverse audiences made up much of the movie-going public. The hashtag, then, moved beyond a discussion of representation to encompass a structural and ideological critique in which whiteness remains (universally) valued despite declining movie sales and television viewership that indicate it is no longer economically viable.[43]

The Oscar's "diversity problem" was not solved by comedian Chris Rock. Early in the broadcast it was clear that his body worked to *stand in* for the black artists not nominated and *stand as* a racial buffer to buttress black flak. Forget Rock as a television host: his main role was to manage and/or mediate race. Rock failed miserably. His so-called truth-telling monologue and off-color jokes actually reinforced racism. For example, Rock introduced three suited and silent Asian children. They were supposed to represent the accountants tabulating votes and the Chinese child laborers whom Rock mocked for making the phones viewers might use to communicate their disgust. Feminist bloggers and columnists echoed Reign by saying the performance not only recalled damaging stereotypes about Asian-Americans as docile bodies and model minorities proficient in math, but the performance also showed the ways people of color are tokenized in popular culture to deflect or shut down meaningful discussions of racism.[44]

Scathing cultural commentary about anti-Asian stereotypes was matched by online criticism about rampant sexism from hip hop generation feminists who recognized that Rock had reserved much of his humorous rancor to ridicule black women. Akiba Solomon and I noted how Rock railed Reign for creating the trending hashtag #Oscarsowhite and chided actor Jada Pinkett-Smith for sharing a video describing why she planned to boycott an awards show that did not value black artistry.[45] In his monologue, Rock likened Pinkett-Smith to an angry spouse upset about an Oscar snub rather than a black actor concerned with the underrepresentation of racial minorities in Hollywood. He dismissed their charges about symbolic annihilation when he suggested the dearth of black people on screen could not compare to the actual deaths of black folks today and historically. Rock recalled how black women have been lynched and raped as a way to remind his mainly white audience of what constitutes a just anti-racist protest. Let's just say his jokes about racial–sexual terrorism were not in the tradition of Ida B. Wells, especially after he reduced Rihanna to a sexual object. Pinkett-Smith, Reign, and black feminist bloggers used social media activism to affirm what Rock actually says in one of his skits: representation matters. Two decades after Pinkett-Smith spoke at the Philadelphia march, she continues to address the significance of representation in shaping the lives of everyday black women.

Cultural commentary in online literary journals and magazines along with Twitter and Facebook campaigns coordinated by Reign, Clemente, and Kendall are recent examples of media activism by the post-civil-rights or hip hop generation that connected a specific event to broader issues affecting women and girls of color (e.g. rape culture). They challenged race and gender privilege within popular cultural and political movements, and they highlighted the creative, productive ways black women have mined media culture to develop feminist media activism. These campaigns call attention to the incommensurability of black womanhood where dominant race, class, and gender discourses continue to render black women's experiences unintelligible.

Digital media have become one site to craft feminist thought on our terms. Through virtual redress, Reign, Clemente, Kendall and other bridge leaders use the language of hip hop to "school" the broader publics about violence, harassment, and discrimination anchored in intersectional analyses, and yet the campaigns that these activists create do so by centering our voices through an affirming ethic of care. This is why when Drexel University Professor Dr. Yaba Blay created the "Locs of Love" digital book for then-suspended 7-year-old natural-hair wearing Tiana Parker, it mattered.[46] This is why when the Crunk Feminist Collective (CFC) began to send virtual care packages about black feminism to wounded women and misogynists in need of recovery, it mattered. With each act these hip hop generation feminists said the lives of black girls and women mattered. Like the Philadelphia marchers before them, they mined networks and relied on grassroots organizing to mobilize groups and raise awareness, adapting old ways for a new time. They are, we are, what afrofuturist soul artist Erykah Badu describes as the analog girls in a digital world.[47]

Conclusion

Contemporary forms of cyberfeminism such as those generated by Clemente, Kendall, and others are steeped in a rich tradition of black women's activism. For the Million Woman March coordinators, the Internet proved to be effective and efficient—and very necessary given the overall silence in mainstream media to address the concerns of girls and women of color. Rather than looking to established civic groups or commercial media, black women turned to each other. Black women turned to a cadre of committed, community-centered folks who could come together to call for social change. This is what we are witnessing with the #BlackLivesMatter movement today. I heard the call nearly 20 years ago when I got on the bus as a budding activist in Philadelphia. This is what I see now as young black women are mobilizing groups to engage in collective action using the language of hip hop and the "make-do" tactics of black feminism. From Philadelphia onward, young black women today are demonstrating, whether online or in the street, whether wired or intentionally unplugged, that in the struggle for self-determination, we are all connected.

Notes

1. Correspondence can be sent to Dr Aisha Durham, Associate Professor of Communication, at the USF Department of Communication, 4202 E. Fowler Avenue, CIS 1040, Tampa, FL 33620-7800. E-mail: aishadurham@usf.edu, Telephone: 813.974.2145, Fax: 813.974.6817.
2. Aisha Durham, "Million-Woman March Means Power to Student," *Commonwealth Times*, 29 October 1997.
3. Hip hop feminism can be defined as a sociocultural, intellectual, and political movement grounded in the situated knowledge of women of color from the broader hip hop or the US post-civil-rights generation who recognize culture as a pivotal site for political intervention to challenge, resist, and mobilize collectives to dismantle systems of exploitation. See Aisha Durham, *Home with Hip Hop Feminism: Performances in Communication and Culture* (New York: Peter Lang, 2014), 3.
4. Anna Everett, "On Cyberfeminism and Cyberwomanism: High-Tech Mediations of Feminism's Discontents," *Signs: Journal of Women in Culture and Society* 30, no. 1 (2004): 1283; Leslie Heywood, Ed., *The Women's Movement Today: An Encyclopedia of Third-Wave Feminism*, 2 vols. (Westport, CT: Greenwood Press, 2006), xix.
5. Belinda Robnett, "Political Mobilization: African American Gendered Repertoires," in *The US Women's Movement in Global Perspective*, Ed. Lee Ann Banaszak (Lanham, MD: Rowman & Littlefield, 2005), 128.

6 Jessie Daniels, "Rethinking Cyberfeminism(s): Race, Gender, and Embodiment," *WSQ: Women's Studies Quarterly* 37, nos. 1–2 (2009).
7 Jessalyn Marie Keller, "Virtual Feminisms: Girls' Blogging Communities, Feminist Activism, and Participatory Politics," *Information, Communication & Society* 15, no. 3 (2012).
8 Anna Everett, "The Revolution Will Be Digitized: Afrocentricity and the Digital Public Sphere," *Social Text* 20, no. 2 (2002); Anna Everett, "On Cyberfeminism and Cyberwomanism: High-Tech Mediations of Feminism's Discontents," *Signs* 40, no. 1 (2014).
9 Anna Everett, *Digital Diaspora: A Race for Cyberspace* (Albany: State University of New York Press, 2009), 61.
10 Everett, "On Cyberfeminism and Cyberwomanism," 1280.
11 Anna Everett, "Platform Issues of the Million Woman March," *The Gainesville Iguana*, www.afn.org/~iguana/archives/1998_01/19980108.html
12 Anna Everett interviewed the webmaster, Ken Anderson, who reported more than 1 million hits on the official site in two months. See "The Revolution Will Be Digitized," 128.
13 Annette John-Hall, "A Gathering Organized at Grass Roots: There Was Strife and Unity Behind the Million Woman March," *The Philadelphia Inquirer*, 19 October 1997, A01.
14 Everett, "The Revolution Will Be Digitized," 65.
15 The Underground Railroad itself was a network (of houses and routes) enslaved Africans used to escape to freedom. Ngozi reported the organizers held press conferences but journalists failed to show. See Karen E. Quinones Miller and Kevin L. Carter, "Leaders: March was just a start. Next, organizers say, is a national organization that will focus on economic empowerment of African American Women," *Philadelphia Inquirer*, 27 October 1997, A01.
16 Robnett, "Political Mobilization," 120–121.
17 Zenzele Isoke, *Urban Black Women and the Politics of Resistance* (New York: Palgrave Macmillan, 2012), 130.
18 Ibid., 131–134. Interestingly, the hip hop agenda highlighted structural inequality as the problem and part of the solution for communities of color; this differed from the Million Man March, which underscored a so-called return to the black patriarchal family.
19 See Jenny Irons, "The Shaping of Activist Recruitment and Participation: A Study of Women in the Mississippi Civil Rights Movement," *Gender and Society* 12, no. 6 (1998): 693.
20 Robnett, "Political Mobilization," 121.
21 Anita Little, "Kimberlé Crenshaw on Sandra Bland and Why We Need to #SayHerName," *Ms. Magazine*, 30 July 2015, http://msmagazine.com/blog/2015/07/30/kimberle-crenshaw-on-sandra-bland-why-we-need-to-sayhername/
22 The keynote speaker for the march was Winnie Mandela, an anti-apartheid activist and former first lady of South Africa.
23 Anita Everett, "Platform Issues of the Million Woman March."
24 Writing about #BlackLivesMatter movement, Frederick Harris said activists in the next civil rights movement also have challenged the politics of respectability, noting that "the politics of respectability is invested in changing the personal behaviours and culture of poor and working class black people, rather than squarely addressing the structural barriers that keep them locked into a perpetual state of marginality." See Fredrick C. Harris, "The Next Civil Rights Movement?," *Dissent* 62, no. 3 (2015): 38.
25 See Donna Britt, "Desperately Seeking Sisterhood," *Essence*, January 1998; Jacquelyn Frazier-Lyde, "Million Woman March an Overwhelming Success

Despite Obstacles," *New York Amsterdam News*, 6 November 1997; Vinette K. Pryce, "Why Are We Marching? For Solidarity!," *New York Amsterdam News*, 30 October 1997.
26 Jennifer Baumgardner, *F 'Em! Goo Goo, Gaga, and Some Thoughts on Balls* (Berkeley, CA: Seal Press, 2011), 199–202.
27 See Jennifer Drake and Leslie Heywood, *Third Wave Agenda: Being Feminist, Doing Feminism* (Minneapolis: University of Minnesota Press, 1997), 3.
28 Baumgardner, *F 'Em!*, 200–201.
29 Shani Jamila, "Can I Get a Witness?: Testimony from a Hip Hop Feminist," in *Colonize This! Young Women of Color on Today's Feminism*, Eds. Daisy Hernández and Bushra Rehman (New York: Seal Press, 2002); Joan Morgan, *When Chickenheads Come Home to Roost: My Life as a Hip-Hop Feminist* (New York: Simon & Schuster, 1999); Gwendolyn D. Pough, "Love Feminism but Where's My Hip Hop?: Shaping a Black Feminist Identity," in *Colonize This! Young Women of Color on Today's Feminism*, Eds. Daisy Hernández and Bushra Rehman (New York Seal Press, 2002); Rebecca Walker, *To Be Real: Telling the Truth and Changing the Face of Feminism* (New York: Anchor Books, 1995). For a detailed discussion about the third wave in relation to hip hop feminism and gender and racial politics in contemporary feminist thought, see Durham, *Home with Hip Hop Feminism*, 1–15.
30 Baumgardner, *F 'Em!*, 196. See also Jennifer Baumgardner and Amy Richards, *Manifesta: Young Women, Feminism, and the Future* (New York: Farrar, Straus and Giroux, 2000); Jennifer Baumgardner and Amy Richards, *Grassroots: A Field Guide for Feminist Activism* (New York, NY: Farrar, Straus and Giroux, 2005).
31 Heywood, *The Women's Movement Today*. There are references to the Million Man March and the Million Mom March in the two-volume encyclopedia. It is important to note there are entries about hip hop culture that contribute to third-wave feminist articulations of contradiction in terms of sexual politics. Rachel Raimist, who is a leading hip hop researcher and filmmaker, includes an entry on hip hop feminism. The entry follows one about Lauryn Hill, who in her groundbreaking album *The MisEducation of Lauryn Hill* (1998) makes a reference to the 1997 Million Woman March in the song "Doo Wop (That Thing)." Raimist is a part of the "We are the 44 percent" coalition challenging rape culture.
32 Everett, *Digital Diaspora*, 65. The digital divide characterizes unequal access to communication technologies, such as computers. See Chris Barker, *Cultural Studies: Theory and Practice*, 4th ed. (Thousand Oaks, CA: Sage, 2012).
33 André Brock, Lynette Kvasny, and Kayla Hales, "Cultural Appropriations of Technical Capital: Black Women, Weblogs, and the Digital Divide," *Information, Communication & Society* 13, no. 7 (2010).
34 Sanjay Sharma, "Black Twitter? Racial Hashtags, Networks and Contagion," *New Formations*, no. 78 (2013).
35 Olivia Cole, "This Is Why We Still Don't Need #WhiteGirlsRock," *HuffPost Women*, 3 June 2015, www.huffingtonpost.com/olivia-cole/this-is-why-we-still-dont-need-whitegirlsrock_b_6999318.html; Max Kutner, "Get Your Fleek On!" *Newsweek Global* 164, no. 12 (2015): 61; Ryan Patrick, "Booty craze bounces up the charts this summer," *USA Today*, 17 September 2014.
36 Janell Hobson, "Digital Whiteness, Primitive Blackness: Racializing the 'Digital Divide' in Film and New Media," *Feminist Media Studies* 8, no. 2 (2008).
37 Sarah Jackson and Brook Foucault Welles, "#Ferguson is Everywhere: Initiators in Emerging Counterpublic Networks," *Information, Communication & Society* 19, no. 3 (2016): 399.

38 Paula Giddings, *When and Where I Enter: The Impact of Black Women on Race and Sex in America* (New York: W. Morrow, 1984), 90–91.
39 Sarah Jackson and Brook Foucault Welles, "#Ferguson is everywhere," 398.
40 dream hampton, "Too $Hort: 'This Is a Wake-up Call for Me'," *Ebony Magazine*, www.ebony.com/entertainment-culture/too-short-interview#axzz3kDr1GFtX
41 Mikki Kendall, "#Solidarityisforwhitewomen: Women of Color's Issue with Digital Feminism," *The Guardian*, 14 August 2013, www.theguardian.com/commentisfree/2013/aug/14/solidarityisforwhitewomen-hashtag-feminism
42 Lilly Workneh, "Meet April Reign, The Activist Who Created #OscarsSoWhite," *Huffington Post Black Voices*, 27 February 2016, www.huffingtonpost.com/entry/april-reign-oscarssowhite_us_56d21088e4b03260bf771018
43 Darnell Hunt and Ana Christina Ramón, "2015 Hollywood Diversity Report: Flipping the Script," *Ralph J. Bunche Center for African American Studies at UCLA*, Los Angeles, California, 2016, www.bunchecenter.ucla.edu/index.php/2015/02/2015-hollywood-diversity-report/
44 Melena Ryzik, "Chris Rock's Asian Joke at Oscars Provokes Backlash," *The New York Times*, 1 March 2016, www.nytimes.com/2016/03/01/movies/chris-rocks-asian-joke-at-oscars-provokes-backlash.html; Sameer Rao, "Chris Rock Swings for Fences, Mostly Misses at This Year's #OscarsSoWhite: Jokes about Asian youth labor exploitation and Stacey Dash left us scratching our heads last night," *Colorlines*, 29 February 2016, www.colorlines.com/articles/chris-rock-swings-fences- mostly-misses-years-oscarssowhite; Akiba Solomon, "8 Reasons Why I Hated Chris Rock's Oscars Monologue," *Colorlines*, 29 February 2016, www.huffingtonpost.com/entry/april-reign-oscarssowhite_us_56d21088e4b03260bf771018
45 Aisha Durham, "Microeditorial: 5 Ways Chris Rock Mocked Black Women For The Amusement Of A White Audience," *Asterix: A Journal of Literature, Art, Criticism*, 1 March 2016, http://asterixjournal.com/microeditorial-5-ways-chris-rock-mocked-black-women-for-the-amusement-of-a-white-audience/; Akiba Solomon, "8 Reasons Why I Hated Chris Rock's Oscars Monologue," *Colorlines*, 29 February 2016, www.huffingtonpost.com/entry/april-reign-oscarssowhite_us_56d21088e4b03260bf771018
46 See the digital care package called "A Care Package for Tiana: Locs of LOVE" by Dr. Yaba Blay at http://yabablay.com/a-care-package-for-tiana-locs-of-love/
47 Erykah Badu, " … & On," in *Mama's Gun*, Motown, 2000.

Index

Figures and tables are indicated by "f" and "t" following page numbers.

access to online information 156; as basic right 166; *see also* digital divide; geoweb
accountability 42, 46, 127, 128
ACLU (American Civil Liberties Union) 95, 155
activism *see* China's online translation activism; crowd-sourced social justice blogs; data activism; feminist activism; geoweb; media at the margins; social movement theory
Adarand v. Pena (1995) 83–4, 89, 96–7n26
Adorno, Theodor 136
affirmative action 82, 83
African Americans: anti-discrimination apparatus of 100; #BlackLivesMatter movement 185, 206, 212, 213n24; black women setting trends in American culture 208; media ownership by 84, 105; Million Man March (DC 1995) 206, 207, 213n18, 214n31; Million Woman March (Philadelphia 1997) 2, 184–5, 205–8; racial profiling 33; *see also* FCC battle over diversity
ageism 42
agency *see* voice and agency
Ai Weiwei 65
Al Jazeera's citizen journalism portal 55
Allen, Donna 108
Allen, Lilly 210
Allied Media Conference 32
amelioration 80, 125, 131
American Civil Liberties Union (ACLU) 95, 155

ancient Greek democracy 18, 26n58
Anderson, Ken 213n12
Anita Borg Institute's Grace Hopper Celebration 203n43
Annenberg School of Communications 90
anonymity of blog contributors 156, 172, 176
"Another Detroit is Happening" mural project 36–7
Anthony, Susan B. 100–1
anti-cnn.com (domain name) 69–70
anti-trust violations 174
Appalachian Media Institute 29
Appalshop 39
application programming interfaces (APIs) 165, 167
April youth (Chinese young nationalists) 70, 71
Arab Spring 54–5, 123
Asia, HarassMap-type of initiatives in 170
Asia-Africa Conference (Bandung, Indonesia, 1955) 58
Asian Americans 210–11; media ownership by 84
Associated Press 108
Association for Progressive Communication (APC) 168; *see also* Take Back the Tech
Atton, Chris 54
authenticity and verifiable information 177
authoritarianism 21, 67, 124
Average Returns Per User (ARPUs) 22

Babbage, Charles 196
Badu, Erykah 212
Baker, Mona 62–3, 65
Baker, Rob 175, 176
Bannon, Steve xvi
barnraisings of community radio stations 189–91
Basilio, Teresa 8–9, 28
Baumgardner, Jennifer: *Encyclopedia of Third-Wave Feminism* 207
BBC Radio 4 178
BBS (bulletin board systems) 4, 69
Beasley, Maurine H. 107
Because of Oxycontin documentary 29
Bechtel v. FCC (1993) 106
Beijing Olympics (2008) 69–70
Beijing Platform for Action 107
Belén de los Andaquíes (Colombia) 50–2
Bennett, W. Lance xiv, 137n4, 140, 142–3, 147
big data *see* data activism
bilibili.com 64, 68–9, 72
#blackgirlsrock 208
#BlackLivesMatter movement 185, 206, 212, 213n24
black press 208
Black Vernacular English 208
black women's activism *see* hip hop feminism; Million Woman March
Blay, Yaba: "Locs of Love" digital book 211
blogs/blogging: defined 141; *see also* bridge blogs; crowd-sourced social justice blogs; *specific blogs*
"Blue Book" ("Public Service Responsibility of Broadcast Licensees") 87
Boggs, Grace Lee 36
bootstrapping 201, 204n65
Borg, Anita 196
Bossip 209
Botello, José, kidnapping of 57–8
Bouazizi immolation and Tunisian uprising (2010) 54–5
Brecht, Bertolt 123
Breitbart xvi
bridge blogs 63, 66–8
bridging the digital divide *see* digital divide
Brill (publisher) 64
British Columbia Civil Liberties Association 172

broadband access: costs to achieve universal access 21; engaging public participation 177; speed increases 18; in United States 13–14, 23n2; *see also* digital enfranchisement
Broadband Technology Opportunities Program (BTOP) 12
broadcasters' free-press rights 81
"broken windows" policing practices (New York) 30
BTOP (Broadband Technology Opportunities Program) 12
"Building the Future: Women, Code and Inclusion" (National Media Reform Conference 2013) 115
bulletin board systems (BBS) 4, 69
Burns, Ryan 166, 176–7
Byerly, Carolyn M. 2, 79, 80, 100, 106–9, 118nn61–2

Cairo University 170
Calabrese, Andrew 125
Cambodia: HarassMap-type of initiatives in 170; National Action Plan to End Violence Against Women 168
Cammaerts, Bart 123, 126
Campbell, Angela 112–13, 114, 118n60
Canada: Bill C-45 171; Charter of Rights and Freedoms 172; geoweb and activist initiatives 171–3; Idle No More movement 171–2; Media Democracy Day 130; media reform movements 108
Canadian Civil Liberties Association 172
Canadian International Development Research Centre (IDRC) 169
Canadian Journalists for Free Expression 172
Carlson, Tucker 94
Carroll, Bill 130, 154
Carter, Dakarai 36–7
Cary, Mary Ann Shadd 208–9
Castells, Manuel 142
censorship: in Canada 172–3; in China 65, 67; digital divide and 14
Censorship Tracker 172
Central Intelligence Agency (CIA) 166; Google access to images collected by 175; In-Q-Tel funding 173
C4D initiatives 58
Chamales, George 175, 176

218 Index

Chiao, Rebecca 169
Children's Audiovisual School of Belén de los Andaquíes *see Escuela Audiovisual Infantil de Belén de los Andaquíes*
children's reconfiguring of identities in EAIBA media program (Colombia) 50–2
China Digital Times: on Chinese media's silence on environmental protests 65; "Grass-Mud Horse Lexicon" 66–7, 72; influence of 66; "Netizen Voices" 66; web site's multiple uses 72
ChinaHush (bridge blog) 67–8
China's online translation activism 1–2, 9, 62–75; anti-cnn.com (domain name) 69–70; anti-domestic violence network 68; bridge blogs 63, 66–8; bullet subtitles, use of 68; citizen translations 65; concept of translation 63; countering Western media's coverage of China 67, 69–71; cyber-nationalists' information and performative politics 69–71, 73; definition of online translation activism 62; "Diba Expedition" 69–73; dissidents in China, reliance on translations 64–5, 67; environmental protest (Ningbo, 2012) 65; importance of new communication technologies 71; information mixed with political functions 72–3; M4.cn (website) 70; online feminist subtitle group 63, 68–9, 72; as part of contemporary online activism 73; political selection of source texts 72; *Southern Weekend* magazine protests (2013) 65; transnational character of 63, 71, 73; two-way translations, Chinese-English 63–6; variety of digital platforms 71–2
Chinese Communist Party 67
Chionesu, Phile 184, 206–7, 209
Chomsky, Noam 120
CIA *see* Central Intelligence Agency
Citizen (formerly Open Constitution Initiative) 74n13
citizens' media 51–2, 54
Citizens United xvi
citizen translations 65

civic engagement 156; *see also* digital enfranchisement; participatory democracy
civil rights: concerns of media justice campaigns 127; in era of big data 155; *see also* #BlackLivesMatter movement
Civil Rights Act (1964), Title VII 108, 109
Civil Rights movement 184
civil society 126, 156, 164, 172
CKAN (open source data portal) 156
Clark, Rosemary 184
classification of media practice 56
class issues 206–7
Clement, Andrew 172–3
Clemente, Rosa 209, 211, 212
Click Obtura Gallo (documentary) 51–2
"clicktivism" 35
Clinton, Hillary xvi
Clyburn, Mignon 92, 94, 117n49
Cole, Harry 97n32
Coleman, Gabriella 195, 204n55
Colombia's EAIBA media program for children 50–2, 54
Colorlines 209
Columbia Journalism Review 94–5
commercialization of personal information 10, 15, 21
common carriage 20, 27n77
communication ecology or culture 55–6, 60n26
communication repertoire 56, 60n29
Communications Act (1934) 82, 105; Section 202(h) 89; Section 257 88–9, 97n27, 97n32; Section 309(j) 89, 97n33
Communications Policy Research Network (CPRN) report 90–1, 93–4
communities of color 34–5, 46; *see also* FCC battle over diversity; hip hop feminism
community role: in youth-led media projects 36–7, 46; *see also* grassroots initiatives
compensation issues in youth-led media projects 42
Computer Technology Center Network (CTCnet) 12
Coney, Asia 184, 205–7, 209
Congress, female members of 110
Congressional Research Service: *Minority Broadcast Station Ownership and Broadcast*

Programming: Is There a Nexus? 83, 96n11
connectivity *see* digital divide
Consumer Federation of America 113
Costanza-Chock, Sasha 1, 8–9, 28, 31, 56, 60n27
Crabgrass network (US) 156
Crenshaw, Kimberlé 206
Crisis in Darfur project 174–5
crisis mapping 165–8
CrisisNET 167
cross-platform media production 40–1
Crow, Barbara 107
crowd-sourced social justice blogs 2–3, 139–50; characteristics of 141–2, 146–7; collective identity and 143, 147–8; considered categories rather than networks 143; cultural genre of 141, 143; evolution of 141–3; framing questions and validation of framing 146; indignation and grievances 147–8; "logic of aggregation" and 140; methodology of case-study analysis 143–4; *No Nos Vamos, Nos Echan* blog, case study of 3, 140, 143–8; "rhetoric of collection" and 140; as social media curators 148; *We Are the 99 Percent* blog, case study of 3, 139, 143–8, 209
crowdsourcing: authenticity and verifiable information as issues for 177; Canadian indigenous rights activitists using 171–2; Crowdmap tool 167; digital humanitarianism and 166; locational content and 164–5; *see also* crowd-sourced social justice blogs
Crunk Feminist Collective (CFC) 209, 211–12
"cryptoparties" 155
cultural and political agency 8
cultural relevance 176–7
cultural translation 63
cyberfeminism 185, 205, 209, 212; *see also* feminist activism
cyber-nationalists' translation activism in China 69–71, 73
cyberstalking, mapping of 168
cyberutopians 19
Cyril, Malkia 113–14

The Daily Caller on FCC policing of news media 94
Darfur, Sudan 174–5
Darnton, Robert 4
data activism 3, 151–63, 161n17; agenda for study of 158–60; algorithm-based methods to study 159; antiprogram 155–8; computational modeling 152; contemporary role of 156–8; datafication process 151; data profiling 152; defined 152, 153–5; proactive 156; reactive 155–6; sociotechnical nature of 158–9
DataCenter 31, 47n1
"data journalists" 161n17
data mining 157
DC Circuit Court of Appeals: *Lamprecht v. FCC* (1992) 96nn11–12, 106
Debian Women 196
de Jong, Wilma 125
della Porta, Donatella 122, 124, 130
de Man, Paul 136
democracy, redefinition of 130
democratic media activism xv, 154, 188
demonstrations *see* protests and demonstrations
demystification of technology 188–9; *see also* feminist activism
deregulation *see* regulation
Detroit Future Youth 36
Detroit Summer collective 36–7
developing countries and digital divide 12, 13
Diallo, Amadou 30
dialogical nature of digital communications 20
Diamond, Sara 187–8
Diani, Mario 122, 124
Diaoyu/Senkaku islands dispute (2012) 27n82
"Diba Expedition" (China) 69–73
DiFranco, Ani 210
digital democracy 19, 21
digital divide 10, 11–17, 214n32; bridging of 11–12, 21–3; definition of access 14; economic implications of 12; political implications of 12–13; speed, reliability, and latency as issues for 15–16; types of 11–12; walled-garden connectivity 14, 16; widening of 13

digital enfranchisement 1, 9, 10–27; approaches to 21–3; costs of 11; definition of 17; democratic implications of 17–21; history of digital divide and digital inclusion 10, 11–17
digital feminism 185; *see also* feminist activism
Digital Globe 166
digital literacy skills 10, 177
Digital Media and Learning Conference 32
discrimination and diversity 9, 10, 16, 100; gender 108; racial profiling 33; Title VII anti-discrimination law 108; *see also* digital divide; FCC battle over diversity; feminist activism; hip hop feminism; media at the margins; *specific ethnic and racial groups*
Dobbs, Lou 33
Dodge, Martin 165
do-it-yourself (DIY) culture 155, 184, 205; technical DIY and FM-radio activism 188–92, 200
Donald H. McGannon award to Cyril 114
Douglass, Frederick: *North Star* newspaper 101
Downing, John 4, 122, 124, 131
Dunbar-Hester, Christina 2, 184, 185–6, 187
Durham, Aisha 2, 184–6, 205

Ebola outbreak 168
Ebony (magazine) 209
Egypt: diaspora protest in London 69; HarassMap to report sexual harassment in 169–70, 177; political cartoons in 69
Ehrensaft-Hawley, Jesse 29–30
Elwood, Sarah 176
email 64, 167, 169, 176, 205
emoji packs 71
empowerment: access to information and 9, 156; big data and 153–4; digital enfranchisement and 17, 21–2; DIY values and technical empowerment 184, 186, 189–90, 200; free software and 196; geoweb and 165; Hollaback and 171; media at the margins and 49, 51, 54; network neutrality and 20; white women and 186, 199; women STEM students and 194; youth-led media projects and 31

encryption 155, 157, 176
Encuentro (immigrant rights organization) 33, 41–2
Encyclopedia of Third-Wave Feminism 207
environmental justice 30–1
environmental NGOs 64
environmental protest (Ningbo, 2012) 65
Enzensberger, Hans Magnus 123
equality 81–2; *see also* media at the margins
equal protection 81–2, 89
Escher, M. C. 136
Escuela Audiovisual Infantil de Belén de los Andaquíes [Children's Audiovisual School of Belén de los Andaquíes] (EAIBA) 50, 54
Essence 209
ethical press concerns 127
European Institute for Gender Equality (EIGE) 103–4
European Union (EU) report on women's presence in proprietary software 194–5
Evans, Faith 207
Everett, Anna 213n12; *Digital Diaspora* 208
Everett C. Parker award to Campbell 113
Everyday Sexism blog 140, 141
exclusion *see* digital divide; discrimination and diversity; FCC battle over diversity; feminist activism; media at the margins

Facebook: as competition to Google Maps 174; CrisisNet monitoring of 167; data amounts handled by 151; Encuentro page 33; HarassMap collecting data from 169; hip hop activism and 211; Internet.org application 14–17, 21, 22, 25n41; monopoly of 149; Resistance workshops 156; Tsai Ing-wen page ("Diba Expedition") 69–73; Tunisia uprising and 55; youth access to 35; Zero Rating program in India 25n40
Fairness and Accuracy in Reporting group 120
Fairness Doctrine 94, 95
FCC *see* Federal Communications Commission
FCC battle over diversity 2, 78–9, 81–99; competing studies 91–4; conflicting

Index 221

responsibilities 82–6; critical information needs, identification of 92–4, 97n26; Diversity Index 87–8; equal employment opportunity rules 82; intermediate scrutiny 83; lack of gender and racial diversity in media ownership 81, 84–6, 105; market entry barrier study 88–91; media ownership rules, revision of 83–4, 92; research methods 86–8; "Review of the Literature Regarding Critical Information Needs of the American Public" 88; right-wing attacks on critical information needs study 94–5; "Statement of Policy on Minority Ownership of Broadcasting Facilities" (1978) 82–3; statistics on minority ownership of media outlets 84, 84–5f; strict scrutiny 83, 89

Federal Communications Commission (FCC): "1960 Programming Policy Statement" 105–6; Barrier Study 88–91; "Blue Book" 87; on broadband access in United States 13–14; CDBS data base 118n60; *Connecting America: The National Broadband Plan* (2010) 23n2; deregulation of media ownership 106; Diversity Index and 87–8; Form 323 statements 118n60; founding of 105; gender-and-race analysis 118n60; MAG-net's effect on policy of (2013) 114; membership of 117n49; Notice of Inquiry (1996) 89; Office of Communications Business Opportunities 90; ownership reports (2012-2014) 86, 101, 112, 112*t*; pirate radio collective shut down by 188; prison phone rates policy 114; Quadrennial Review (2010) 113; Report and Order on new ownership rules (2003) 113; Section 257 reports 89, 97n27, 97n32; Universal Service Fund 12; women as members of 110; women ownership and 100–4; *see also* FCC battle over diversity; *specific casenames*

Federal Radio Commission (FRC) 105
Federal Trade Commission (FTC) 174
Feigenbaum, Anna 52–3, 55, 56
feminist activism 2, 79, 100–19, 184–215; China's online feminist subtitle group 63, 68–9, 72; flashpoints in 209–12; hip hop feminism 184, 205–15; history of 110–14; marginalization through public policy and court action 114–15; media activism and 110–14; neoliberalism and 109–10; in open-technology cultures 192–9; regulation, gender biases in 104–6; research on women's relationship to media 106–8; technical DIY and FM-radio activism 2, 185, 188–92, 200; technology as site of gender production and maintenance 187–8; theoretical framework based on feminist political economy and media activism 108–9; wave model of feminism and 207–9; women's media ownership 79, 100–6; *see also* hip hop feminism; Million Woman March
feminist political economy 108–9
feminist social studies 204n63
Fenced OUT documentary 29, 37, 39
FIERCE! (NYC LGBTQ youth organizing group) 29, 30, 37
#firevanessasatten 209
First Amendment 81–3, 89, 95, 97n26; *see also* freedom of speech
FM-radio activism 2, 185, 188–92; *see also* low-power FM radio
Fonda, Jane 169
Forbes Magazine on gender composition of corporate boards in media sector 103
For Harriet 209
F/OSS *see* free and open source software
Foucault, Michel 126
4th Media website 70
fourth wave of feminism 207
Fox News on FCC policy to police newsrooms 94
Fratrik, Mark 91–2
FRC (Federal Radio Commission) 105
free and open source software (F/OSS or F/LOSS) 2, 187, 192, 194–7, 201n2, 203n32, 203n38, 203n43, 204n56
Freedman, Des 2, 79–80, 120
freedom of speech 9, 81–2, 172–3; *see also* censorship
Free Press 108, 114–15, 125
Free Software Foundation (FSF) 196, 203n35

222 Index

French Revolution: *cahier de doleances* and 140, 147; underground publications 4
Frenzel, Fabian 52–3, 55, 56
Friends of Nature 64
FSF (Free Software Foundation) 196, 203n35
FTC (Federal Trade Commission) 174
Fukuyama, Francis: "The End of History?" 26n67
Funders' Collaborative on Youth Organizing 29; 2013 report 30
funding: In-Q-Tel funding from CIA 173; for job training 30; Universal Service Fund (FCC) 12; for youth-led media projects 42

Gallagher, Margaret 107
Gamson, William: *The Strategy of Social Protest* 122–3
G.A.P. *see* Global Action Project
Geek Feminism project 196, 198
Genachowski, Julius 91
gender diversity and gender production: social identity and 201n4; social structure's role in 201n5; *see also* FCC battle over diversity; feminist activism
Gender Links 107
genres' form and purpose 2
GeoEye 166
geographic information *see* geoweb
Georgetown Law Center 113; Institute for Public Representation 114
geoweb 137, 164–82; access, diversity, and data literacy issues 176–7; censorship/freedom of speech in Canada, mapping of incidents 172–3; crowdsourcing issues of authenticity and verifiable information 177; defined 164–5; digital humanitarianism and crisis mapping 165–8; indigenous rights in Canada, mapping of initiatives 171–2; platform ownership and political economy of 173–5; security, privacy, and surveillance issues 175–6; social justice activism challenges for 173–5; uses of 165; violence against women, mapping of 168–71
Gerbaudo, Paolo 2–3, 136, 139
Gibbons, Sheila 107
Gibson, William 12–13

Gillham, Patrick 3
GIMP (GNU Image Manipulation Program) 204n56
GitHub 159
Gitlin, Todd 4, 121–2
Giuliani, Rudy 30
glass ceiling 109
Global Action Project (G.A.P.) 30, 31–41, 47n1; Media in Action report 46–7
globalization 110, 194
Global Voices (Chinese bridge blog) 66, 68
GNOME project 204n56
GNU Image Manipulation Program (GIMP) 204n56
GNU-symbol 196
Gómez García, Rodrigo 58
Google: data amounts handled by 151; "Empowering Entrepreneurs" webpage 194; Google Earth 164, 173–5; Google Maps 145, 164, 165, 171–6; Google Translate 71; "Google Women, Our Work" webpage 203n26; https proxies for 176; Keyhole Inc. purchase by 173; monopoly of 149, 174
Gordon, Jessica 171
GPS 164, 174
Grace Hopper Celebration (Anita Borg Institute) 203n43
grassroots initiatives: feminist activism and 109, 111; media at the margins and 1, 50, 51, 56, 58; social movement theory and 122, 123, 127; *see also* Million Woman March; protests
Green Earth Volunteers 64
Greenpeace 120
the Grio 209
group solidarity 136, 140, 143; digital solidarity, emergence of 148–9
Groves, Tim 171–2
Gurstein, Michael 16–17
Guyer, Jonathan 69

Habermas, Jürgen 19, 27n75, 185, 192
hackers 128, 154–6, 161n17
Hackers on Planet Earth (H.O.P.E.) Conference (NYC 2006) 193
Hackett, Bob 130, 154
Hacks/Hackers global network 154
Haddad, Aitza 118n61

Haiti earthquake (2010) 151, 156, 166
Hamilton, Evan 3, 137, 164
hampton, dream 209
harassment initiatives: HarassMap 168, 169–70, 177; Hollaback 168, 170–1, 176
Harris, Frederick 213n24
hashtags: #blackgirlsrock 208; #BlackLivesMatter movement 185, 206, 212, 213n24; #firevanessasatten 209; #itsbiggerthantooshort 209; #Oscarsowhite 210–12; #RapeinSyria 176; #SayHerName 206; #SolidarityIsForWhiteWomen 185, 209–10; #whitegirlsrock 208
hate speech 33
health issues, media tracking of 168
Health Map 168
Hellerstein, Joseph 151
Herfindahl-Hirschmann Index 87
Herman, Edward 120
HHNPC (Hip Hop National Political Convention) 206
Hidden Harmonies (Chinese bridge blog) 67–8
Hill, Lauryn 214n31
hip hop feminism 2, 184–5, 205–15; as counter model 207–9; defined 212n3; from (post-)hip hop generation 209–12; #Oscarsowhite 210–12; #Solidarityisforwhitewomen 185, 209–10; "We are the 44 Percent" campaign 184, 185, 209, 214n31
Hip Hop National Political Convention (HHNPC, 2004) 206
Hispanic/Latino media ownership 84, 85f
Hollaback 168, 170–1, 176
Hong Kong pro-democracy protests 165
Honig, David 91–2, 105
Honig study 91–2
hooks, bell 45, 100
H.O.P.E. (Hackers on Planet Earth) 193
Hopper, Grace 196
House of Representatives, US 18, 26n59
Howard Media Group (Howard University) 118n62
Hoynes, William 120, 123
Huff, Mickey: *Project Censored* 125
Hughes, Cathy 106
humanitarian management through digital technologies 165–8;
"Humanitarianism in the Network Age" (OCHA) 165–6; Humanitarian OpenStreetMap Team (HOT) 166; Humanitarian Tracker 167–8
human rights abuses, exposure of 65
Human Rights in China (NGO) 64
HushMail 176

ICT4D experts 27n83
ICTs *see* information and communication technologies
Idle No More movement (Canada) 171–2
IDRC (Canadian International Development Research Centre) 169
imagination 10
imagined communities of resistance 155
Independent Media Center 110–11
indigenous rights (Canada) 171–2
indignados movement (Spain) 139; *see also No Nos Vamos, Nos Echan*
individualism 123, 143, 154
Indymedia Center 117n50
inequality 125, 148, 213n18; *see also* discrimination and diversity; FCC battle over diversity; feminist activism; media at the margins; *specific ethnic and racial groups*
information and communication technologies (ICTs): access to 11; digital divide and 10, 11–17; digital enfranchisement and 17–21; equitable access to 16–18; violence against women, mapping of 168
In-Q-Tel 173
intellectual property rights 175
intergenerational relationships 36–7, 42
International Network of Crisis Mappers 168
International Telecommunications Union statistics 13, 24n20
Internet.org application on Facebook 14–17, 21, 22, 25n41
Isoke, Zenzele 206
#itsbiggerthantooshort 209
IXmaps.ca mapping of NSA interceptions of internet traffic 172

Jamieson, Kathleen Hall 82
Jamila, Shani 207
Japan: Diaoyu/Senkaku islands dispute (2012) 27n82; HarassMap-type of initiatives in 170

job training, funding for 30
JoinFeministSubtitleGroup 69, 72–3
Juris, Jeffrey 59, 140
juvenile detention centers 28–9
Juventud Sin Futuro [Youth Without a Future] activist group 140; *see also* No Nos Vamos, Nos Echan blog

Karaganis, Joe 127
Karanovic, Jelena 196
Kavada, Anastasia 56, 60n26
Keeble, Richard 128
Kendall, Mikki 209–12
Kennard, William 89
Kenyan election crisis (2008) 167
Keyhole Inc. 173
KGFX-AM (Pierre, South Dakota) 105
Khasnabish, Alex 59
Kitchin, Rob 165
KML (standard for geospatial data notation) 174
knowledge economy 12, 16

Ladies' Home Journal sit-in (1970) 107
Lamar Broadcasting Co. v. FCC (1965, 1969) 105
Lamprecht v. FCC (1992) 96nn11–12, 106
Landale, Jeff 1, 9, 10
Langlois, Ganaele 154
language, rules of 125
Lego company 120
Leszczynski, Agnieszka 173, 176
Leveson Inquiry into press standards 128–9, 130
LGBTQ: Hollaback and 170; Queer, Trans*, and/or People of Color (QTPOC) 46; within technical cultures 199; white privileging excluding 186; youth and Two-Spirit activists 1, 9; *see also* youth-led media projects in United States
Libert, Timothy 78
Lievrouw, Leah 2
Lim, Merlyna 54–5, 56
LinuxChix 196
Lloyd, Mark 2, 78–9, 80, 81
Lo, Puck 8–9, 28
Local Community Radio Act (2011) 111
locational content *see* geoweb
"Locs of Love" (digital book) 211
Londoño, Duvan 51–2

Lorea network (Spain) 156
Los Angeles 28–9
Lovelace, Ada 196
low-power FM radio (LPFM) 110–12, 118n60, 188, 189
low-power TV stations (LPTV) 84, 101, 112
Luxemburg, Rosa: *Reform or Revolution* 131

MABs (multi-author blogs) 139, 141; *see also* crowd-sourced social justice blogs
MacKinnon, Rebecca 66
Magdalena Medio region (Colombia) 57
MAG-net (Media Action Grassroots Network) 113–14
mainstream media 78, 95, 121, 123; blogging compared to 141; limitations of, as impetus for radical media activism 127
Makhlouf, Zouhayr 55
Malina, Anna 17
Mandela, Winnie 213n22
Mansell, Robin 110
mapping 164–5, 168–71; crisis mapping 165–8; violence against women 168–71; *see also* geoweb
March on Washington (1963) 206
Marea Granate activist group 146
marginalization 127; *see also* media at the margins
Marinescu, Valentina 107
Martin, Kevin 86
Martín-Barbero, Jesús 8, 51
Mattoni, Alice 53, 56, 58
May, Emily 170
McAdam, Sylvia 171
McCurdy, Patrick 52–3, 55, 56
McDermott, Meghan 8–9, 28
McGill, Kim 28, 34
McLean, Sheelah 171
McLuhan, Marshall 136
McNeil, Ida 105
Medellín (Colombia) 51
Media Access Project 111, 112
Media Action Grassroots Network (MAG-net) 113–14
media activism: China's online translation activism 1–2, 9, 62–75; complexity of media and 53, 55; defined xiv–xvi, 120; digital

enfranchisement 1, 9, 10–27; feminist activism and 110–14; as intent and transformative practice 9; legacy of xiv; media at the margins 1, 8, 49–61; media consolidation, pposition to 202n8; radical media activism 127–9; scholars in and studies of xv; social media, access to 157–8; temporalities and 58; of Trump xvi; types of 1; youth-led media projects in United States 8, 28–48; *see also* China's online translation activism; crowd-sourced social justice blogs; feminist activism; media at the margins; youth-led media projects in United States
Media Alliance 113
media at the margins 1, 8, 49–61; Botello, José, kidnapping of 57–8; classification of media practice 56; Colombia's EAIBA media program for children 50–2, 54; communication needs 57–9; complexity of 54–6; invisibility of 49–50; media ecology and 55–6, 58, 59; rhizospheres and 56, 58, 59; tactical knowledge, creative use of 56; terminology to explain chaos within 56; Tunisian uprising and 54–5, 56; women's rights and 53f, 53–4
media bridging 56
media democracy *see* democratic media activism
Media Democracy Day 130
media ecology 55–6, 58, 59; FCC community econology study 92–3
Media in Action report 46–7
Media Lens 120, 128
mediation framework in activism 8
Meehan, Eileen 109
Meier, Patrick 166–8
Meinrath, Sascha 1, 9, 10; "The New Network Neutrality: Criteria for Internet Freedom" (with Pickard) 20
Melucci, Alberto 122
metadata 151, 157, 175
Metcalfe's Law 11, 13, 22, 24n12
Metro Broadcasting v. FCC (1990) 83, 96n11
M4.cn (website) 70
microblogging 157
microphones, use at protests 52–3

Middle East, HarassMap-type of initiatives in 170
Milan, Stefania 3, 123, 137, 151
military aerial photographs 166
Million Man March (DC 1995) 206, 207, 213n18, 214n31
Million Mom March (DC 2000) 214n31
Million Woman March (Philadelphia 1997) 2, 184–5, 205–8, 212, 214n31
Minority Broadcast Station Ownership and Broadcast Programming: Is There a Nexus? report 83
Minority Media and Telecommunications Council (MMTC) 91–2
minority ownership of media 84–5; *see also* FCC battle over diversity; *specific minority groups*
"Missing Home" (Chinese song) 71
MMTC (Minority Media and Telecommunications Council) 91–2
mobile phones 169, 175; *see also* smartphones
Molotch, Harvey 122
Morgan, Joan: *When Chickenheads Come Home to Roost: My Life as a Hip-Hop Feminist* 207
Morgan, Robin 169
Mosca, Lorenzo 122
Mouffe, Chantal 51
multi-author blogs (MABs) 139, 141; *see also* crowd-sourced social justice blogs
murals, community involvement in 36–7
Murdoch, Rupert 128

NAACP (National Association for the Advancement of Colored People) 205
NAB (National Association of Broadcasters) 91–3, 94
Nafus, Dawn 203n32
Nardone, Michael 52
National Action Plan to End Violence Against Women (Cambodia) 168
National Association for the Advancement of Colored People (NAACP) 205
National Association of Broadcasters (NAB) 91–3, 94
National Broadband Plan (US) 23n2, 92
national conversation, right to contribute to 82

National Media Reform Conferences 114–15, 118n62
National Organization for Women (NOW) 108, 112, 114
National Reconnaissance Office 175
National Security Agency (NSA) 172
National Telecommunications and Information Administration's "Falling Through the Net: Defining the Digital Divide" (report 1999) 12
Nation of Islam 205
Native American media ownership 84
neoliberalism 110, 126
NetHope 168
net neutrality 20, 27n77, 38, 121, 193
network access *see* digital divide
New Civil Movement (China) 74n13
new media dialectics 136–8
New Mexico, digital divide in 41–2
new political genres: crowd-sourced social justice blogs 2–3, 139–50; data activism 3, 151–63; geoweb 137, 164–82; *see also* crowd-sourced social justice blogs; data activism; geoweb
New World Information and Communication Order (NWICO) 107
New York City 29, 30, 52
New York Times 64, 108
NGOs (non-governmental organizations) 21, 64, 124, 175
Ngozi, Tabiyah 206, 213n15
Nielsen's Law of Internet Growth 26n60
Nixon, Richard 34
non-governmental organizations (NGOs) 21, 64, 124, 175
No Nos Vamos, Nos Echan [*We Don't Go, They Kick Us Out*] blog 3, 140, 143–8
NOW (National Organization for Women) 108, 112, 114
NSA (National Security Agency) 172
NSA.gov 21
NVidia (chip manufacturer) 173
NWICO (New World Information and Communication Order) 107

Oaxaca TV station takeover 55
Obama, Barack xvi, 202–3n25
Occupy Data 156
Occupy Wall Street movement and protests xv, 3, 52, 55, 123, 156–7, 209;
We Are the 99 Percent (Tumblr blog) 3, 139, 143–8, 209
OCHA (UN Office for the Coordination of Humanitarian Affairs) 165–6
Okolloh, Ory 167
old media, as one-way distribution of information 18–19, 20, 21, 26n63
on-demand entertainment 19
One Laptop Per Child 16
online feminism 184–5; *see also* feminist activism
Open Constitution Initiative 74n13
open data and open source 27n77, 151, 155, 156, 165, 167, 177; *see also* free and open source software (F/OSS or F/LOSS)
Open Geospatial Consortium 174
Open Knowledge Foundation 156
OpenSpending platform 154
OpenStreetMap 164, 165, 168, 175, 176; Humanitarian OpenStreetMap Team (HOT) 166
open-technology cultures 192–9
O'Rielly, Michael 117n49
#Oscarsowhite 210–12
ownership of media: deregulation of 104–6, 111; gender-and-race analysis 100, 101–4, 118n60; lack of gender and racial diversity in 81, 84–6, 105; by minorities 84, 85f; by women 100–4

Pace, Jonathan 136
Pai, Ajit 117n49; "The FCC Wades Into the Newsroom: Why is the Agency Studying 'Perceived Station Bias' and Asking About Coverage Choices?" 94
Paper Tiger TV 38
Parker, Tiana 211
Parks, Lisa 175
participatory democracy 9, 10, 17–19, 26n67
participatory media 51, 189–90
Pasolini en Medellín (PeM) 51
Patriot Act 173
Pei Wu, Diana 30–1
PEN Canada 172
People's Global Action (PGA) 58
Philadelphia Million Woman March *see* Million Woman March
Pickard, Victor 1; "The New Network Neutrality: Criteria for Internet Freedom" (with Meinrath) 20

Pilger, John 128
Ping (emergency system) 167
Pinkett-Smith, Jada 207, 211
policy advocacy 78–80; FCC battle over diversity 2, 81–99; feminist activism 100–19; social movement theory 2, 4, 120–33
political economy 4, 79; feminist political economy 108–9; of geoweb 173–5
political movements 52–3; *see also* China's online translation activism; social movement theory
political sociology 158
Portalatin, Krystal 30, 37, 38–9
Pough, Gwendolyn 207
Powell, Michael 86; Diversity Index and 87–8
Pozner, Jennifer 111, 112
presidential politics and journalism xvi
prime-time activism *see* social movement theory
privacy 20, 152, 156, 176; *see also* data activism; security, privacy, and surveillance
Progressive Era 19
Project Unbreakable blog 141
Prometheus Radio Project (Philadelphia) 111, 191
Prometheus Radio Project v. FCC (Prometheus I, 2004) 87, 111–13
Prometheus Radio Project v. FCC (Prometheus II, 2011) 113
promiscuity of ideas 52–3
protests and demonstrations: effectiveness in achieving social change through 130; Hong Kong pro-democracy protests 165; *Ladies' Home Journal* sit-in (1970) 107; Mexico, Istanbul, and Athens street protests 129; WIMN-led protests against deregulation of media ownership 111; WTO meeting protests (Seattle, 1999) 110–11; *see also* Arab Spring; China's online translation activism; Million Man March; Million Woman March; Occupy Wall Street movement and protests
"Public Service Responsibility of Broadcast Licensees" (FCC "Blue Book") 87

public service system 124
Puget Sound, Washington, emergency response system 167
PyLadies 196, 197–8

Qiu, Jack 69
Queer, Trans*, and/or People of Color (QTPOC) 46
Quiroz-Martinez, Julie 30–1

racial diversity *see* FCC battle over diversity; hip hop feminism
RAD.cat *see* Research Action Design
Radio Act of 1912 104
Radio Act of 1927 104, 105
Radio One 106
radio stations: gender-and-race analysis of ownership 101, 113; low-power FM radio (LPFM) 110–12, 118n60, 188, 189; *see also* FCC battle over diversity; Federal Communications Commission
Raimist, Rachel 214n31
RAND Corporation study on digital divide (1995) 24n16
Rao Jin 69–70
rape culture 209, 211; *see also* violence against women
#RapeinSyria 176
Reapportionment Act (1929) 26n59
Red Lion Broadcasting v. FCC (1969) 86
Reese, Stephen D. 66
Regan, Leslie 108
regulation: deregulation of media ownership 104–6, 111; procedural focus of 125; *see also* Censorship; FCC battle over diversity; Federal Communications Commission
Reign, April 210–11
remote sensing 173, 177
Renzi, Alessandra 154
repertoire of communication 56, 60n28
Research Action Design (RAD.cat) 31, 47n1
Resource Guide for Media Activists 111
rhizospheres/rhizomes 56, 58, 59, 159–60
Rihanna 211
Riordan, Ellen 108–9
Ristovska, Sandra 8
Rivera, Sylvia 38
Rock, Chris 210–11
Rodríguez, Clemencia 1, 8–9, 49

Rogers, Simon 151
Roggeband, Conny 62
The Root 209
Rosenworcel, Jessica 117n49
Ross, Karen 108, 109
Rucht, Dieter 124–5
Ryan, Charlotte: *Prime Time Activism* 123

Sandberg, Sheryl: *Lean In* 195
Sandvine Inc. 19
Sandy Hook Elementary School shooting (2012) 34
Santa Rosa Estéreo community radio station 57–8
Sarikakis, Katharine: *Feminist Interventions in International Communication* (with Shade) 107
Sassaman, Hannah 111, 112
satellite imagery 173; *see also* geoweb
Satten, Vanessa 209
Sawchuk, Kim 107
#SayHerName 206
SBTF (Standby Volunteer Task Force for Live Mapping) 168
SBZone (Sidi Bouzid events, Tunisia) 55
Schwartzman, Andrew 112
Schweidler, Chris 8–9, 28
Schwyzer, Hugo 209–10
Science, Technology, Engineering, and Math (STEM) 194–5, 202–3n25, 203n31
science and technology studies (STS) 153, 159, 161n19
"Searching for an Appalachian Accent" documentary 39
security, privacy, and surveillance issues 20–1; defending against government and corporate surveillance 157; geoweb 3, 175–6; opposition to state surveillance 124; state surveillance's role 128; *see also* hackers
Segerberg, Alexandra 140, 142–3, 147
sexual harassment, mapping of 168
sexual orientation 68–9
Shade, Leslie Regan 3, 108, 137, 164; *Feminist Interventions in International Communication* (with Sarikakis) 107
Shanley, Lea H. 175, 176
Shaw, Martin 125
Shaw, Todd ("Too Short") 209

Shell Oil 120
Sidi Bouzid (Tunisia) 55
Silverstone, Roger 125
Simon, Sherry 62
Sina Weibo network 64, 72
Sister Souljah 207
SLAPP suits 172
smartphones 16, 46, 55, 164
Smith, Harrison 3, 137, 164
SMS 167, 169, 170
Snowden, Edward J. 152
social change *see* data activism; media activism; social movement theory
social experiments, crowd-sourced blogs as 148
social justice 126, 130; *see also* crowd-sourced social justice blogs; geoweb; policy advocacy
social media 157, 176, 184; *see also* Facebook; Twitter
social movement studies 158, 162n30
social movement theory 2, 4, 79–80, 120–33; diversity of approaches as goal of 129; features of radical media policy activism 127–9; four "A's" of abstention, attack, adaptation, and alternative media 124–5; hierarchy within activism and 121; mobilizing citizens to seek preogressive media policies 121; relationship to media's role 121–7; sufficiency of reform 129–31
Social Solutions International, Inc. (SSI) 90–4
solidarity *see* group solidarity
#SolidarityIsForWhiteWomen 185, 209–10
Solomon, Akiba 211
Sony's Broadband Entertainment 173
Southern African partnerships in Gender Links 107
Southern Weekend magazine protests (2013) 65
Spaces of Their Own: Women's Public Sphere in Transnational China 68
Spangler, Ben 29, 30, 39
Spanish activism 139; *see also* No Nos Vamos, Nos Echan
Squires, Catherine R. 100
SSI (Social Solutions International, Inc.) 90–4
Stammers, Neil 125

Standby Volunteer Task Force for Live Mapping (SBTF) 168
Steinem, Gloria 169
STEM (Science, Technology, Engineering, and Math) 194–5, 202–3n25, 203n31
Sterpka, M.K. 58
Stevens, Ted 193, 202n24
storytelling 10, 35, 36f, 44, 171
Straight Outta Compton (film) 210
street harassment 168, 170–1
strict scrutiny 83, 89
STS (science and technology studies) 153, 159, 161n19
Sudan and Crisis in Darfur project 174–5
Summerhayes, Catherine 174
Supreme Court, US: *Adarand v. Pena* (1995) 83–4, 89, 96–7n26; *Bechtel v. FCC* (1993) 106; *Metro Broadcasting* decision (1990) 83, 96n11; *Red Lion Broadcasting v. FCC* (1969) 86
surveillance *see* security, privacy, and surveillance
Swiftriver (emergency support system) 167
Syria: documenting sexual violence in 169, 176; HarassMap-type of initiatives in 170; mapping violence in 167, 168
Systers (mailing list) 203n43

tabloid press 128–9
Tactical Tech Collective 156
Tahrir Square (Cairo) 55
Take Back the Tech (APC campaign) 165, 168
Tarrow, S. 56
technical expertise vs. DIY 188–92, 200
technological-fascinaton bias 53
technological studies 158
Technology Opportunity Program (NTIA) 12
techno-utopians 19
Telecommunications Act of 1996 106, 114
television: gender-and-race analysis of station ownership 101, 102t; low-power TV stations (LPTV) 84, 101, 112; and student activism 4; *see also* FCC battle over diversity; Federal Communications Commission

Teune, Simon 56
Thawar, Tasleem 172
Third Circuit Court of Appeals: on FCC ownership rules 83–4, 96n26; *Prometheus Radio Project v. FCC* (Prometheus I decision, 2004) 87, 111–13; *Prometheus Radio Project v. FCC* (Prometheus II decision, 2011) 113
third wave of feminism 207, 214n29, 214n31
Thucydides 26n58
Tilly, Charles 143
Title VII anti-discrimination law 108
Tongia, Rahul and Wilson, Ernie: "The Flip Side of Metcalfe's Law" 13, 24n10
Tor network 156, 176
translation activism *see* China's online translation activism
transmedia mobilization 56, 60n27
transnational character of translation activism 63, 71, 73
Treré, Emiliano 53, 56, 58
TrGen software 172
Trump, Donald xv–xvi
Tsai Ing-wen 69–72
TTR: Traduction, terminologie, redaction (journal), special issue on "Translation and Social Activism" 62
Tufts University 167
Tumblr 139, 141; *see also* We Are the 99 Percent
Tunisian uprising (2010) 54–5, 56
Turner, S. Derek 92
Twitter 64, 65, 72, 149, 151, 211; HarassMap collecting data from 169; Trump's use of xvi; Ushahidi collecting data from 167, 175; *see also* hashtags
two-way translations, Chinese-English 63–6

Ubuntu Women 196
Umbrella Movement Visual Archives and Research Collective 165
UN Declaration of Human Rights, Article 19 113
Underground Railroad 206, 213n15
Underhill, Helen 69
UNESCO 107
United Church of Christ 105, 113

United States Holocaust Memorial Museum (USHMM) 174
Universal Service Fund (FCC) 12
universal service provision *see* digital enfranchisement
University of New Mexico 41
University of Oklahoma 53
University of Southern California's Annenberg School of Communications 90
UN Office for the Coordination of Humanitarian Affairs (OCHA) 165–6
urban/rural divide 12
Usenet discussion group 203n43
Ushahidi software 151, 164; Haiti Crisis Map using 167; Take Back the Tech using 168; Twitter as data source for 167, 175; Women Under Siege using 169

The Vagina Monologues (play) 68
Vazquez, Candelario 32–3, 41–2
vendor lock-in 10
VillaNiza, documentary on 51–2
violence against women: Chinese anti-domestic violence network 68; mapping of 168–71
virtual feminism 185, 205; *see also* feminist activism
voice and agency 8, 51, 55; advocate change agents 109; in media policy activism 127; moral voice 155
volunteered geographic information (VGI) 164, 176

Walder, Andrew 4
Walker, Angus 65
Walker, Rebecca 207
walled-garden connectivity 14, 16–17, 20–1
Wall Street Journal 64
Washington Post 95, 108
wave model of feminism 207–9
Waze, purchase by Google Maps 174
"We are the 44 Percent" campaign 184, 185, 209, 214n31
We are the 99 Percent blog 3, 139, 143–8, 209
web 2.0 era 141, 157–8
wechat 64
Wedes, Justin 52
Weibo platform (China) 27n82, 64

WELL discussion group 203n43
Wells, Ida B. 208–9, 211
Wheeler, Tom 94, 95, 117n49
"When You Are a Girl Questioning Your Sexuality" video (China) 68–9
#whitegirlsrock 208
whiteness, privileging of 186, 210; *see also* #SolidarityIsForWhiteWomen
WIAE-AM (Vinton, Iowa) 104
Wiki pages 198
Wilson, Nina 171
"WIMN's Voice Blog" 111
Wolfe, Lauren 169
women: alternative media to defend against social expectations for 54; congressional members who are women 110; corporate governance role of 101–4, 103–4*t*, 109–10; geoweb content, contribution to 176; mapping of violence against women 168–71; ownership of media by 101–6, 110, 112, 112*t*; protests against government regulation of reproductive rights of 53*f*, 53–4; suffrage rights 100–1; women's programming 96n12; *see also* feminist activism; hip hop feminism; Million Woman March
Womeninfreesoftware listserv 196–7
Women in Media and News (WIMN) 108; *Resource Guide for Media Activists* 111
Women's Institute for Freedom of the Press 108
Women's Media Center (New York) 168; Women Under Siege project 169, 176
World Social Forum 58
World Summit on the Information Society (WSIS) 107
World Trade Organization, protests against (Seattle, 1999) 110–11

Xu Zhiyong 65, 74n13
XXL (online magazine) 209

Yahoo: https proxies for 176; Yahoo Maps 164
Yang, Guobin 1, 9, 62
Youth Justice Coalition (YJC) 28–9, 34–5
youth-led media projects in United States 8, 28–48; accountability,

demand for 42, 46; ageism problem of 42; barriers and challenges 41–3; challenges for 45; communication as a right 35; communities of color 34–5, 46; community and intergenerational connections through 36–7, 46; compensation issues 42; cross-platform media production in 40–1; digital media education for 45–6; organizational media work, youth involvement in 32, 34*f*; partnerships, advantages of 38; political education and youth leadership development through 38–9; priorities of media work 36; research design and participation 31–2; social change as result of 35*f*, 35–6; stereotypes challenged by 39; storytelling and media control for 32–4, 36*f*, 44; supports needed for success 42, 43*f*; target audiences of 39–40; transformative media for 32–41, 43*f*; "transformative media organizing" approach 44–5; youth engagement through 32, 37–8, 38*f*; *see also We Are the 99 Percent*
Youth Media Council (YMC) 30
Youthville (Detroit, Michigan) 36
YouTube 26n65, 54, 68, 72, 146, 167, 208

Zambia 25n41
Zero Rating program (Facebook) 25n40
zero tolerance: in drug laws 34; in sexual harassment 169, 170
Zheng, Nan 66
Ziemke, Jen 168
Zimmerman, Marie 30–1, 104–5
Zuccotti Park (New York City) 52, 55, 144; *see also* Occupy Wall Street movement and protests
Zuckerberg, Mark 15–16
Zuckerman, Ethan 66

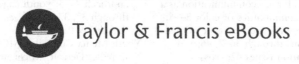

Helping you to choose the right eBooks for your Library

Add Routledge titles to your library's digital collection today. Taylor and Francis ebooks contains over 50,000 titles in the Humanities, Social Sciences, Behavioural Sciences, Built Environment and Law.

Choose from a range of subject packages or create your own!

Benefits for you
- » Free MARC records
- » COUNTER-compliant usage statistics
- » Flexible purchase and pricing options
- » All titles DRM-free.

Benefits for your user
- » Off-site, anytime access via Athens or referring URL
- » Print or copy pages or chapters
- » Full content search
- » Bookmark, highlight and annotate text
- » Access to thousands of pages of quality research at the click of a button.

REQUEST YOUR FREE INSTITUTIONAL TRIAL TODAY

Free Trials Available
We offer free trials to qualifying academic, corporate and government customers.

eCollections – Choose from over 30 subject eCollections, including:

Archaeology	Language Learning
Architecture	Law
Asian Studies	Literature
Business & Management	Media & Communication
Classical Studies	Middle East Studies
Construction	Music
Creative & Media Arts	Philosophy
Criminology & Criminal Justice	Planning
Economics	Politics
Education	Psychology & Mental Health
Energy	Religion
Engineering	Security
English Language & Linguistics	Social Work
Environment & Sustainability	Sociology
Geography	Sport
Health Studies	Theatre & Performance
History	Tourism, Hospitality & Events

For more information, pricing enquiries or to order a free trial, please contact your local sales team:
www.tandfebooks.com/page/sales

 Routledge Taylor & Francis Group | The home of Routledge books

www.tandfebooks.com